ADVANCE PRAISE FOR

Nurture, Care, Respect, and Trust: Transformative Pedagogy Inspired by Janusz Korczak

"It is indeed heartening to see such a wonderful exposition of the life and work of Janusz Korczak published for today's generation of students and teachers."
—*Peter McLaren, Distinguished Professor in Critical Studies*
Attallah College of Educational Studies, Chapman University

"In our increasingly diverse and interconnected world, bringing the life and work of Janusz Korczak into the classroom is of vital importance to teachers and students. As we advocate for students' social, emotional, and academic needs, Korczak provides innovative ideas and strategies for developing compassionate and culturally responsive classrooms. After participating in a recent Korczak educators' workshop, I am now empowered to use his ideas to effectively educate the whole child and promote student agency and self-advocacy."
—*Ryan Hauck*
Director, Global Classroom Program at World Affairs Council, Seattle, WA
Social Studies Teacher, Glacier Peak High School, WA

"Children's rights issues that Korczak pioneered are even more relevant today than they were in his lifetime. This volume's mission is not just to acknowledge and celebrate his groundbreaking legacy but also to expand on it in current thinking and practice."
—*Jerry Nussbaum*
President, Korczak Association of Canada

"Korczak reminds us that the children we are educating are not 'potential' people, but are already people with their own needs, ideas, and concerns. Listening to them and including them in the decisions about their learning makes our teaching more powerful, and, most importantly, more human. This compelling book will allow educators to become familiar with Korczak's inspiring legacy, and use it to transform their practice."
—*Nance Morris Adler*
Internationally Acclaimed Educator for "We are Here! – Foundation for Upstanders"
USHMM Museum Teacher Fellow,
Holocaust Center for Humanity Powell Fellow, Seattle, WA

"In American schools today we are just rediscovering the concept of student-centered instruction and teaching the whole child. These ideas were foundational for the Polish physician and educator Janusz Korczak. If we followed Korczak's principles here, our schools would become humane learning centers where all children could study and flourish."
—*Michele Anciaux Aoki, Ph.D., P.M.P.*
International Education Administrator,
Seattle Public Schools, Seattle, WA

Copyright © 2020 | Myers Education Press, LLC

Published by Myers Education Press, LLC
P.O. Box 424
Gorham, ME 04038

Myers Education Press is an academic publisher specializing in books, e-books, and digital content in the field of education. All of our books are subjected to a rigorous peer review process and produced in compliance with the standards of the Council on Library and Information Resources.

LIBRARY OF CONGRESS CATALOGING-IN-PUBLICATION DATA AVAILABLE FROM LIBRARY OF CONGRESS
13-digit ISBN 978-1-9755-0131-0 (paperback)
13-digit ISBN 978-1-9755-0130-3 (hard cover)
13-digit ISBN 978-1-9755-0132-7 (library networkable e-edition)
13-digit ISBN 978-1-9755-0133-4 (consumer e-edition)

Printed in the United States of America.

All first editions printed on acid-free paper that meets the American National Standards Institute Z39-48 standard.

Books published by Myers Education Press may be purchased at special quantity discount rates for groups, workshops, training organizations, and classroom usage. Please call our customer service department at 1-800-232-0223 for details.

Cover design by Sophie Appel.

Visit us on the web at **www.myersedpress.com** to browse our complete list of titles.

Nurture, Care, Respect, and Trust

Photo of Janusz Korczak used with permission of Jerry Nussbaum

Nurture, Care, Respect, and Trust

Transformative Pedagogy Inspired by Janusz Korczak

EDITED BY

Tatyana V. Tsyrlina-Spady and Peter C. Renn

Myers
Education
Press

Gorham, Maine

EARLY YEARS & YOUTH STUDIES

Gaile S. Cannella, Editor

The **Early Years & Youth Studies** series is a set of volumes designed to focus on the multiple life experiences, forms of representation, relations, changes, and issues facing those who are identified (usually by those who are older in years) as child or youth in the 21st Century. The content is cross-disciplinary, but unique in that each volume always folds back to direct applications for care and/or education. Further, while lived experience, cultural studies, and research in the social sciences have demonstrated that there is no universal childhood or human development, diversity and multiplicity remain to a large extent unrecognized. Authors are encouraged to consider one or more of the following: children and youth as diverse beings and becomings in the 21st Century (e.g. childhood and youth studies after 50 years of the critique of human development, hybrid and indigenous childhoods, youth as refugee and immigrant entanglements, transgendered childhoods); complexities of being young in the digital age (e.g., bullying, digital identities, use of media by those who are younger); critical pedagogies (e.g., of affect; of collective activism, social justice, environmental justice; with/of the more-than-human like forest pedagogies, youth and critical animal studies, educational practices that avoid human/nonhuman and curricular dualisms); and/or activist movements and public policy (e.g., youth activism, parent activism to counter neoliberal education, research methods and practices directly employed to impact childhood public policy).

Books in the Series

Nurture, Care, Respect, and Trust: Transformative Pedagogy Insprired by Janusz Korczak
Edited by Tatyana Tsyrlina-Spady and Peter C. Renn (2020)

Authors interested in having their manuscripts considered for publication in Early Years & Youth Studies are encouraged to send a prospectus, sample chapter, and CV to the series editor, Gaile Cannella (gaile.cannella@gmail.com). For instructions and advice on preparing a prospectus, please refer to the Myers Education Press website at http://myersedpress.com/sites/stylus/MEP/Docs/Prospectus%20Guidelines%20MEP.pdf.

Gaile S. Cannella (EdD, University of Georgia) is an independent scholar who has served as a tenured full professor at Texas A&M University–College Station and at Arizona State University–Tempe, as well as the Velma Schmidt Endowed Chair of Education at the University of North Texas.

To Vicki, Max, and Sophia Minakov
and
To Sylvia, Bonnie, Bob, and Lorrie—
four educators who had a
profound impact in my life

Acknowledgments

The editors want to thank Dr. Nyaradzo Mvududu, dean of the School of Education at Seattle Pacific University, for her continued support of this project; Mr. Jerry Nussbaum, president of the Janusz Korczak Association of Canada, for his encouragement and friendship; every author who contributed to the book and their national Korczak Associations. We are very grateful to the eagle-eyed Dr. Donna Rafanello for helping us to edit the manuscript, and SPU students Amanda and Elizabeth for their help with reformatting the lesson plan and activity pages.

Tatyana is also very grateful to her husband, John, for his patience and to her daughter, Vicki, and grandchildren, Sophia and Max, for providing constant inspiration and positivity, and to all her students who have chosen to follow Korczak's theory and implement it in school practice.

Contents

PART II
Advocate and Win:
Korczak as a Champion of the Rights of the Child

PART III
Nurture and Care:
Early Childhood Support as a Basis for a Happy and Successful Life

PART IV
Respect and Inspire:
From School Years to College

PART V
Transform and Play:
Creating Different Educational Realities Inspired by Korczak

Marta Santos Pais

JANUSZ KORCZAK IS a well-known writer, pediatrician, pedagogue, journalist, and social activist. Throughout his tireless efforts and courageous life, he was an inspiring child rights advocate, promoting a paradigm shift in the way children are perceived by society; sensitizing families and communities to treasure and respect children as citizens of today, rather than adults in the making; motivating professionals to respect the mystery and difficult uncertainties of growing up, to empower children and always act in their best interests; and very importantly, galvanizing young people to feel confident and believe in themselves, to nurture hope in times of despair, and to experience democracy, as real agents of change.

Korczak's vision and commitment are powerfully captured in his writings and throughout his daily action, in Poland and abroad, in times of peace and in times of war, in the children's home of Dom Sierot, during the difficult times of the Warsaw ghetto, and certainly in his dramatic journey to the Treblinka concentration camp.

As he powerfully stressed, "every caregiver must be a spokesperson for child's rights!" Children are people too; they have the right to enjoy and influence the present, rather than being a vague promise for tomorrow; "give them the right to be children"; they are the princes of emotion, poets and thinkers, and must be respected as experts and partners, as they guide us in our reflections and support the discovery of new truths.

Korczak's legacy knows no time or geographic borders. Indeed, having called for a Magna Carta for the rights of the child, he later became one of the promoters of the 1924 Declaration on the Rights of the Child, the first-ever international agreement on this topic, adopted in Geneva by the League of Nations, and also signed by him. As he noted then, the Declaration conveyed a strong message of persuasion, an appeal to good will and a request for kindness.

More than six decades later, his vision gave birth to the groundbreaking provisions of the Convention on the Rights of the Child. Adopted by the United Nations in 1989, the Convention provided the world with a binding, comprehensive charter of children's rights which is the most widely ratified treaty in world history.

The Convention helped to bridge distinct legal systems, cultural contexts, and political agendas, and made it imperative to respect and protect children, not as passive beneficiaries of services or adults in the making, but as full-fledged citizens and real partners in the consolidation of cohesive and democratic societies.

In 2019, as the international community commemorates the 30th anniversary of the adoption of the Convention, Janusz Korczak's vision remains as relevant and inspiring as ever!

Children's agency and participation in decision-making lie at the heart of the Convention. And yet, thirty years after its solemn adoption, the translation into practice of these far-reaching principles remains demanding and challenging for nations around the world. But in this endeavor, Korczak's work provides a constant source of inspiration: time and time again, we learn from the model of democracy through which he ran the children's home, with the engagement and consultation of children on all major decisions; with children's own parliament and their own newspaper; as well as through the establishment of the Children's Court, to recognize the right of the child to be taken seriously and considered fairly, and to promote children's evolving emancipation and release from the dependency on adults.

The right of the child to grow up free from violence is another fundamental dimension of the Convention. In essence, it is recognition of the right of the child to be respected in his or her human dignity and integrity, a principle Janusz Korczak pursued with perseverance throughout his life. As he highlighted: "I am a ruthless, inexorable opponent of corporal punishment. Whips, even for adults, will only be a drug, never a means of education!"

Sadly, however, in striking contrast with this vision and the binding provisions of the Convention, violence against children remains pervasive, concealed and socially condoned.

In many nations, incidents of violence are still perceived as a social taboo, as a needed form of discipline, or as an entirely private matter that needs to be kept within closed circles. Neglect, abuse, and exploitation are seldom reported; and official statistics do not fully capture the true scale and extent of this phenomenon.

Violence affects children of all ages and it often starts in early childhood. Children are intentionally targeted in politically driven processes, manipulated by organized crime, forced to flee community violence, sold and exploited for economic gain, groomed online, disciplined by violent means, sexually assaulted in their homes, neglected in institutions, abused in detention centers, bullied in schools, and tortured because of superstitious beliefs or harmful practices.

In several countries, there has been significant progress, as legislation has been enacted to protect children from violence, including within the privacy of the home and behind the walls of institutions. This is key to express states' accountability for children's rights. Furthermore, it conveys an unequivocal message of condemnation of any form of violence against children, while calling for the upbringing and education of children through non-violent means—promoting, as Korczak stresses, the "democratization of childrearing."

With strong legislation, society gains clarity about what is acceptable and what is non-negotiable. It provides clear guidance to state officials, professionals working with and for children, as well as families and common citizens. More importantly, with clear legislation, child victims feel they matter: they can enjoy protection from neglect, abuse, and exploitation, and can gain access to effective tools of redress and to genuine recovery and reintegration.

Thirty years after the adoption of the Convention, only 60 countries have a clear legal prohibition of all forms of violence, including corporal punishment of children. Inspired by the vision and work of Janusz Korczak, it is high time to leverage action and support to ensure freedom from violence for all children around the world.

This is also the vision of the new global development agenda, adopted by the United Nations in 2015.

The 2030 Agenda for Sustainable Development, as it is known, has an ambitious goal: to build a world that invests in its children and where every child can grow up free from want, from fear, and from violence—a world where no one is left behind.

As Janusz Korczak showed throughout his life, the best way of leaving no child behind is placing children first! First, when policies are shaped, when laws are enacted and enforced, when budget allocations are made. First, when professionals are recruited and strengthened in their skills and capacity to always uphold the best interests of the child. First, when children are compelled to leave their homes or communities in the search for a place of safety and protection. And first also, when children are empowered to confidently participate in decisions, as agents of change and as citizens of today.

Janusz Korczak showed an extraordinary courage and determination to never leave a child behind: younger or older, privileged or poor, sick, abandoned, or victim of war. Fearlessly, he sacrificed his life, refusing to abandon the children when they were sent on their final journey from the Warsaw ghetto to the Treblinka death camp.

Inspired by Janusz Korczak's vision and legacy, and with the energy galvanized by all those who continue to promote his vision and the cause of children's rights, we can secure a world of respect for human rights and peace for children, and a world of peace for all! This publication is a critical contribution to this process and will stand as a strong reminder of the urgency of safeguarding the right of every child, never leaving anyone behind.

Marta Santos Pais,
UN Special Representative of the
Secretary General on Violence against Children
April 2019, New York

Amy N. Spangler

I HAVE SPENT the past 33 years in public education, serving schools and communities as a teacher, principal, and consultant in six states across the country as well as in Tokyo, Japan. It is my strong opinion that Janusz Korczak's legacy is not only timely to utilize in American public education, but essential to the advancement of our society as a whole.

The lack of civility that we are seeing play out in our nation today stems from childhood being slowly squeezed down to a nub from both home and school. Children are experiencing isolation at an all-time high that is impacting their ability to interact, solve problems, and learn. Our fast-paced/high-output society has left our children stuck in strollers looking at cell phones instead of being held and spoken to by loving care providers. Public schools have become institutions where the standard for academic achievement completely outweighs most things having to do with developing happy adults who possess social competency.

In the past, public school systems were able to support positive societal outcomes by bridging perceived gaps prevailing at home, but the gap is now a cavern and it is too large to bridge without a substantial shift in educational thinking.

Specifically, how students are treated through the lens of equity and how students react to the environment through bullying and emotions' management top the list in most American schools as the largest challenges identified to reaching and teaching all students. Yet few systems are willing to recognize and tackle this as a true obstacle. Test scores, ratings, and graduation rates drive most of the economic decision making in public education, with scraps often thrown toward the true purpose of public school: to support the positive advancement of society. Terms such as unconditional love and acceptance, developmentally appropriate practice, play, fun, and joy are missing from our educational dialogue and landscape. The majority of our curricula lack thinking, compassion, real problem solving, and opportunities to engage students' hearts and minds.

Many outsiders in education will point to this being the "fault" of teachers, yet nothing could be further from the truth. Teachers are still closing their doors, trying to create happy and encouraging learning environments for children while also sticking to the adopted curricula and required standards. Until systems, states, and our government support what teachers know in their hearts to be essential to student growth and learning, by focusing goals, resources, and outcomes on restoring Korczakian approaches, teachers will continue to attempt these efforts with huge headwinds and conflict, leading to inconsistent and poor outcomes, and major teacher burnout.

In my opinion, staying focused on Korczak's principles as foundational is a great way to begin shifting our focus toward the human child. As an elementary school principal, I challenged my staff to think about all of the reasons why our students were showing signs of stress, sadness, and anxiety at school. And, as I look at the most effective solutions we developed in order to address this reality, they ALL took on Korczak's principles, with love being the central theme throughout our school.

Let us remember that children have the right to *be* children especially at school, where highly trained, loving professionals know and understand what they each require in order to thrive. Reading this volume of stories and ideas is a step in the right direction toward making Korczak's dream for all children a reality today.

Amy N. Spangler, M.Ed.,
School Principal and Education Consultant

PART I
Learn and Follow:
Korczak, a Life Story of
Dedication and Love

A Letter from the Editors: Ten Reasons to Read This Book

Tatyana Tsyrlina-Spady and Peter C. Renn

A HEARTY WELCOME to the teacher, school administrator, college instructor, student, librarian, children's rights advocate, parent, and simply curious persons!

By opening this book, something caught your attention—the unusual name or perhaps the intriguing promise of a transformative pedagogy. You probably started questioning yourself:

- Who is Janusz Korczak? What makes him so special?
- If I read this, how will it enrich and enlighten me?
- What are the groundbreaking innovations he's credited with?
- Are these innovations really effective? Don't we have enough of them already?

These questions are all understandable. You are uncertain and about to return the book to the shelf where you found it. . . . But please, before you do so, give us just a couple of minutes to explain. Predicting your doubts, we have composed our top ten reasons to read this book:

1. The first and most simple reason is to discover a new name—**Janusz Korczak** (Henryk Goldszmit, 1878–1942), a Polish Jewish educator, doctor, writer, and orphanage director who experienced several wars and other misfortunes but managed to survive all of them, giving his heart and wisdom to the children in his care. He was the first to formulate the *Declaration of Children's Rights,* and what is more, to create different children's self-governing bodies. For educators and parents he wrote *How to Love a Child, When I Am Little Again,* and many others. For children he composed *King Matt the First, Kaytek the Wizard* (a true

Harry Potter of his time), and more. He is best known as the Old Doctor who, on August 5, 1942, in Warsaw, marched together with his charges in a silent demonstration of protest against Nazism that ended in the Treblinka extermination camp. This legendary final act of love, commitment, and sacrifice to his children came to define Korczak, but there is much more to learn about him.

2. The message to respect children's rights comes from TV screens, newspapers, journals, books, politicians, and human rights' advocates, but all over the world children still suffer from mistreatment and abuse. Written almost a century ago, the following words from Korczak (2018) are timely and accurate in our world today. They implore us to respect children's rights in the best possible way:

    > Years of work have made it even more clear that children deserve respect, trust, and kindness; that they enjoy a sunny atmosphere of gentle feelings, cheerful laughter, lively first efforts and surprises; of pure, bright, loving joy; where work is dynamic, fruitful, and beautiful. (p. 317)

3. Are you struggling to understand your students and/or your own children? Does it feel like each time you learn something new about them, either pleasant or concerning, it becomes more difficult to make sense of the increasingly complex tapestry of their lives? Again, Korczak (2018) speaks to us: "We are not miracle-workers—and we do not wish to be charlatans. We renounce hypocritical longing for the perfect child" (p. 329).

4. You may be just starting your career in teaching, full of high expectations but feeling unprepared for the disappointments and reality of the classroom. Then this is for you to remember:

    > A child is a foreigner, ignorant of the language, of where the roads lead, and of laws and customs. Often, she prefers to explore for herself, asking for directions and advice when she finds herself in difficulty. She requires a guide to courteously answer her questions. (Korczak, 2018, p. 321)

If you are new to teaching, you are looking for some interesting and unusual approaches to engage all of your students and make them feel excited about the subject matter you teach. The Korczak-inspired projects of a Human Library and Found Poetry will speak to you.

5. Or maybe you are an experienced teacher? With educational policymakers continuing to de-professionalize the work of teachers, undoubtedly you have questioned yourself many times about your role in the classroom. Additional words of wisdom from a short Korczak book, *The Child's Right to Respect* (1992), serve as a reflective prompt and a call to action:

> What is our teacher's role? A storehouse of admonitions, a dispenser of moral platitudes, and a retailer of denatured knowledge which intimidates, confuses, and lulls rather than awakens, animates, and gladdens. Agents of cheap virtues, we have to force from children respect and obedience; we have to stir up sentimental feelings in adults, prod warm emotions from them. . . . The doctor rescued the child from the hands of death; the teacher's job is to let him live, to let him win the right to be a child. (p. 184)

6. Perhaps you are in a leadership position, wanting to positively head your school community while battling the voices of reform that demand accountability and dehumanize the schooling experience. Giving students a distinct voice in their own educational experience was one of many strategies Korczak used to practice respect for a child's individual rights. Sometimes it is necessary to think outside the box to resist mandated schooling practices (i.e., testing, testing, and more testing) to provide children with meaningful and growth-filled experiences. Read more about Korczak's pedagogical approach and encourage teachers to listen to the needs and interests of the children in their care and model the curriculum around them.

7. You are a parent, and you are trying to figure out your son or daughter; why are they so different from what you have expected? And why have they stopped sharing their lives with you? Again, read Korczak (1992) to hear the voices of the children:

> Maybe that is why we tell things to grownups reluctantly, because they're always in a hurry when we talk to them. It always seems that they are not interested, that they respond only to be rid of us faster, to be free of us sooner. Well, of course, they have their own important affairs, and we ours. And we also try to be brief so as not to confuse them, as if our problem is unimportant. If only they would answer yes or no. (p. 30)

8. You are none of the above. You work at the university and teach future teachers. Then please surprise yourself with Korczak's wisdom, as have many of the contributors to this book. "One of the most egregious mistakes is to think that pedagogy is a science about a child, not a personality" (Korczak, 2018). You say, you knew this; you have always thought this way. Great! But do your pre-service teachers grasp this concept? Do they understand the pervasive influence of fear in the classroom and its ability to limit and damage a child's concept of self? Read about Korczak's use of an X-ray machine to demonstrate the rhythm of the heart of a frightened child and the hidden emotions residing in all of us.

9. You work in a field unrelated to education but have developed a keen interest in history and the lessons it holds for the future. This book provides personal insights of the Holocaust; its effects on children; how Korczak and his team and supporters managed to provide some semblance of normalcy and even joy for their charges, and physically saved many of them from death. His work serves as a testimony to the human spirit and the ability to withstand any difficulties and remain a true human being: responsible and caring, a moral exemplar whose life teaches and inspires.

10. Lastly, you are probably a student, and you are considering a career as a teacher or a school counselor, or a social worker. You want to make a difference and search for ways how to do this. This book is for you as well. Consider how Korczak (2018) defines the teacher or tutor:

> Not how to demand and what to demand of a child, not how to impose or forbid, but instead to find out what the child lacks, what

she has in excess, what she demands, what she can give. A childcare institution, as well as a regular school, is both a research territory and a child-raising clinic. (p. 252)

Your journey *deeper* into the book can be unpredictable, and because of its complicated nature (like any journey to an unknown land) we decided to make it easier by providing a roadmap to guide you to the appropriate section based on your interests or needs:

- If you are curious to know more about Korczak as a personality, his life, and what he is famous for, start with Part I to better understand the historical background of the man and his times.

- If you want to explore the development of children's rights advocacy from Korczak to today, begin your journey with Part II.

- If you are more interested in Korczak's philosophy and pedagogy, then proceed to Parts III and IV for different perspectives on his approach and educational interventions in working with children.

- If you are unsure how to translate Korczak's ideas into your own classroom routine, start with Part V and also carefully examine the appendices.

We appreciate your interest in learning more about Janusz Korczak. In a world where children continue to suffer unspeakable trauma—from Rohingya to Syria to the US/Mexican border, his words are needed now more than ever. As Korczak (2018) explained: "A child is not a soldier, he does not defend the homeland, though he suffers along with it" (p. 312).

References

Korczak, J. (1986). *King Matt the first.* (R. Lourie, Trans.). New York: Farrar, Straus and Giroux.

Korczak, J. (1992). *When I am little again and The child's right to respect.* Lanham, MD: University Press of America.

Korczak, J. (2012). *Kaytek the wizard.* (A. Lloyd-Jones, Trans.). New York: Penlight Publications.

Korczak, J. (2018). *How to love a child and other selected works. Vol. I.* (B. Platoff, D. Borchardt & S. G. Bye, Trans.). Chicago: Vallentine Mitchell.

CHAPTER ONE

The Good Doctor of Warsaw,
A Historical Novel about Janusz Korczak

Elisabeth Gifford

As a young teacher and mother, I had a lot of questions about the best way to care for children—and a lot of anxiety. I came across some of Korczak's quotations at a teaching seminar and they burst across the landscape like a ray of sunshine.

Here was a man who advocated not a prescribed best way to raise children but a relationship based on knowing who the child really was, on respecting them as an individual, and working out what they needed from that understanding. In other words, *how to love a child*. Getting to know more about Korczak brought joy back to my teaching and mothering. To this day, I turn to his insights to realign my values with a more rewarding way of relating to both children and adults.

The tutor in charge of that seminar also told us about Korczak's life and his courage. I was surprised that I had never heard about such a remarkable man and decided to write a book to bring his ideas and story to more people, a book that would help to know Korczak the man, to see him as he worked and cared for children, relating to each individual person with empathy, understanding, and respect.

I had two problems, however. To begin with, I knew very little about Korczak's life, and more fundamentally, I did not know how to write a book. I attended writing classes and published three other books. Only ten years later did I finally begin to write *The Good Doctor of Warsaw* (Gifford, 2018).

The research for the book was a journey into some of the darkest history of the 20th century. I read intensively, including the Warsaw Ghetto diaries and accounts of Janusz Korczak (2003), Mary Berg (Schneiderman & Pentlin, 2009), Adam Czerniakow (Hilberg, Staron, & Kermisz, 1979), Michael Zylberberg (1969), Halina Birnbaum (McQuaid, 2013), Janina David (2005), Yitzhak

Zuckerman (1993), etc., and various firsthand accounts from the Oneg Shabbat archives published in the book *Words to Outlive Us* (Grynberg, 2003). I visited the British Library, the Weiner Library, the Polish Library in London, and the Bodleian in Oxford, searching for any books I could find on Korczak. I read biographies of Korczak by Betty Jean Lifton (2018), Adir Cohen (1995), and many others. I also managed to source some of Korczak's works including *How to Love a Child* (Korczak, 2018a and 2018b), *When I Am Little Again and The Child's Right to Respect* (Korczak, 1992).

I contacted some of the various Korczak Associations worldwide for information and wrote to Misha Wroblewski, head of the Korczak Association in Sweden. His son, Roman Wroblewski-Wasserman, replied to say that Misha had recently passed away, but that he could help. I travelled to Sweden to meet Roman, and over the following years he became a friend and trusted adviser on the book, providing a constant stream of information on Korczak and on the Warsaw ghetto years. The book would not have been possible without his hard work and kindness in sharing his parents' story. Roman's parents, Misha and Sophia, worked with Korczak both before and during the war, living in the ghetto with Korczak and the children. Misha and Sophia were among the less than 1 percent out of a population of over half a million who survived the Warsaw ghetto. The book I finally wrote about Korczak was their story also.

During my initial research, I travelled to Warsaw to visit the Warsaw Korczak Museum housed in a room of Korczak's original orphanage on Krochmalna Street, now Jaktorowska Street. I visited the POLIN Museum of the History of Polish Jews and read accounts of pre-war Jewish Warsaw by Isaac Bashevis Singer. Roman was also in contact with Barbara Engelking, and I referred to her book, *The Warsaw Ghetto* (Engelking & Leociak, 2009), extensively to re-create the details of the ghetto.

Warsaw was all but razed to the ground in the war. The medieval center of the Polish capital today is an almost perfect reconstruction that is in fact no more than 50 years old. The ghetto and many of the Jewish areas are now gone, covered by Soviet-era housing and modern office buildings, but it is possible, still, to find parts of the original buildings, and to reconstruct the area mentally by following historical locations on a map.

My big question after completing the first stages of research was, How do you write a book about the Holocaust? I decided to focus on documented facts about

Korczak and the war years and to fill in the background details, such as food and transport, from research. I watched Andrzej Wajda's 1990 film about Korczak for its wonderful poetic evocation. The Nazis were avid film documenters of the Warsaw ghetto and this material is available online. The book aims to give a cinematic reconstruction of Korczak's life and crucial war years in the hope that a wider audience would get to know Korczak and want to learn more about his work and writings. A novel, rather than a biography, seemed appropriate to Korczak's method of using plays and stories to help children explore ideas.

Janusz Korczak was a pen name, acquired before he became a famous writer in Poland. Born Henryk Goldszmit in 1878 (or 1879, which is not clear to this day), he was the son of a wealthy Jewish lawyer and his wife, who mixed freely with both Polish and Jewish friends in fin de siècle Warsaw. Korczak did not realize he was Jewish until his canary died when he was five, and, burying it in the courtyard, was told by a Polish boy that he couldn't put a cross on the grave because it was a Jewish bird. Poland in those days was divided between three superpowers: Germany, Russia, and the Austro-Hungarian Empire.

Korczak's first taste of school was at a Russian establishment where the beating reduced him to nervous terror and this memory led to his lifelong quest to give children a voice and to foster a better understanding between children and their care providers. Korczak's beloved and brilliant father died in the Tworki Lunatic Asylum when Korczak was just 17, and Korczak's impoverished mother and sister relied on his income as a tutor, while hoping he would soon graduate as a doctor. Korczak later became a sought-after pediatrician, also famous for his novels charting the lives of the street children he worked with in his spare time—when not dodging the tsar's police for his involvement in the seditious "Flying University," whose groundbreaking lectures on observational psychology enthralled Korczak. Eventually, he decided to follow his heart and leave medicine to work full time with children at a neglected orphanage run by a remarkable young woman called Stefania (Stefa) Wilczyńska. He and Stefa formed a lifelong partnership dedicated to children.

Poland gained independence after WWI. The following decade was a golden time for Korczak's expansion of the kingdom of the child. He wrote and lectured extensively about and for children, made child-centered broadcasts, founded a children's newspaper, and served as a court advocate for teenage delinquents. With the advent of the economic depression in the 1930s, a fascist

spirit spread through Europe, and as a Jew in an increasingly nationalistic
Poland, Korczak's work was curtailed. He lost everything except his Jewish
orphanage on Krochmalna Street.

Korczak was an early pioneer of child welfare and psychology. As a young
man at the beginning of the 20th century, Korczak looked around and began to
ask why so many children were unhappy. There were vast numbers of slum children in Warsaw, neglected and unloved. Even the children of the rich seemed
frustrated and resentful in spite of their material wealth. It felt as if adults had
forgotten what it was like to be a child. Adults had to learn to communicate with
children and speak their language again. It was a lesson he understood from
experience. As a young doctor in training, he wanted to heal not only children's
physical ailments, but also their souls and lives.

Determined to make children's lives happier in his first summer camp for
slum children, he set out with a full knowledge of books on children, a bag full
of games, good intentions, and a carnation in his buttonhole. The week was
chaotic. Korzcak found himself at odds with the boys, shouting at them to go
to sleep and even resorting to threats. Ashamed and confused, he decided to
ask the boys what they thought was going wrong. It soon became clear that his
one-size-fits-all policy on childcare was missing the mark with children who
had different needs for sleep and food, and different clothes sizes and interests.
He realized that only by really listening to and knowing the children could he
begin to devise creative ways to lead them towards who they were meant to be
as people. Each child was a person to be respected in terms of their thoughts and
feelings. The following summer, with a hefty dose of preplanning for a group of
30 boys—lists, schedules, and a lot of effort in getting to know each boy—he
and the children had a wonderful experience in the countryside. He realized
that childrearing practices drew on knowledge developed from failed attempts,
an ongoing quest to find out what works for an individual.

For this reason, Korczak always put respecting and getting to know a child
far higher than relying on books by child experts—although these were useful. "No book, no doctor can replace your own careful observation of a child."[1]
Mothers and fathers should trust their instinct about their own child, based
on years of watching and getting to know who their child is. And above all,
he saw childrearing as a relationship, not an exercise in control. The adult was
charged with the responsibility of the child's safety and happiness, but this

meant accountability, not a free pass to lose one's temper or be unfair for one's own convenience. He loathed physical punishment, viewing it as wrong and completely ineffective. He understood that an adult has to be a grown-up: "Before you start laying down the law to children and bossing them about, make sure that you have brought up and educated the child inside yourself." And he saw no merit in treating childhood as if it were a mere preparation for the more important time of adulthood. Korczak believed, "Children are people today, not people tomorrow," and they deserve the right to their happiness.

He taught children and adults to treat each other with empathy. He was quite happy to point out to a child that he was busy working or reading or simply tired, and that the child could perhaps amuse herself for a while—while always remaining close at hand and available for needed help and comfort. He taught social responsibility through the court of peers where children brought their grievances against each other and debated the rights and wrongs of each case, considering the feelings of others, and developing a sense of justice and fairness. Punishments were mostly written warnings.

Korczak knew that children take comfort from the religion they were raised in and gave both Jewish and Christian children the chance to pray or go to services if they so wished. He was not a practicing Jew, but had been brought up in the tenets of the religion, and though he did not follow a specific creed, he believed in a loving God and read widely from wisdom literature. His religion, he said, was the sacred duty to protect children. He believed that a child belongs to herself and that it is the duty of not only parents but the whole community to care for the children in their midst. He had no children of his own, yet he was a beloved father to hundreds of children. Korczak firmly believed that children held the world together and that the basis of nationhood was not an ethnic or cultural group, but the decision of a people irrespective of creed or race to come together to care for their children. He understood that where nations decide not to care for the child then civilization is on the verge of flying apart, which is precisely what happened when the Third Reich decided to murder thousands of children in 1942, in Warsaw, in Poland, and across Europe. There can be no greater contrast to this terrible decision than Korczak's will to protect the rights and happiness of his children, even to the very end when he accompanied them to a death camp.

The Nazis razed the Treblinka death camp to the ground in the war's closing days in an attempt to hide the evidence of their genocide. A total of 900,000 people were gassed there in the space of 14 months. After the war, a monument was erected on the site of the gas chambers and a trail of smaller stones laid to represent the people of the 1,700 Jewish towns and village communities killed in Treblinka. Only one boulder was inscribed with an individual's name. It read: Janusz Korczak and the Children. The real monument to Korczak, however, is his call to make the world a better place for children from all backgrounds and the many people who continue to follow his example in working for the rights of children everywhere.

In Canada, Israel, Poland, Russia, the United States, and all over the world, Korczak's teachings and his principles of respect and empathy are still followed and taught in schools, and universities, and at education conferences. His plea to treat all children with fairness, and to consider the welfare of the child, remains as important today as it did when he first wrote *How to Love a Child* over a century ago. Perhaps the best observation of Korczak comes from a child in care who was given some of Korczak's work. He said, "I wish all parents could read Janusz Korczak, because then children would be happier" (Joseph, 2007).

References

Cohen, A. (1995). *The gate of light: Janusz Korczak, the educator and writer who overcame the Holocaust*. Cranbury, NJ: Associated University Presses.

David, J. (2005). *A square of sky: A wartime childhood from ghetto to convent*. London: Eland Books.

Engelking, B., & Leociak, J. (2009). *The Warsaw ghetto: A guide to the perished City*. New Haven, CT: Yale University Press.

Gifford, E. (2018). *The good doctor of Warsaw*. London: Corvus.

Grynberg, M. (Ed.). (2002). *Words to outlive us: Eyewitness accounts from the Warsaw ghetto*. New York: Picador.

Hilberg, R., Staron, S., & Kermisz, J. (Eds.). (1979). *The Warsaw diary of Adam Czerniakow: The prelude to doom*. New York: Stein & Day.

Joseph, S. (2007). *Loving every child: Wisdom for parents*. New York: Algonquin Books.

Korczak, J. (1992). *When I am little again and The child's right to respect*. Lanham, MD: UPA.

Korczak, J. (2003). *Ghetto diary*. New York: Yale University Press.

Korczak, J. (2018a). *How to love a child and other selected works, Volume 1*. Elstree, Herts, England: Vallentine Mitchell.

Korczak, J. (2018b). *How to love a child and other selected works, Volume 2*. Elstree, Herts, England: Vallentine Mitchell.

Lifton, B. J. (2018). *King of children: The life and death of Janusz Korczak.* Elstree, Herts, England: Vallentine Mitchell.

McQuaid, E. (2013). *Halina: Faith in the fire.* Westville, NJ: The Friends of Israel Gospel Ministry.

Schneiderman, S. L., & Pentlin, S. L. (Eds.) (2009). *The diary of Mary Berg: Growing up in the Warsaw ghetto.* London: Oneworld Publications.

Zuckerman, Y. (1993). *A surplus of memory: Chronicle of the Warsaw ghetto uprising.* Berkeley: University of California Press.

Zylberberg, W. (1969). *The Warsaw diary, 1939–1945.* Elstree, Hertshire, England: Vallentine Mitchell.

Endnote

1 All Korczak's quotes in this chapter are taken from the book by Sandra Joseph (2007). *Loving Every Child: Wisdom for Parents,* and used with permission from Sandra Joseph and Algonquin Books USA.

CHAPTER TWO

The Home for Orphans during WWII: A Micro-History of Perseverance and Care

Agnieszka Witkowska-Krych

Introduction

STUDYING HISTORICAL EVENTS that took place nearly 80 years ago is always charged with a high level of uncertainty and research risk. Different sources that document distant reality and specific events within it are often incomplete, inaccurate, and, sometimes, contradictory. The same applies to personal biographies. Pieces of information, memories, or preserved documents are not sufficient to fully restore the life and experience of another person. Historical events and the lives of those who came before are immersed in a context that is inaccessible for modern researchers; this complicates the task of reconstructing micro-history even more. Despite these limitations well known to seasoned historians who try not to recapture this lost world but at least to study the discourse that it describes, it is, nevertheless, worth revisiting the past. At the very least it allows us to get closer to what was happening *hic et nunc*.

Exploring the world that through the years remains on the margins of the main research trends, is particularly tempting. Especially interesting is the fate of people or groups that were socially excluded (e.g., national or religious minorities, women, children, the sick, or the poor). A good example is Janusz Korczak, a medical doctor, writer, and pedagogue who is known as a loyal, responsible educator, and director of the most popular Jewish orphanage in Warsaw between the two world wars.

The Home for Orphans: General Characteristics

The Home for Orphans was the residence of 107 Jewish children ages 7 to 14. Originally, it was built with the support of the Relief for the Orphans Association and generous personal donations from its members. The Home for Orphans was opened in 1912 at 92 Krochmalna Street in Warsaw. Just about three years earlier Korczak joined the association and—at its invitation and request—started working with them as an educator, implementing his innovative pedagogical methods in close cooperation with Stefania Wilczyńska, who came to the orphanage prior to him.

From the very beginning, the Home for Orphans was considered and planned to be a research institute, which, apart from providing its charges with all necessary things, served as a unique laboratory to study children's growth and development. For Janusz Korczak, Stefania Wilczyńska, and other educational and non-educational staff, it was a place of methodically documented daily observations of the children. For the future co-workers, including future social workers and schoolteachers, it was also an opportunity to closely evaluate their desire to stay in education or to move on and change their profession. For the children and youth, it was undoubtedly a place where they felt at home and could grow and develop surrounded by understanding, love, and respect.

The orphanage, subsidized by the Relief for the Orphans Association, was largely independent from the state, ministerial branches, city council, and the Jewish community of Warsaw. This independence allowed the orphanage to introduce and successfully implement numerous innovative pedagogical methods. In his most famous book, *How to Love a Child* (Korczak, 2018a), in the part devoted to the organization of the orphanage, Korczak provides a detailed description of the functioning of this facility.

It is important to mention here that there existed another, very similar, institution for Polish children called Our Home, which was co-founded by Janusz Korczak and Maryna Falska (Maria Rogowska-Falska, 1877–1944) that was located first in Pruszków and then in Warsaw, in the Bielany neighborhood. At this site, Korczak refined a number of very useful, effective, and efficient methods that were aimed at making the life of abandoned and/or orphaned children more comfortable and more appreciated. The everyday practices and methods used in Our Home helped to create the atmosphere of trust which allowed his charges to grow into conscientious adults ready to meet different challenges.

Every Korczak home could be characterized by a few specific and, without exaggeration, unique features that had a long-lasting effect on the children. On average, a child lived there about seven years. This was a long period of time that allowed for the systematic pedagogical work of providing all the charges with an emotionally and physically safe environment where they could grow, develop, and mature physically, mentally, and—above all—socially. Internal institutions (like the court of peers, parliament, newspaper, shared responsibilities, and others) regulated the relations between the children, teachers, and staff members. The Home lived by the rule that everyone engaged in its work, whether a child or a teacher, was co-responsible for the atmosphere there. This situation in the Home for Orphans remained relatively undisturbed from 1912 until the outbreak of World War II in September 1939.

If we were to assess the situation of the orphanage in August 1939, a moment before the cataclysm of war, we could say that in the facility lived about 100 Jewish children, among them orphans, semi-orphans, and so-called social orphans, those children who had parents who were unable to support them due to unemployment or other deleterious conditions. Living with these children included about a dozen or so workers and a rich collection of materials documenting the daily life of this institution.

How Did WWII Affect the Home for Orphans?

At the very beginning of World War II, Korczak was in Warsaw, and historians assume that he probably stayed in the apartment of his sister on Złota Street. In September 1939, he moved to live at the orphanage on Krochmalna Street. As he wrote a few months later, he proclaimed "the state of emergency" there (a kind of internal "martial law") to provide safety to the children and to protect the material goods of the orphanage that were prone to destruction by military actions. He trained the children how to behave during the bombing, and how to save water and other resources. At the same time, Korczak tried to maintain typical institutional routines; the children were still allowed and even encouraged to visit their families, play games, and have fun.

Remembering his previous war experience, he tried to use his position as director to keep the orphanage functioning. With the great help of Stefania Wilczyńska, he managed to do this by reorganizing the schedule and distributing all the usual work similar to the pre-war mode. More so, all of the Home's self-governing institutions, such as the parliament, the newspaper, and even theatre productions, continued to operate.

Unfortunately, the orphanage building was partially destroyed during frequent Warsaw bombings, and one of the young workers, Józef Sztokman, died of an illness contracted while staying on the roof for hours in order to protect the building from incendiary bombs.

The war situation left more children parentless or displaced, and the number of the children in his care increased up to 150. But even all these hardships did not prevent Korczak from taking the children out of Warsaw into the countryside for a summer camp as was tradition, and what is more, dozens of charges from other Jewish institutions joined them there as well. This wouldn't be that surprising if not for the time period—summer of 1940.

After returning from summer camp and a few relatively calm weeks, Korczak, together with his staff and the children, was forced to move from their home on Krochmalna Street in November 1940 and relocate to the area of a newly created ghetto. They resettled in the building of Józef and Maria Roesler Trade School for Boys, at 33 Chłodna Street, switching places with the latter. But during this relocation, Korczak was arrested and jailed for about a month, which put Stefania fully in charge of the orphanage—a role she previously filled in 1914 when Korczak was drafted into the army as a medical doctor.

Although the inner structure of the orphanage was fully maintained, its financial situation dramatically changed; the Relief for the Orphans Association was not as active as it had been before. In order to raise additional funds, Wilczyńska and Korczak organized charity shows. Additional funding came also from the Jewish Council and the Jewish Social Self Help that was largely supported by the American Jewish Joint Distribution Committee, also known as the Joint.

In October 1941, because of the changes in the borders of the Warsaw ghetto, Korczak's orphanage had to relocate once again, this time to the building right at the corner of two streets, which explains its address—16 Sienna/9 Śliska Street. It was the place where Korczak and the children spent the last months of their lives. The number of the children increased, and their living conditions worsened.

While faced with innumerable challenges, there existed places where the situation looked much more tragic. Korczak was fully aware of it, and apart from working in his orphanage, he made a decision to provide help to another institution for children called the Main Home of Refuge, located at 39 Dzielna Street, very close to the St. Augustine Church. At the beginning of 1942, he even briefly moved there trying to understand the life of this institution from inside, and importantly, in an attempt to improve its terrible state. Unfortunately, his efforts were in vain and he returned to the Home for Orphans, where he felt more useful.

The last months of Korczak's life are well documented in his "Diary" (Korczak, 2012), where he regularly took notes from May to August 1942. There, in this poignant document, we can find many details about the ghetto period of the orphanage existence. The diary also serves as a register of different ways the prewar style was sustained. Apart from this very important source and other documents composed by Korczak in the Warsaw ghetto, known today as "new sources," many other testimonies and documents show that despite worsening financial conditions, a growing number of charges, and disheartening prospects for the future, Korczak, Stefania Wilczyńska, and other employees and volunteers tried to provide the children with the feeling of normalcy and safety.

Korczak, who had survived prior wars and revolutions, and his staff persevered and devoted themselves to their everyday work, which in today's discourse would be undoubtedly considered civil resistance. As conditions worsened, the Old Doctor rejected any opportunity for personal rescue and turned down offers to leave the Warsaw ghetto in order to go into hiding. On August 4, 1942, Korczak (2012) wrote in his diary, "What I am living through now, already happened" (p. 140). He was thinking about his previous war experiences, but was unaware of what was about to happen to him and his children.

References

Engelking, B., & Leociak, J. (2013). *Getto warszawskie. Przewodnik po nieistniejącym mieście [Warsaw ghetto. The guide to the non-existent city]*. Warszawa, Poland: Instytut Filozofii i Socjologii.

Korczak, J. (1992). *Janusz Korczak w getcie. Nowe źródła [Janusz Korczak in the ghetto. New sources]*. Warszawa, Poland: Oficyna Wydawnicza Latona.

Korczak, J. (2012). *Pamiętnik i inne pisma z getta [The diary and other sources from the ghetto]*. Warszawa, Poland: Wydawnictwo WAB.

Korczak, J. (2018). *How to love a child, Volume 1*. Elstree, Herts, England: Vallentine Mitchell.

Olczak-Ronikier, J. (2012). *Korczak. Próba biografii [Korczak. An attempt of a biography]*. Kraków, Poland: Wydawnictwo WAB.

Sakowska, R. (1993). *Ludzie z dzielnicy zamkniętej [People from the closed district]*. Warszawa, Poland: Wydawnictwo Naukowe PWN.

Witkowska, A. (2010). *Ostatnia droga mieszkańców i pracowników warszawskiego Domu Sierot [Last march of the inhabitants and workers of the Home for Orphans]*. Warszawa, Poland: Zagłada Żydów. Studia i materiały.

Witkowska-Krych, A. (2015). *Janusz Korczak (1878[9]–1942)*. Warszawa, Poland: Wydawnictwo Instytutu Pamięci Narodowej.

CHAPTER THREE

Janusz Korczak: Sculptor of Children's Souls

Marcia Talmage Schneider

IN 1972, I first heard of Janusz Korczak and Stefania Wilczyńska. At that time there was only one chapter in one book written in English about Korczak, emphasizing his heroism but saying nothing about his innovative educational methods with children. I was especially struck by his love for children. As the years ensued, the world discovered Korczak, and now a growing body of literature dedicated to his philosophy and pedagogical teachings exists.

Upon my visit to Treblinka in 1992, I viewed the memorial stone honoring "Janusz Korczak and His Children" and noted a small memorial candle next to a card written by one of my former students. A full circle . . . Tears rolled down my cheeks. I realized then that I had to do something to kindle others' interest in Korczak.

In 2001, while in Israel, I went to the Ghetto Fighters' Museum and obtained names, addresses, and phone numbers of 10 persons who had lived in the Polish orphanage, Dom Sierot, in Warsaw, before the Holocaust. They all were living in Israel. I took my old-fashioned tape recorder and set out to visit with them. Most were in the autumn of their lives, but their memories were still fresh. Many chose their life professions based upon Korczak's influence and their time spent at the orphanage. At this writing, only one interviewee is still alive. These interviews are the basis for my book, *Janusz Korczak: Sculptor of Children's Souls* (Talmage Schneider, 2015).

They were unmarried, yet "Pan Doktor" was the father and "Pani Stefa" was the mother to thousands of children, deeply loving, respecting, and showing kindness to them. They understood that childhood was preparation for the future, and thereby they were influencing the lives of future families as well.

In the introduction to Korczak's *Ghetto Diary* (2003), Betty Lifton, author of the first comprehensive Korczak biography, mentions what Korczak once said to his friend: "I am a doctor by education, a pedagogue by choice, a writer by passion and a psychologist by necessity" (p. xvii). You will be able to see this unfold as we explore his life's journey.

Korczak was a visionary, far ahead of his time. Decades before Lawrence Kohlberg[1] and terms like moral education, rights for the child, journal writing, behavior modification, social mores, communal living, self-government, and peer counseling were popular, Korczak and Stefa used *all* these approaches.

As a doctor, Korczak weighed and measured each child each week. He wrote information in a small notebook that he kept in the breast pocket of his khaki green lab coat. He monitored who gained or lost weight; mostly it was the latter. There were bathtubs in the basement of the orphanage. One of the interviewees, Erna Lador, who had become head of psychologists in a small city in Israel, remembered, "Every week, Doctor would wash the children down to their bare bones. He often would cut their nails and shampoo their hair. He even shaved their heads when necessary, because he was especially worried about lice and other diseases."

Mira Caspi related, "As we got dressed in the morning, we stood in line near the two sinks in order to wash our upper bodies in the morning, and of course brush our teeth." She started singing in Polish, "I brush my teeth so I will have my teeth for 100 years. By brushing my teeth twice a day, I will have teeth as strong as a wolf. If you don't do that when you get older, you will put them on the dresser." She said it in a rhyme originally created by Korczak. She added, "And I learned it so many years ago and still remember it today!" Mira Caspi was the interviewee who had an exotic bird in a cage in her apartment. She told me that because of Korczak she had this bird. She recalled, "He used to feed the sparrows and even call them by names, some by the same names as a few of the children."

Klara Maayan, a peer counselor and not an orphan, remembered that Stefa poured daily doses of cod liver oil for the children in nicely decorated cups, some with gold rims, and Korczak would go around making sure the children drank up.

Sarah Kremer told me of small pieces of bread that were on the tray to "help with the awful strong taste of the cod liver oil. And, God forbid, you didn't drink it up! I actually think we were kept healthy by drinking that awful stuff." Sarah became a teacher of young children because of Korczak. Her daughter did as well, and she advised her daughter to give out rewards like candy to her students "like Korczak did to us." She told me of the time she remembered that the "Doctor would give a child who had lost a tooth a reward for it—candy, chocolate, or even money . . . But, if it didn't fall out, he'd help pull it out. He built a model of 'our home' with the lost teeth. It was a shame if the tooth got lost and we couldn't use it for the model."

Shmuel Nissenbaum relates that when he was taken into the orphanage he had been sick, homeless, and very young. He whistled like a bird, begging for money. At first, Korczak separated him from the other children, letting the boy sleep in his attic room. This enabled Korczak to closely watch over Shmuel. Nissenbaum recalled, "He took care of me as though I was his own child. He was like a mother and father to me."

Another innovation was the radio talk show called *The Old Doctor*. The program avoided using his real name, which was Jewish. He was like a Dr. Phil of today . . . a pediatric consultant addressing problems of parents with children, children with parents, and children with their peers. His talks were humorous and warm, like Korczak himself. But due to the rise in anti-Semitism in the mid-1930s in Poland, the program was cancelled. I often wonder what Korczak would say about Facebook and social media today and their effect on children.

Korczak always appreciated the written word and wrote numerous children's books (e.g., Korczak, 1969; 2012). He also made another innovation—the *Mały Przegląd* (*Little Review*) newspaper. It was the first children's newspaper, written mostly by the children, with a short story or article by Korczak. The paper was read aloud on Saturdays in the orphanage after the children ate breakfast and before the children who lived nearby went home for a family visit.

Korczak instituted peer counselors; university students were provided with room and board in lieu of four hours of daily work with the children, serving as big brothers or sisters while playing games like chess, playing sports, and helping with homework. It was a win-win situation. Erna Lador, whom I mentioned above, arrived at the orphanage early for her intake interview. She recalled putting down her suitcase and wandering around interacting with the children. "I noticed tables with children playing games and then the tables changed into dining tables. There was order and detail. Later I found Stefa and Korczak. He told me, 'It's not necessary for us to talk. We've been watching you. The job is yours! Put your name on the Bulletin Board.'"

The Bulletin Board was another of Korczak's methods of announcing activities and news within the orphanage. It was placed where everyone could easily see it.

There were two columns posted: One read *Disagreements* and the other *Expression of Thanks*. If a child was too short or did not know how to write, another taller or older child would help by writing for him or her. This idea fostered Korczak's belief in employing older children to assist in the care of the younger ones.

Korczak himself did not follow religious practices. However, he did want the children to have a positive feeling of their cultural heritage, so he created a room called the Quiet Room, where the children could pray if they desired. There was a poster of the main Morning Prayer. Since many of the children were orphans, they wanted to say the memorial prayer of Kaddish. He would sometimes be there for support. He wanted the Jewish holidays with historical significance, like Chanukah and Passover, to be taught. The counselors who had Jewish backgrounds also taught prayers and holiday songs in Hebrew.

Shlomo Nadel told me an amazing story from his Passover experience. In order to complete the Passover ceremony of a Seder ritual, one needs a small piece of matzo bread, called the afikomen. At the beginning of the meal, it is hidden, generally by the leader, and later on, "searched" for by the children, found, and presented at the end of the ceremony. With 100 children that would be too chaotic! So Korczak devised a way for the afikomen to be a walnut, concealed in one of the dumplings (matzo balls) in the soup. As Nadel was telling me this story, he took out of his pocket a disheveled and browned handkerchief with the walnut he had found in his soup some 60 years prior. "It was my good luck charm," he said.

Everyone had a job to do, even Korczak himself. This taught social and moral responsibility. Korczak's job was to clear away the dishes. That way he could see who was eating too much or not enough and he also could see which plates were chipped and needed to be replaced.

Sarah Kremer remembers her experience in the orphanage; her memories are full of gratitude and love:

> The best years of my life were spent with Korczak. It was my HOME. The whole seed of my interest in children was planted from my time with Korczak. I used many of his methods with my own children and those in my school. I told my daughter who became a teacher, too, to use rewards in her classroom.

Mira Caspi relates how, upon first coming to the orphanage, she played alone on the sidelines. She had no friends. Korczak noticed this and put her up onto a tree branch. Mira recalls,

> I was so frightened and did not know what to think. I started crying and screaming: "Put me down!" The children gathered around the tree. He did not take me down. The children started shouting, "Take him to Court!" He then did take me down finally. The children shouted vehemently, "Take him to the Court of Justice!" How could I take him there? But they kept shouting, so I did. I wrote his name on the Bulletin Board too. He was "tried" and the punishment was the most lenient, 100 or *setka* in Polish. After that, the children started playing with me. Surely, he knew that would be the outcome.

Korczak had a rare psychological insight into children. He knew just what to do. After that incident, he was given the fond nickname of *setka*. In one of his illustrated books, Itzhak Belfer (2016) made a sketch of this incident.

Another time Korczak was brought to the Court of Justice was when he disobeyed the rule of never sliding down the bannister that was on the stairs from the first to the second floor where the dormitory rooms were. He forbade that, as pants would be ripped, or even worse, bottoms were splintered. He did it for the attention and as a fun-loving gesture. When I visited the orphanage in 1998, I just had to see that bannister!

There were also clubs at the orphanage. Dov Netzer attended the chess club, where Korczak taught him to play chess. Dov explained that he hadn't played chess for more than 50 years. Since Dov was recuperating from surgery and was well advanced in age, he relied on the care of a caretaker from the former Soviet Union. He explained, "This afternoon, he will come to take care of me and also play a game of chess. I just love to play!"

There was a photography club where Nadel learned to take and develop photos. It was Shlomo's peer counselor who introduced him to photography and took him into the darkroom where film was processed and developed. He was always interested in this process, which became his profession later in life. He took numerous prized photos of children and events at the orphanage and summer camp and miraculously saved them across his life's adventures and travels. His two sons have been very involved in activities of the second-generation Korczak Association. They recall that there was a portrait of Korczak on their living room wall all their lives. Shlomo's wife, at the time of my interview, mentioned that when a significant decision needed to be made, she and Shlomo would ask themselves, "What would Korczak say or advise us to do?"

Yitzhak Belfer, who is alive at this writing, has become a famous and highly respected Israeli artist whose many drawings and bronze sculptures depict Korczak (Belfer, 2016). As a boy, Belfer was given crayons and paper, and a small space in which to draw. This enabled him to develop self-confidence and to expand his experiences with his natural talents and interests.

Summer camp was another of Korczak's methods. Nadel said, "I just loved walking around barefoot and in short pants all the time. We learned how to kayak too. It was a great sport then, not only in present days." Mira Caspi shared her memories with me:

> We walked into the forest one night with Doktor and had pretended that there was a break into the pantry. It was our secret! We had so much fun! We met a gypsy girl in the forest and she tried to trick us, but Korczak, in the end, taught *her* a real moral lesson.

His ideas and methods enabled the development of morals and self-discipline. The children had cubbies where they could put their private "treasures." They did not have locks or even covers. No one stole from the cubbies or from each other. Korczak helped expand the children's morality and sense of responsibility. He encouraged personal initiative, good citizenship, and human relations, and strengthened the children's character. He and Stefa had an amazing ability to touch a child's soul with *love* and *respect*, which they believed would eventually make for *a better world*.

References

Belfer, I. (2016). *White house in a grey city: A child of Janusz Korczak*. Toronto: Provincial Advocate for Children and Youth of Ontario.

Korczak, J. (1969). *The stubborn boy: The life of Louis Pasteur* (Hebrew edition). Transl. by Sh. Meltzer. Tel-Aviv: M. Neuman.

Korczak, J. (2003). *Ghetto diary*. New Haven and London: Yale University Press.

Korczak, J. (2012). *Kaytek the wizard*. [Trans. by A. Lloyd-Jones]. Brooklyn, NY: Penlight Publications.

Lifton, B. J. (1988). *The king of children: A biography of Janusz Korczak*. New York: Farrar, Straus & Giroux.

Talmage Schneider, M. (2015). *Janusz Korczak: Sculptor of children's souls*. New York: Child Development Research & The Wordsmithy, LLC.

Note

1 Lawrence Kohlberg (1927–1987), a famous American psychologist and educator, best known for his theory of moral development.

CHAPTER FOUR

On Becoming Korczak:
A Short Reflection

Lillian Boraks-Nemetz

DR. JANUSZ KORCZAK is and has always been my hero. My father knew and admired him in the Warsaw ghetto. I grew up with the stories of the Old Doctor and his love for children. After the war this was the light that helped to guide me out of the darkness of war-torn Europe. I view Korczak as a man who listened to children as people not only with his ears but his whole being.

Korczak (as cited by Lifton, 1988) wrote: "You cannot even understand a child, until you achieve self-knowledge: you yourself are a child whom you must learn to know, rear, and above all enlighten" (p. 80).

How many of us know ourselves that way? Many people barely look deeply into their own lives for answers but judge themselves and others by the most recent event and never stop to ask questions, never dig to the bottom of the problem. We often arrive at erroneous conclusions and messages sometimes harmful both to ourselves and to those we judge.

Imagine the Old Doctor in the Warsaw ghetto as he sits at night in a semi-dilapidated building on Dzielna Street, hungry and tired, with a glass of vodka and a piece of black bread. Blackout shades drawn, Korczak bends over his paper in the dim light of a kerosene lamp. He will begin writing, he says, by digging a well:

> I shall try to do something different with the story of my own life.
> Perhaps the idea is good, perhaps it will work. Perhaps this is the
> right way. When you dig a well, you do not start at the deepest end.
> First you break up the upper layer, throw the earth aside, shovelful

after shovelful, not knowing what is underneath, how many tangled roots, what other obstacles, how many stones forgotten and buried by yourself and by others .... Roll up your sleeves. A firm grip on the shovel . . . Let's go! . . . This final work of mine—I must do myself. (Korczak, 2003, pp. 6–7)

In his diary, Korczak reveals his most profound self as he digs towards his well of life from the present to the past, from his adult to childhood years, revealing that child self still residing within him. He uses self-examination as a blueprint for understanding children.

Thus, to understand children, we need to apply his pedagogical approaches and principles of unselfishness, kindness, responsiveness to the needs of others, empathy, and tolerance to our lives as adults to learn more about Korczak; we need to use his example to become better teachers and human beings.

Considerate and so incredibly human in the way he beheld children's lives: listening to what they had to say; watching their body language; paying attention to what they wrote in their diaries from the heart—their own truths, putting together the whole person, not just a part. He listened to and heard their questions and words seemingly unimportant to an adult, but all-encompassing to the child; allowing him or her to be who they were meant to be and not what critical, and sometimes bossy, adults would have them become.

He envisioned the child from the bottom of their own well of feelings and thoughts, taking into account their circumstances and the suffering that was imposed upon them. As Hartman (2009) put it, "It was the children who had to carry the burden of history's atrocities" (p. 13).

Many such children of war bear scars which only grow deeper if not attended to. When children suffer violence in childhood it often affects how they cope as adults. Using myself as an example of a war child, I suffered persecution, physical and mental abuse, abandonment, and loneliness. When other child survivors and I arrived in Canada, nobody was interested or wanted to listen to our devastating experiences. I will never forget how as a child I hung on to my mother's arm in the line-up for the dreaded Umschlagplatz in the Warsaw ghetto where cattle cars stood waiting to send Jewish people—men, women, and little children—to the Treblinka death camp where most would be gassed on arrival. "Mommy, you won't leave me?" I begged my mother, squeezing her arm. "How could I leave you?

Of course not," she replied. Miraculously we were able to escape that deadly line, into a building during a shooting chaos. And we were saved.

Not so Janusz Korczak, and yet we walked along the same road as he did with his 200 orphans to their deaths. When offered a reprieve, he refused, saying that his children needed him. They all perished in the Treblinka death camp, the dire consequence of the most grotesque form of anti-Semitism and racism ever experienced by a civilized society. Korczak still lives in the light that was kindled the day he died a hero.

After we emigrated, I tried to live like my peers whose childhoods in Canada seemed much more peaceful. I squelched within me the child who was racially persecuted, considered low as vermin, and sentenced to death by Hitler, as was every European child in Poland of 1939. As an adult woman, I married, raised children, and yet when something triggered the memory of that violent past, my world fell apart.

Childhood trauma can be unforgiving if not dealt with. Therefore, prevention is necessary in the careful upbringing of children, being mindful of their beginnings and helping them before they become embittered adults. If only we, as adults, could become more like Janusz Korczak by listening to children and adults alike, using the Korczak way. If we re-learned to put our self-interests and judgmental presumptions on the back burner and stopped ignoring those who need a sympathetic listener, and listen to one another with compassion, we would become a fine model for all children. And we could help to heal their wounds before it is too late.

In conclusion, imagine the teacher's classroom as the microcosm of Korczak's orphanage where this great man shaped children's souls. There, the teacher could do the same by treating her pupils with respect and care, and at the same time endowing their minds with the kind of knowledge that is necessary to their well-being and to the well-being of the world—just like Korczak.

References

Hartman, S. (2009). Janusz Korczak's legacy: An inestimable source of inspiration. In Janusz Korczak. *The child's right to respect Janusz Korczak's legacy. Lectures on today's challenges for children* (pp. 13–21). France: Council of Europe Publishing.

Korczak, J. (2003). *Ghetto diary*. New Haven, CT: Yale University Press.

Lifton, B.J. (1988). *The king of children*. New York: Schocken Books.

CHAPTER FIVE

Korczak: From Dijon to Seattle— an Odyssey

Mark Bernheim

JANUSZ KORCZAK WAS unknown to me in 1978. It was the centennial year of what was thought to be his birth and already had been proclaimed by the United Nations as "The Year of Korczak," with postage stamps and ceremonies. It took meeting a pediatrician and a blind refugee in Dijon, France, to begin learning about this extraordinary man and to develop my commitment to writing about him, a goal still active and alive four decades later.

Together with my family, I went to Dijon on a Fulbright academic exchange in late 1977, and, halfway through our year there, welcomed a second daughter born in January 1978 at a maternity clinic in the suburb of Chenove, just outside the city. Like her sister before, this baby needed some immediate orthopedic attention, and we were referred to a local pediatrician who provided the care our daughter needed. By chance, the doctor mentioned that he knew an elderly man living in Dijon who had come from Poland before the Second World War, survived the German occupation as a Jew in hiding, and, now blind, still had some important papers in his possession relating to the wartime atrocities committed in the region. He had lived as a child at a particular orphanage in Warsaw directed by a heroic pediatrician whom our doctor greatly admired from historical knowledge. The doctor suggested I might wish to meet and possibly assist this elderly man with the preservation of the papers.

Thus I came to meet Benjamin Rozenberg. He was small and frail, but animated. He lived alone in a modest apartment in central Dijon, where the neighborhood children took turns helping and guiding him, while others aided in his shopping, meals, and medical care. Dijon had a small Jewish community, but as I am not observant, I had not established contact with them during my stay. With a history in Dijon of nearly 900 years, this community persevered through great struggles and lingering anti-Semitism, something I unfortunately also experienced firsthand with a supervisor at my university.

By the time I met Mr. Rozenberg I had learned to ignore the hostility and simply go about the work I had been sent to do. My sensibilities were heightened by the moment and the cast of characters, and when I met Mr. Rozenberg, I was ready to be enlightened. We spent several afternoons together in his small flat as he told me about Korczak and the Warsaw orphanage where he had been placed as a child. His sight gone, he came to "know" me by touching my face carefully with his hands and holding my shoulder as we spoke, or my elbow when we took a walk outside. Forty years later I have not forgotten the lightness of his touch and the trust he revealed in my willingness to help him.

Korczak was a total novelty to me. I listened as Benjamin told me about the self-governing life the children had, the openness and respect the doctor showed them all. He narrated for me the workings of the children's store, where they managed their own paltry funds and learned thrift and management. He spoke of the wondrous Children's Court where disputes were settled through listening and compromise, treating the children's needs and demands with respect and taken seriously, so that they could rebuild their belief in the remote possibility of justice in a world in which they had learned that the odds would be stacked against them.

He told me about the doctor's assistant, Stefania Wilczyńska, who brought a sense of maternal love and care. She supervised much of their education too, being deeply patient with the needs of each child. Benjamin repeated words he could still remember from those days long past about the need to be autonomous and self-reliant but also tied in duty and obligation to the fellow residents. Every child knew he or she could turn to the doctor or staff at any time day or night.

He remembered the important lessons of learning by doing, observing and practicing and not by passive or rote instruction. What Korczak wished the children to do, he did himself first so that they would see the power of active work well done and mastered first before being expected of others. Benjamin was not religious but absorbed the respect shown by Korczak for those who were, and the sense that although the Jewish children were mandated separate care from Polish Catholic children in other homes, they knew that what they shared was far more important than what kept them apart.

Benjamin still had some frayed papers and notebooks from his previous life there, before he, along with thousands of other Polish Jews, immigrated to France. But more gripping for me was the dusty box of typed and photocopied papers he had me pull out from under his bed. After the war and the liberation of Burgundy by the Allies, the small surviving community had regrouped and one day discovered a cache of materials the retreating Germans had left behind. Pages and pages of records of the roundups and executions of the Dijon community were stapled neatly together, untouched for many years, and entrusted to Mr. Rozenberg to keep. He had one single copy, perhaps 50 pages, many of varying degrees of legibility, some faded and torn, others perfectly clear from the careful typing of 35 years before. He had no family or others to entrust them to. He lived an isolated existence, and the small survivor community also had no idea what to do with the papers. He knew me as a Jewish scholar and academic with a family name familiar in Paris and other metropolitan areas. He entrusted the papers to me to read and pore over, asking me to remember that the present year, 1978, was being commemorated in Poland as Korczak's centennial and in France as well by the many descendants of Polish refugees.

I did take the box carefully, aware of the precious nature of the documents. I read every page and entry over the next weeks. It was clear that in the German occupation of Burgundy, Dijon as its capital had served as a central roundup point for those seized and bound for deportation or worse. We lived in a rental on a main street in town, across the road from an elementary school and playground named for Jules Ferry, a great French educational pioneer and reformer. I saw that it had been used as the holding ground (as known in German, the Umschlagplatz) for people taken from their homes and likely destined for Drancy and Auschwitz.

My three-year-old daughter went to preschool there, learning French in a few weeks and singing the charming songs and rounds every French child knows. Her tiny sister slept in a carriage, loaned to us by a kindly neighbor, on the balcony overlooking the schoolyard. I read the French text transcribed from the German records. In that location, just below my peacefully sleeping daughter, people were forcibly brought, interrogated, mistreated, and tortured, all of it reflected in the papers I held in my hands. One entry was even for a woman, Rose Bernheim (my last name), who had been shot for an unspecified infraction. That was enough for me . . . .

When I returned the papers to Rozenberg, he could not tell which were the originals and which the photocopies, but he had my solemn word I would take them back with great care to the US. Now that I had read what he could recall in his memory from the papers he could no longer see, he continued telling me about the Korczak orphanage of his youth and life there, the level of love and care for children that he never forgot in his darkest days in hiding. I promised him to secure support for the research that would be needed to write a book.

His hands were light and cool on my brow as I bid him farewell en route back to America in the summer of 1978, and he had my word Korczak would not be forgotten. As my own children grew and matured in the safety of our home, they would be treated to that same respect and care, and wherever my career would take me, I would write the book about the life of Korczak as Benjamin Rozenberg had introduced me to it.

Many years later, I gave a copy of the papers to Beate Klarsfeld, the famous Nazi hunter, when she came to our university to speak about the work she and her husband, Serge, did for remembrance and Holocaust history. I gave an additional copy to the US Holocaust Museum in Washington and learned that the Klarsfelds had deposited their copy with the French Holocaust Museum in Paris. Benjamin Rozenberg lived some years after I knew him. A friend, who had spent time in Dijon well after my stay there, later shared with me that Mr. Rozenberg had died peacefully, still cared for by the community until the end.

In the early 1980s I contacted various Korczak Associations in the US and abroad to learn more about the life of the man and those around him. Lacking any knowledge of Polish and holding no contacts in Poland is not the best approach to begin an inquiry or obtain financial support, but I knew I would find a way to stay true to my word to Benjamin. A turning point came in 1988 with another Fulbright award, which sent me to Vienna. I arrived with a manuscript completed in New York with the research assistance of several Polish American and Jewish refugee and medical organizations. In Austria, I found an active Korczak Association, which welcomed me at its meetings, and connections to similar groups in Germany and Holland. My network expanded with associations in France and Switzerland, especially in the French-speaking Geneva region, where the Halperin family became, and still is, a major source of information and linkage to other people working in the field. Meeting them in Geneva led me to important new sources of knowledge and contacts.

My time in Vienna into the early 1990s was stimulating for numerous reasons, as it was the era of the Waldheim presidency and controversy over this diplomat's hidden Nazi connections, which were being unearthed to much resistance. While celebrating the publication of my book, *Father of the Orphans* (1989), I experienced the turmoil of the Waldheim era and its attendant ugliness. Local tabloids proclaimed "another war against Austria by the Jews," and on several occasions I was subjected to hostility from students and others. One evening, at the famed State Opera house, an elderly occupant of the adjoining box suggested that it was time I returned to, as he snarled it, my "home in Israel." Such memories remain, and, although I am not Polish, nor observant, and a third-generation American, the idea of holding fast to the promise made to Rozenberg and the memory of the executed Jews of Dijon took on uninterrupted, even stubborn significance.

I remained as active as I could in Korczak-related scholarship, welcoming the end of the Communist era in Poland. I was pleased to see my biography of him reviewed favorably and its place noted as a more popular and accessible work alongside the masterful and indispensable *The King of Children* by Betty Jean Lifton (1988), which is considered the gold standard for knowledge on him. With university support, I managed a trip to the Kibbutz Lohamei Hagetaot in Israel where memories of Korczak's sole trip to Mandate-era Palestine remain. This site continues to serve as an important resource center for artifacts in connection to Korczak, Stefa Wilczyńska, and the children.

In my own career, I took on other responsibilities related to our university study abroad programs, which came to eclipse my work in the US for long periods of time. We spent years in Italy seemingly far from the subject, but my long-delayed plans came to fruition with an invitation in 2015 to speak on Korczak in Paris at a lycée of the Alliance Israelite. Sadly, the event was scheduled within days of the murderous terrorist attack in January of that year, but the program went on as scheduled. The school building was located just across the street from the scene of the attack, a market now adorned with flowers placed in memory of the lives lost to unspeakable violence. The large groups of French Jewish high school students and the school staff had a deep response to my address. My host teacher had just left the market minutes before after doing her Sabbath shopping; some of the students narrated their own experiences having been hassled on the Metro for wearing Stars of David and covering their heads. Korczak and his work with young people seemed to resound deeply with them.

Later that year, I was invited by the Polish cultural attaché in Washington to visit Warsaw and Krakow on a 10-day research tour sponsored by the government. In the new Poland and reconstituted Warsaw, I spent a remarkable time visiting the new POLIN museum on a private tour, meeting with government officials including Marek Michalak, the Ombudsman for Children's Rights. I spent inspirational time with Marta Ciesielska, Director at the Korczakianum, in the restored orphanage itself. She knew and had read *Father of the Orphans*, and shared with me engrossing materials of all sorts.

One item in particular stood out from our conversation. The famous photo of Korczak outside under trees with the children—included in my biography as well as most other books on him—shows him with one somewhat older girl who stands at the center of the picture and has become an iconic image. Speaking in the dining hall, Marta Ciesielska opened my eyes to another picture of the children seated at a meal. It is one of the last photos ever taken there, and significant because many of the faces can be identified. She showed the same girl seated and recognizable, and explained that she had miraculously survived the war, having left the orphanage with her birth mother before the final round-up in August 1942. They went to Israel, and she lived to old age there under a different name. Late in her life, she agreed to meet with Marta and speaking in Polish, provided a record about her life and times. It is such episodes that make the entire story far more than a legend, but a reality.

After an absence of many years from scholarly gatherings for simple lack of time and other commitments, I took the opportunity to participate in 2018 at the Seattle meeting of Korczak scholars emphasizing his pedagogy in practice. This Seattle conference brought together in North America for the first time a great number of committed people worldwide (Australia, Brazil, Canada, England, France, Israel, Netherlands, Poland, Russia, Switzerland, Tunisia, etc.) for intense discussion and planning. The welfare of children everywhere in the world was on our pages and screens daily. Orphaned by warfare, weakened by starvation and disease, political pawns in struggles to define borders and immigration, matured beyond their years by new standards in media behavior and exposure—a need exists for reflection and action based on standards enunciated by Korczak and put into practice at the Children's Homes a century ago. If adults are resistant to new definitions of identity and diversity, we know that children are the most open to them.

Almost no one who knew or lived with Korczak is alive in the second decade of this millennium. Old borders and systems of government are now down, but new challenges to tolerance and acceptance make their own lines in the sand. I have tried here to sketch an odyssey over 40 years, and it is both personal and I hope more universal than that. I have found it impossible to be objective about Korczak or to stand too far from the subject. His story and his achievements are not about us, but the immense passion and dedication that motivated his life make it impossible—for me—to stand apart, nor am I sure anyone can. That is, the story of Korczak *is* about us and involves us in the world that, in a century since he created the orphanages, still demands that we not separate ourselves lest we end in emptiness. The biography I committed to writing so many years ago continues to develop and will include all the precious information absorbed since the first volume was inspired by the blind immigrant in Dijon. It is, as if seeing in a single photograph a face that now has a name, such that I can and will give other shades and shadows their names too.

References

Bernheim, M. (1989). *Father of the orphans: The story of Janusz Korczak*. New York: E.P. Dutton.

Korczak, J. (2003). *Ghetto diary*. New Haven and London: Yale University Press.

Korczak, J. (2009). The child's right to respect (1928), in *Janusz Korczak's legacy: Lectures on today's challenges*. Strasbourg: Council of Europe.

Korczak, J. (2017). *Les colonies de vacance*. [The holiday colonies.] Paris: Fabert.

Lifton, B. J. (1988). *The king of children: A biography of Janusz Korczak*. New York: Farrar, Straus & Giroux.

Part I: Assignments

1. Review Korczak's life as discussed in this section and identify the most important periods that defined his decision to switch from medicine to education.

2. After you learned about Korczak, what changes do you anticipate in your own approach to students and teaching?

3. What were the main life lessons that Korczak's pupils received in the orphanage? Give examples from interviews with some of his pupils and explain why those lessons were so powerful and personality shaping.

PART II
Advocate and Win:
Korczak as a Champion
of the Rights of the Child

CHAPTER SIX

Starting with the Rights of the Child

Kenneth Bedell

AS WE APPROACH the end of the first quarter of the 21st century, American teachers, administrators, and education policymakers find themselves at odds, with children caught in the middle. This dilemma exists even though there is a clear consensus in each of the three groups regarding the goal of providing all American children, irrespective of family circumstances or history, with the knowledge and skills to contribute to society as engaged and productive citizens. This is the key objective of policymakers from the US Department of Education and a message to every local school board. It is also the desire of every classroom teacher and principal. However, the rhetoric often fails to match the reality of schooling in America. The vast disparity in equal and equitable educational opportunity for children continues to undermine a school system desperately in need of reform, but seemingly resistant to comprehensive change.

This chapter explores how the seeds of our society's continued inability to address these issues is in part a legacy from the progressive educators of the beginning of the 20th century and contrasts these approaches with Korczak's philosophical and pedagogical beliefs.

The Foundational Education Policy—Rights of the Child

Immediately after World War I, progressive leaders like Jane Addams (1860–1935) in the United States and Eglantyne Jebb (1876–1928) in Europe worked hard to relieve the suffering of children. One result of these efforts was the creation of the World Child Welfare Charter, published in 1923 by the International Save the Children Union in Geneva. It emphasized five key principles:

1. The child must be given the means requisite for its normal development, both materially and spiritually.

2. The child that is hungry must be fed, the child that is sick must be nursed, the child that is backward must be helped, the delinquent child must be reclaimed, and the orphan and the waif must be sheltered and succoured.

3. The child must be the first to receive relief in times of distress.

4. The child must be put in a position to earn a livelihood, and must be protected against every form of exploitation.

5. The child must be brought up in the consciousness that its talents must be devoted to the service of its fellow men. (Buck, 2011, p. 89)

Korczak supported the Charter because it described what children are entitled to, as well as the responsibilities of adults, however, it was not a comprehensive statement of the rights of the child. Except for Section 4, a child living in slavery could receive the benefits of all the other sections. Often mistakenly identified as the first statement of the rights of the child, the document is exactly what the title says, a child welfare charter.

Korczak's understanding of the rights of the child was quite different from the adult's responsibility to protect children. Of course, adults need to provide for children; he did this at his orphanage. But that was a responsibility of adults, not a right of the child. Korczak summarized his views on the matter:

> Children, depending on their age, mental development and experience, have certain individual rights, which are uncomfortable for adults, and—therefore—most often not recognized by them. Apart from nourishment and hygiene, children demand freedom to release their excess of vital energy, demand the right to undergo a whole series of experiences, methodically incorporating them into their lives, as well as the right to take initiative when it comes to their own needs. Adults' roles should be limited in many cases to that of understanding guardians, protecting children against any excessively painful results or their experiments. (Medvedeva-Nathoo & Czernow, 2018, p. 158)

Friedrich Froebel, the creator of the kindergarten and an educator admired by Korczak, once said, "Come let us live for our children" (as cited in Hartman, 2009, p. 13). After World War II, most progressive educators adopted Froebel's perspective. They saw the horror of the Nazis putting children to death, but they did not recognize Korczak's message that children should have equal standing with adults.

These are rights of each individual child rather than generalized rights of children. The way Korczak administered the orphanage was based on the rights of the child. And the methods he used as the person responsible for the development (education) of the orphans depended on his understanding of their rights. All of Korczak's teaching and writings make sense only when viewed through the lens of his unswerving commitment to the rights of the child.

Student or Child?

American progressive education focused on the role of the teacher in delivering to the student an experience that would be professional, effective, and egalitarian. After World War II this professionalization of the educator resulted in a focus on curriculum, supervision, and a more efficient schooling process. Korczak had a different approach, which focused on the *child* rather than the student. Unfortunately, the byproduct of these reforms created schools more aligned to the needs of the adults running them, with students efficiently packaged and moved through a factory model year after year. Instead of developing home-school partnerships, parents took on the role of supporting educators in this model. This approach ran contrary to Korczak's advice, as he believed parents and teachers filled complementary roles in the life of a child. He challenged parents and teachers alike to love and respect each child. In fact, it is important to remember Korczak's lack of distinction between what parents do and what teachers or caregivers do. In the 1930s under the alias of "Old Doctor," he gave advice to parents on a radio program that was the same advice he gave in lectures to teachers (Lifton, 2018, pp. 199–208). For Korczak, a child was never a student turned over to professional educators by a parent.

Most importantly, Korczak proposed that our work in education and with children, in general, should grow out of a clear understanding that children deserve to have equal standing with adults. Specifically, he proposed that children have rights deserving respect. Starting with this insight, there are implications for the way we teach, the way educational institutions are structured, and the development of educational policies. Studying Korczak in the 21st century is helpful because he was an innovator in the three areas that correspond to the roles of American educators: classroom teacher, administrator, and policymaker.

Classroom teacher—Child-centered pedagogy. John Dewey (1899) believed that students learn by doing and the desire to learn must come from the child and cannot be imposed by the teacher. He encouraged schools to provide curricula relevant to a student's life while criticizing the schools of his era for dismissing exploration and curiosity (Dewey, 1899, Kindle Edition, sec. 308). Because Dewey (1916) starts with the assumption that "the teacher already knows the things which the student is only learning" (Kindle Edition, sec. 2956), he gives the responsibility for directing learning to the teacher. This contrasts with Korczak's understanding of the relationship between the teacher and the child. Korczak wrote, "Children are not the people of tomorrow, but are people of today. They have a right to be taken seriously, and to be treated with tenderness and respect" (as cited in Hartman, 2009, p. 13).

Korczak directly challenges the role of classroom teachers that American teachers inherited from Dewey and the progressives. Dewey (1899) wrote, "When engaged in the direct act of teaching, the instructor needs to have subject matter at his finger's ends; his attention should be upon the attitude and response of the pupil. To understand the latter in its interplay with subject matter is his task" (Kindle Edition, sec. 1288). Korczak agreed that teachers should give their full attention to the child, but the purpose of the observation is not in order to deliver curriculum effectively. Rather, Korczak wants the teacher to pay attention to the child because "they should be allowed to grow into whoever they were meant to be." He says this because "the unknown person inside each of them is our hope for the future" (Korczak, 2009, p. 19).

School administrators—School discipline. In America, governance and discipline are primarily the responsibility of administrators who determine the style of discipline and the extent to which classroom teachers have a say in what happens in the school. However, individual classroom teachers may have unique approaches to establishing expectations for student behavior within limits. These rules and expectations serve to create a healthy and respectful learning environment. Yet the unspoken message of conforming to a top-down system of management is an ever-present reality for children in schools. Many schools require students to walk through the halls in a single file while maintaining complete silence. In these schools it would be unthinkable if a teacher regularly led students in cheers as they walked through the halls or had races to see who could get to the next activity first.

Like Dewey and other progressives, Korczak observed that if a child feels that the school is imposing unjust or arbitrary expectations, then the child will not engage or learn (Dewey, 1899, Kindle Edition, sec. 1236). Dewey (1916) discussed the need to "direct" students. He stated: "Speaking accurately, all direction is but re-direction; it shifts the activities already going on into another channel. Unless one is cognizant of the energies which are already in operation, one's attempts at direction will almost surely go amiss" (Kindle Edition, sec. 3706–3708). The role of the educator is to manage the redirection of energies to improve behavior. For Dewey (1916), the experience of being part of a school community with others also results in learning proper behavior: "The mind in this sense is the method of social control" (Kindle Edition, sec. 3828).

Korczak empathized with children who rebelled. In part, he saw his pedagogy as a remedy for rebellion. If each child is treated with love and respect, he argued, there is less inclination to rebel. However, as he observed, sometimes a child has experiences outside of the school environment which create rebellion: things like discord at home or insufficient nutrition, insufficient sleep, or illness. Addressing the same issue, Dewey and Korczak came to radically different conclusions regarding rebellious students. Korczak recognized that the problem was not with the child, but with the organization of the institutions that children inhabited. His solution was to treat children "as people of today."

The children played a critical role in managing the day-to-day operation of Korczak's orphanage. There was an elected Children's Parliament and Court. The Collegial Court Code determined possible offenses and punishments. Forgiveness was always a preferred option when the court of child judges determined the verdict. Even the adults, including Korczak himself, could be brought to the court by any child, and be subject to its judgments (Medvedeva-Nathoo & Czernow, 2018, p. 338).

Every effort was made to encourage the administration of the orphanage to share their responsibilities with the children. For example, when new staff came to the orphanage, they were placed on probation. After three months, the orphans voted on whether the staff member would be retained. Korczak promoted his democratic practices when he visited other institutions and in his lectures. He hoped that, in time, these practices would spread to all schools. For Korczak, empowering the child to manage the institutional environment was as important as empowering the child to participate in her own development.

Conclusion

Should Korczak be considered an interesting thinker and a heroic figure in response to the atrocities of the Holocaust? Or should we carefully consider Korczak's ideas and actions as guides for solving the issues facing American education in the 21st century? Another way to phrase the same question is: Are children deserving of love and respect? or Are children immature humans in need of protection and direction by adults?

One way to answer these questions is to consider whether by adopting Korczak's approach to education, the problems with American education could be solved. The internal logic of his educational practices suggests that there is a way forward. His approach, in which parents and teachers both participate in supporting the child, would change parents from consumers of what professional educators offer to full participants in the educational process that requires their support of their children. Classrooms, where children are full participants in their own education, offer the opportunity to motivate children to achieve an education that is relevant to them. Involving students in the maintenance, rulemaking, and discipline of schools addresses a number of issues facing schools. Among them is the problem of disruptive or rebellious students. Reducing the burden of discipline gives adults more time to participate in practices that support children.

Establishing the rights of the child as the foundation for local, state, or national education policy is a project that concerned teachers, administrators, and parents can join forces to accomplish. Since education policy is a political process, political action is necessary to change the foundational assumptions of policy-makers. Because of their training in pedagogical theory and their frustration with the demands placed on classroom teachers, teachers have a unique opportunity to bring leadership in their local setting to a "rights-of-the-child movement."

In the final analysis, a decision to work on a project of convincing school policymakers to make a commitment to the rights of the child is an expression of hope for the future. As Korczak (2009) said in his most famous defense of the rights of the child,

> Years of work have confirmed for me more and more clearly that children deserve respect, trust, and kindness, that it is pleasant to be with them in a cheerful atmosphere of gentle feelings, merry laughter, an atmosphere of strenuous first efforts and surprises, of pure, clear, and heartwarming joys, that working with children in such an atmosphere is exhilarating, fruitful, and attractive. (p. 31)

References

Buck, T. (Ed.). (2011). *International child law* (2nd ed.). New York: Routledge.

Dewey, J. (1899). *The school and society*. (Kindle Version). Retrieved from Amazon.com

Dewey, J. (1916). *Democracy and education* (Kindle Version). Retrieved from Amazon.com

Hartman, S. (2009). Introduction. In *Child's right to respect: Prawo Dzieka do Szacunku* (1929). Strasbourg Cedex, France: Council of Europe Publishing.

Korczak, J. (2009). *Child's right to respect: Prawo Dzieka do Szacunku* (1929). Strasbourg Cedex, France: Council of Europe Publishing.

Lifton, B.J. (2018). *The king of children: A biography of Janusz Korczak*. London and Portland, OR: Vallentine Mitchell.

Medvedeva-Nathoo, O., & Czernow, A.M. (Eds.). (2018). *How to love a child and other selected works* (Vol. 2). London and Chicago: Vallentine Mitchell.

CHAPTER SEVEN

The Rights of the Child and the Order of the Smile: Korczak's Influence in Today's World

Marek Michalak

THE INCREASINGLY COMPLICATED modern world of groundbreaking discoveries has provided enough evidence that science, information technologies, and artificial intelligence alone are insufficient to meet the needs of society. In addition to the vast array of technological advancements, there remains a pronounced need to appreciate the role of moral values. Mahatma Gandhi and Mother Teresa helped to remind us of our purpose on Earth by treating those around them with respect and dignity. Janusz Korczak, too, served as one of these quintessential moral leaders through his strong advocacy for the rights of children and his willingness to sacrifice his own life while remaining true to his principles. His paramount legacy still prevails today.

It was Korczak who, in the period between two world wars in Poland, developed an original concept based on the belief that any child is an autonomous person with his/her own interests, needs, and rights. He also promoted the idea that each child is the subject of care and respect, and that the child's rights and well-being should be honored and protected by law. This concept is the foundation of the modern Convention on the Rights of the Child (1989) initiated by Poland. The Convention is a set of standards for the legal, social, and cultural conditions under which children should develop, and how the relationships between children and adults should be created. Dignity, support, help, care, cooperation with children, recognition of the child's voice and perspective—these values are spelled out in international law enshrined in the Convention, and until this day it remains the most important legal document to protect the rights of all children.

It was also Korczak who helped to transform the understanding of children's rights as a type of human rights, equally significant and important, and dealt with as independent issues of a social, moral, and legal nature. In my opinion, it is one of the most relevant ideas of the past century that has made an impact on nearly all fields of human activity. The Convention has developed into a source of inspiration and has significantly influenced a range of actions taken in order to improve the situation of children around the world. However, it is still not sufficient to cure all the pain that children endure. Rather, the Convention serves as an international framework to effectively oversee activities of various nations to address the needs of children today and tomorrow.

An important element in the fulfillment of Janusz Korczak's legacy was the creation of the only award which young people could grant to adults. Children received a true voice in matters that concern them. It is no coincidence that this distinction was named the Order of the Smile. Everyone knows, although children especially understand, the significance of a genuine smile: honest, kind, joyful, and supportive. Children thirst for a smile as they might thirst for air. A smile costs nothing but gives so much energy, provides optimism, strengthens one's self-esteem, and mobilizes good work. The child needs a smile and has a smile, and it is often the most beautiful and precious gift that children are capable of giving. The importance of smiles is preserved in the people's wisdom in different cultures and lives on through their proverbs and sayings (Czerwińska-Rydel, 2018). For example, "Nothing defends us better than the warmth of a smile" (Mexico); "Everyone smiles in the same language" (United Kingdom); "When you have nothing to offer, give a smile" (China); or " "With a smile on his face a man doubles his capabilities" (Japan).

Janusz Korczak, in referring to the meaning of a smile, gave it a special rank, saying: "When a child smiles, the whole world smiles back."[1] These words can be interpreted differently and imbued with different meanings, such as a special message to adults stating that, by providing a child with a happy and joyful childhood full of smiles, we help this child to develop the best in him/herself; we also help this child to grow into a good and wise adult who is able to create a happy world. Korczak made direct connections between one child's happiness and the happiness of the entire world. After all, it is well known that Korczak looked hopefully to children for the renovation and repair of this world.

The Order of the Smile was initiated in 1967 in an interview with Wanda Chotomska, an outstanding Polish poet and writer, on the occasion of the fifth anniversary of her popular bedtime story *Jacek and Agatka*.[2] The author recounted talking to a sick boy being treated at the rehabilitation sanatorium in Konstancin-Jeziorna near Warsaw, who asked her a question: "Why doesn't the Order of Smile actually exist? It should" (Zdanowska, 1967a). A little later there came an initiative undertaken by a few journalists from "Kurier Polski"[3] and Polish National Television, who together announced a competition for artwork: projects of the Order of the Smile. The most popular and frequent image turned out to be a bright and smiling sun, and the winner was nine-year-old Ewa Chrobak (Zdanowska, 1967b). In addition to the decoration itself, the Chapter of the Order of the Smile was also established, which served as a commission to consider children's nominations. Soon enough the first Knight of the Order of Smile was chosen. It was Doctor Wiktor Dega from Poznań, a world-famous orthopedist, who was recommended as a person who managed to bring back children's smiles even in the midst of their suffering and pain.

An important moment in the history of the Order was the speech of its Chancellor, Cezar Leżeński (1978), at the United Nations Plenary Session in New York, where, among other things, he said:

> I am here before you on the eve of 1979, the International Year of the Child, which will undoubtedly become embedded in the consciousness of all nations as the first step towards the establishment of a universal convention that guarantees a broad spectrum of rights for all children.... Polish children have already made the first step in this direction.... For the first time on such a scale the youngest evaluate their teachers, doctors, parents ... all those who look after them. From among them, they choose those who are their true friends, bring them joy, happiness, best understand their thoughts and the beatings of children's hearts. (Michalak, 2009, pp. 228–229).

The consequence of this speech was the United Nations' decision to internationalize the Order of the Smile and keep it as the only decoration in the world awarded to adults but submitted by children. The composition of the Chapter was extended to include representatives of all continents. This beautiful idea, based on Janusz Korczak's legacy, continues to this day.

The Order of the Smile is an institution and a phenomenon. There are parks, streets, squares, and most importantly, schools and other organizations named after the Order of the Smile or its Knights. There is a monument to the Order of the Smile and the Order of the Smile Museum, which was opened in Rabka, Poland, in 1996. In 2003, after an International Charter of the Order of the Smile session took place outside the Warsaw headquarters in Swidnica, the Child Friendship Center was founded there while the town itself was officially proclaimed the "Capital of Children's Dreams," and September 21, 2003, was declared The Order of the Smile Children's Day.[4]

The Order of the Smile has now been awarded to over 1,000 personalities from all over the world: the popes—John Paul II and Francis, the 14th Dalai Lama, Queen Sylvia of Sweden, Nelson Mandela, Mother Teresa of Kolkata, Oprah Winfrey, Steven Spielberg, J.K. Rowling, Peter Ustinov, Astrid Lindgren, Marta Santos Pais, and three surviving (at the time) "Korczak's children": Itzchak Belfer, Szlomo Nadel, and Izaak Skalka, to name just a few.

In fact, I had the pleasure of meeting the last three in Israel in 2013 during the ceremony awarding them the Order of the Smile.[5] They all reminisced that their Dad, as they used to refer to Korczak, probably never slept or rested. He was always working. Yet he always had time for each of them. More so, when spoken to, every child got the impression of being the center of the world. It was Korczak's method to fully focus his attention on *his* children. Another pupil, Alina Edestin, remembers, "Janusz Korczak was certainly a wizard, who easily won children's hearts. Each gesture and look was radiant with deep, peaceful, and true love. Children immediately felt safe and trusting" (Edestin, 1981). He was consistent and demanding, and yet full of understanding and respect for children and their needs. First and foremost, he challenged himself before challenging others.

More and more often today, children fall victim to complex social changes, as indicated by the growing number of conflicts involving them. This includes matters on an international scale, such as the provision of health care, means of sustenance, violence, kidnapping, and intricate matters related to property ownership. Of great concern is the lack of effective action taken in defense of children, who are victims of armed conflicts, genocide, or ethnic cleansing. Regrettably, in many parts of the world children are still the subjects of trafficking and economic and sexual exploitation.

The types and scale of children's problems have caused the protection of children's rights internationally to become heavily exposed to the forum of the United Nations. Hence, the proposal submitted by the Polish Ombudsman for Children was to equip the Committee on the Rights of the Child to receive and process individual complaints. As a result of these efforts, the United Nations General Assembly adopted the Third Optional Protocol to the Convention on the Rights of the Child (OP3 CRC; 2011) on a communications procedure in December 2011. The Convention itself is a living instrument and may not be treated as the last stage in the development of the rights of the child and his/ her protection. As such, it does not contain a comprehensive catalogue of the rights of the child, which are continuously developed. The Convention remains a living document not only to protect those rights but also to make adults recognize the value of their own childhood, and thus the humanity in the process of peaceful and friendly coexistence.

One recommendation is to form institutions of children's rights—essentially, appointing ombudspersons for children to serve as independent bodies equipped with the authority to effectively protect the rights set out in the Convention on the Rights of the Child. I strongly believe that the thoughts and ideas of Janusz Korczak will become a lesson for us all—a moment of contemplation about the rights of the children; the condemnation of crimes, violence, and exploitation; and that we should better grasp the meaning of what he had once said: "Childhood years are real life, and not merely a preamble."

References

Czerwińska-Rydel, A. (2018). *Medal for a smile . . . and something more—children have a voice!* Lodz, Poland: Lodz Publishing.

Edestin, A. (1981). Uśnij, moja córeczko [Sleep, my little daughter]. In *Wspomnienia o Januszu Korczaku [Memoirs about Janusz Korczak]*. Warsaw: Nasza Księgarnia, p. 43.

Michalak, M. (2009). With bowl and silence made sense. In C. Leżeński & W. Piątek, *Life Is Full of Punch Lines*. International Chapter of the Order of Smile, Warsaw.

UN Human Rights Council. (2011, July 14). *Optional Protocol to the Convention on the Rights of the Child on a Communications Procedure : resolution / adopted by the Human Rights Council*, 14 July 2011, A/HRC/RES/17/18, available at: https:// www.refworld.org/docid/4e72fbb12.html.

Zdanowska, Z. (1967a). Five years of a cheerful smile. *Kurier Polski*, 30.09 / 1.10.1967, No. 231, p. 4.
Zdanowska, Z. (1967b). 44 thousand submitted projects. Order of Smile. Ewa Chrobak—laureate of the competition. *Kurier i Telewizji, Kurier Polski*, 28 / 29.10.1967, No. 255, p. 1.

Endnotes

1 These words were commonly attributed to Janusz Korczak, but no confirmation was found in the Korczak archives.
2 Jacek i Agatka [Jacek and Agatka] is the first nighttime television show for children in Poland, which was broadcast every evening at 7:20 PM (Television Poland) from 1962 to 1973. The author of the program was a well-known writer, Wanda Chotomska (later she, herself, was awarded the Order of the Smile). The title characters are two puppets, which had heads made of wood and were put on the animators' black-gloved index fingers. The designer of the puppets was Adam Kilian (he also became Knight of the Order of Smile). Jacek and Agatka were voiced by Zofia Raciborska.
3 *Kurier Polski* was created in 1957 and was considered the key mass media body of the Democratic Party of Poland.
4 For more details check the following link: https://en.wikipedia.org/wiki/Order_of_the_Smile
5 See more in Michalak, M. (2013). Ma moc serdeczności [A whole host of warmth]. In T. Belerski, *Kawalerowie Orderu Uśmiechu* [Knights of the Order of the Smile]. Warsaw: Meissner & Partners, pp. 11–13.

CHAPTER EIGHT

Two UN Conventions and Their Fathers: Janusz Korczak and Raphael Lemkin

Ewa Łukowicz-Oniszczuk

Introduction

THE PRIMARY AIM of this chapter is to compare two outstanding personalities of the 20th century who outlined the new standards of human rights' understanding: Janusz Korczak (1878–1942) and Raphael Lemkin (1900–1959). Both were ahead of their times, proposing a novel perception of human rights. Korczak questioned the traditional conviction that a child was owned by his or her parents, and that consequently children's rights were limited by parental power. He introduced the concept of a child as an autonomous person with a full range of rights. As is now well known, Korczak's teachings, publications, and work inspired the current shape and content of the UN Convention on the Rights of the Child (1989).

Raphael Lemkin is said to have expanded the idea of human rights from individual rights to group rights. It was Lemkin who coined the term "genocide" and drafted the text of the UN Convention on the Prevention and Punishment of the Crime of Genocide (1948).

Using comparative analysis and close reading of primary and secondary sources,[1] I present several striking similarities between their concepts in an attempt to find common roots or inspirations for their way of thinking and acting. I also strive to show how to unravel and counter some present-day tendencies that constitute a real threat to global peace and, finally, how to use Korczak's and Lemkin's legacy in this regard.

In the Beginning

Let me take you back to the Jan Kazimierz University of Lvov (now Lviv, Ukraine) around the year 1920, when a young law student wondered why a murderer would be considered a criminal and prosecuted, while representatives of state authorities who exterminated millions of human beings were not charged with any crime. The reason, indisputable to most law theoreticians at that time, remained the following: there was no such crime indicated in the international law due to the principle of sovereignty of a state which consequently allowed the state authorities to own the right to determine the lives and deaths of their own citizens. Evident to almost everyone else, this explanation was not so obvious to the young and idealistic man, Raphael Lemkin. Starting from the early 1930s, and on many occasions, he voiced the need to redefine international law and argued: "Sovereignty of state implies conducting an independent foreign and internal policy, building schools, construction of roads, all types of activities directed toward the welfare of people. Sovereignty cannot be conceived as the right to kill millions of innocent people" (Lemkin, 2013, p. 20).

At almost the same time Janusz Korczak (2018a) questioned another traditional principle, obvious to people throughout the centuries, that children "belong" to their parents as some sort of property, stating:

> The cruel but candid law of Greece and Rome permitted killing children… In seventeenth century Paris, older children were sold to beggars… Not so long ago. To this day children are cast aside if they get in the way. The quantity of illegitimate, abandoned, neglected, exploited, depraved, and abused children is growing. (p. 320)

Korczak was deeply disappointed with the Declaration of the Rights of the Child (1924) adopted by the League of Nations as he expected to see real guarantees of children's rights there, including respect for their dignity and physical integrity. Korczak (2018a) clearly explained his position: "The lawmakers of Geneva confused obligations and rights. The tone of the Declaration is one of persuasion, not of insistence" (p. 320).

As indicated in the chapter title, I call Korczak and Lemkin fathers of these two UN Conventions, but not in the same way. Lemkin was the driving spirit and the author of the text of the so-called Genocide Convention and its main advocate,[2] whereas Korczak was an inspiring soul for the UN Convention on the Rights of a Child (besides, the latter being a Polish initiative). In one of his articles, Korczak (2018a) expresses his conviction that "a court can become the seed of a child's equal rights, it leads toward a constitution . . .—a declaration— of the rights of the child. The child has a right to have its affairs taken seriously, to have them weighed fairly" (p. 207).

Entering Common Ground

Except for the obvious connection that both Korczak and Lemkin were Polish Jewish intellectuals, there were other numerous striking similarities between them. It is not only that their views, dreams, and fears followed the same path in spirit, but their actual paths in Warsaw in the 1930s could have crossed as well. We can imagine them walking the same streets, entering the same libraries, cafes, and parks. Both gave lectures at the Free Polish University, worked in the municipal judiciary, visited Warsaw University, and published.

Another common point is that they both devoted their lives to one consuming passion. As a result, both remained single—consciously deciding to never set up a family. In his autobiography Lemkin (2013) explains: "I have no time for married life, or the funds to support it (p. 163)." He confessed: "I was condemned to loneliness . . . for I felt that only the lonely person can reach the borders. I will devote the rest of my life to my work—outlawing the destruction of people" (p. 66).

Life mission. The formative event in Lemkin's life was his debate with a law professor at John Casimir University, where he raised the question: "How could killing 1.2 million Armenians by a state go unpunished? If killing one man is a crime, why is killing of millions legal?" The professor explained that: "Rule of state's sovereignty gives it the right to do whatever it wishes with its citizens, and any interference from the outside would be treated as meddling in state's internal affairs" and added: "If you knew something about international law . . ." (Lemkin, 2013, p. 163). Lemkin decided not only to learn more but also to act on his new knowledge.

Korczak's life mission was evolving gradually—his first bewilderment at the world's injustice started when, as a boy, he witnessed discrimination towards the weakest and unprotected part of mankind. However, according to his biographer, Joanna Olczak Ronikier, a final decision to sacrifice his life to children was made after a visit to a Warsaw orphanage in 1909 where Korczak met Stefa Wilczyńska, his future supporter and partner in creating and managing "Dom Sierot." Much later, in a letter to Mietek Zylbertal Korczak (2008) recollected the exact moment when he "decided not to set up a family. . . . A slave has no right to his own children. A Polish Jew under Russian tsar rule . . . For a son I've chosen an idea to serve a child and its needs" (p. 222). The culmination of this idea is clarified in his *Ghetto Diary*: "I exist not to be loved and admired, but myself to act and love. It is not the duty of those around to help me but I am duty-bound to look after the world, after man" (Korczak, 2003, p. 69).

Lemkin's lonely crusade against barbarism, lasting from 1930 until his death, gained momentum after he successfully completed a degree in law, wrote his doctoral thesis, and became involved in a global movement to codify international penal law. It came to his attention that in order to protect civilians, the existing law penalized only crimes committed during wartime, thus, for example, blocking any possibility to persecute the Nazis for their actions in 1933–1939 in prewar Germany. As a Polish member of the Codification Commission, Lemkin proposed a new jurisdiction in international law to prevent and punish "mass destruction of millions." Being also involved in the works of the Polish committee on Codification of Laws (Penal Section), he insisted on introducing an article prosecuting hate speech and propaganda inciting violence.

In 1946, residing in the United States after his escape from Poland, Lemkin coined a new term, "genocide"—mass murder with "an aim of annihilating the group or nation."[3] Aware of the existing law shortcomings, Lemkin (1946) provides explanations in his paper in *American Scholar*: "It would be impractical to treat genocide as a national crime, since by its very nature it is committed by a state or by powerful groups. . . . A state would never prosecute a crime instigated by itself" (p. 228).

Not far from Lvov, where young Lemkin was observing the tragedy of the Polish-Soviet War in 1920 and even working as a volunteer in a sanitary unit, Korczak was participating in the same war drafted as a doctor and facing horrible military atrocities mainly affecting civilians: children and women.

The acknowledgment of power of education. This is another shared belief between Korczak and Lemkin, who both cherished wisdom and learning. As educators, they promoted and practiced an interdisciplinary approach and a dialogue (similar to Socrates) as a primary type of communication between students/children and teachers/adults.

Korczak (2018b) promoted child-friendly pedagogy and education based on participation, believing that ethics was more important than mere facts. As a veteran of several wars, he kept questioning why education was of less value than any armed conflict: "Everywhere armies cost more than schools, scrap iron more than future citizens, future people" (p. 112).

Criticizing contemporary education, Korczak (2018b) described schools as "educational prisons of 'civilized' Europe" where "children wait for years for a piece of paper which is to prove their loyal maturity," whereas "schools ought to be a smithy where the holiest watchwords are forged, all that is life-giving ought to flow through them—it should clamour the loudest for human rights, condemn . . . the quagmire of humanity" (p. 113).

Addressing pedagogues, he called for an interdisciplinary approach and the necessity to search for answers "not merely in psychology, but rather in books of medicine, in sociology, ethnology, history, poetry, criminology, in the prayer as well as training manuals" (p. 318). His belief in the false nature of one-size-fits-all approach was never shaken.

Similarly, when recalling his experience as a tutor at Yale University, Lemkin (2013) stated: "Although my class was for law students, I took an interdisciplinary approach and introduced concepts from psychology, sociology, anthropology and even economics…. I didn't impose my knowledge upon them. They arrived at their ideas by themselves under my direction" (p. 181). While drafting the text of the Genocide Convention, Lemkin included in it a requirement that contracting parties should

> take certain measures in the education and cultural fields to prevent antagonisms and tensions which may lead to genocide. The undefined measures were to include instruction in the schools and the systematic use of the mass media such as press, radio and films. (as cited in Korey, 2001, p. 41)

Lastly, both Korczak and Lemkin shared their admiration and knowledge of Johann H. Pestalozzi's pedagogical approaches. More so, Lemkin's own up-bringing was inspired by this great Swiss luminary as his mother was a follower of Pestalozzi's ideas.

On culture. Another common feature is their understanding of the role of culture. Korczak and Lemkin highly valued culture and cultural diversity, considering the latter one of the world greatest treasures. Korczak was seeking inspiration not only in Judaism, but also in ancient Greek humanities, Hin-duism, Christian thought, and theosophy. In the most tragic moments of his life, he looked for hope in the depths of culture: when seeking refuge in an imaginary planet Ro, or approaching the philosophical drama "Post Office" by Rabindranath Tagore. (For more details see the chapter by Shlomi Doron.)

As much as Korczak, Lemkin also treated culture as a hallmark of human-ness, while both believed that the world would survive only if culture prevailed in it. Lemkin considered cultural needs as vital, no less important for people than their basic physiological needs. Thanks to his knowledge of other cultures and the ability to speak 11 languages, Lemkin could find common ground with people from all over the world.

In his autobiography Lemkin stated that the destruction of any particular group's art and cultural heritage would result in this group's spiritual death. His paper "Genocide" (Lemkin, 1946) has the following revelations:

> [H]ow impoverished our culture would be if the peoples doomed
> by Germany, such as Jews, had not been permitted to create the
> Bible or to give birth to an Einstein, a Spinoza; if the Poles had
> no opportunity to give to the world a Copernicus, a Chopin, a
> Curie; the Czechs—a Huss, a Dvorak; the Greeks—a Plato and
> a Socrates. (p. 3)

Against discrimination. Korczak perceived a psychosis of detecting dif-ferences between races and peoples as an entirely anti-scientific uproar that resulted in dividing, stirring up discord, and setting people against each other. In an article published in *Jewish Monthly* he wrote:

I've read about attempts to study intelligence of Negroes and Europeans on one island; the Whites had no particular advantage. But the Dark Ages may go on a long time, with their lack of understanding, their passions and wars . . . . Such simple thing is . . . the hardest to explain: that all people are equal that they are all brothers. (Korczak, 2018b, p. 174)

In accord with the above come Lemkin's notes taken immediately after his arrival in the United States:

I saw for the first time, in the restrooms of the station, the inscription: "For Whites" and "For Colored." These intrigued me, and I innocently asked the Negro porter if there were special toilets for Negros. He gave me a puzzled look, mixed with hostility, and did not answer . . . . I understand now that he must have thought I was making fun of him . . . . I remembered that in Warsaw there was one Negro who was employed as a dancer in a popular nightclub . . . . Everyone enjoyed his dancing and tried to invite him for drinks . . . . But toward the Jews, there was not the same friendliness; there were three million of them—in the trades, in the professions, and their competition was felt. (Lemkin, 2013, p. 100)

Double identity. Both Lemkin and Korczak cherished and preserved their double identity, being ready to fight for their country, although remaining pacifists. Neither of them renounced their roots, even when it could become a life-saving decision. They regarded themselves as Jews and Poles, emphasizing the fact that they were Polish citizens of Jewish descent. In his writings and pedagogical work Korczak tried to empower Poles to study and understand Jewish culture, just like his father and grandfather tried to close the gap between Poles and Jews. Korczak (1994) believed in the necessity to raise a new generation free from racial bias, in the spirit of tolerance. Happy to work with both Polish and Jewish children, he announced: "We are all brothers, sons of the same soil . . . . Why not work together?" (p. 222).

In the spirit of democratic, enlightened thought. Another common ground is Korczak's and Lemkin's upbringing in the humanistic, open spirit. Both

could be called the children of an enlightened democratic spirit of their time—
driven by works and ideals of contemporary progressive thinkers. Both worked at
the Free Polish University in Warsaw, together with many outstanding academics,
Lemkin being a lecturer in Comparative Law at the Institute of Criminology,
while Korczak taught in the School of Education and Social Work. Both were
also strongly impacted by the university's basic principles: to respect the dignity
of every human being and to display solidarity with any human suffering.

Another interesting similarity is their talent to communicate, convince,
and empathize. Korczak is known to perceive and describe reality from the
point of view of a child, while Lemkin identified himself with the oppressed
ones. Both were extremely sensitive, one might even call them "oversensitive";
and both cherished nature in all its forms. In his autobiography Lemkin (Freize,
2013) wrote: "I did not differentiate at that time among human beings, animals
and birds .... The conviction that I was saving a life made me happy" (p. 18).

Last but not least, both are said to have been skillful actors with a good
sense of humor which they used as a helpful tool in life and work. Korczak
engaged humor in many of his writings, radio programs and articles, and in his
work with children. Lemkin made use of his sense of humor when championing
for the Genocide Convention. His talent for acting saved his life when he was
in the custody of the Bolsheviks.

Prophecies and Lessons to Learn

Looking back on what happened in Korczak's and Lemkin's lifetime and in
how many ways they predicted it, we have all the rights to call them "prophets."
Korczak tried to alarm the world as early as the 1930s. Predicting a disaster, he
wrote a drama, *Senate of Lunatics*, a prophetic warning showing that humanity
was on the verge of a catastrophe since the madmen ruled the world. In 1937,
Korczak (2008) bitterly stated: "It hurts so much when in our times a poison is
oozing its venom [of hatred].... Evil is growing and I'm so powerless. Isn't there
any chance to extinguish the world fire? (p. 222).

Being called an insistent prophet, Lemkin (2013) is also full of grave mis-
givings about the future, as he was well aware of the Nazis' theory and barbaric
practice. He clearly expressed it in his autobiography after the Nuremberg Trial:

"The Allies decided their case against a past Hitler but refused to envisage future Hitlers... to prevent and punish future crime." He is said to "possess a vision that could grasp the potential of the Nazis to inflict unprecedented enormities upon ethnic minorities" (p. 118).

When in the United States, he continued his fight to stop genocide. During WWII Lemkin (Lemkin, 2013) wrote: "Hitler was one of the few statesmen in history who proclaimed his intentions many years before he took power. Yet the statesmen of the democracies either did not read him or did not believe him" (p. 76). He explained the reasons why genocide was so easy to commit and so difficult to prevent: "because people do not want to believe it until after it happens" (p. 113) and also due to the fact that "reality of genocide is against nature, against logic, against life itself" (p. 52).

Lemkin (Lemkin, 2013) wondered why the Allies refused to make known that "the execution of nations and races had already begun" and called it "the silence of murder" (p. 117). Indeed, cases of the 20th and 21st centuries' genocides show that even after the crime was committed, it happens to be denied and suppressed—there is no readiness to call it genocide.

More recently, we keep hearing numerous warnings about the growth of dangerous trends. For example, Andrew Nagorski (2012) claims that words do have a meaning, and it is a grave mistake to disregard extremists. Similarly, Timothy Snyder (Snyder, 2017) emphasizes that people need to realize the rulers who came to power through certain institutions may change or destroy those very institutions. An increasing number of voices are alerting the world to the growing danger of fascism and calling for a dialogue as a primary way of countering nationalism and inequalities (e.g., Bauman, 2017; Levitsky & Ziblatt, 2018; Riemen, 2018).

Conclusion

Legal, international institutionalization of the progressive visions of Korczak and Lemkin, which influenced our perception of human rights, enabled the next stage in the attempt to develop a humanistic approach toward individuals, as well as groups of people and nations. It is our role to work out contemporary standards and mechanisms of an implementation of those standards, since peace is unimaginable without a respect for human rights.

In summing up what these two heroes did while introducing the concept of human rights, we can recognize their fundamental role. Their contribution still serves as a powerful inspiration to advocates of human rights and researchers. With their own examples and lives they proved that openness to other cultures and education for peace can protect the world from violence and war. This message is especially meaningful now with the revival of nationalism and xenophobia. Nationalism, which triggers the desire to restore an extreme notion of state's sovereignty and promotes a supranational interest over universal values was a target of Lemkin's lifelong fight. Similarly, Korczak (2018a) steadily confronted nationalism and also an extreme understanding of parental custody expressed in the phrase: "My child is my property: hands off!" (p. 310).

The concepts and work of Janusz Korczak and Raphael Lemkin can be perceived as specific peace projects rooted in the conviction that there is no other way to lay foundations for a better society than through changes in law and education for peace—education providing young generations with good living conditions and raising them in a humanistic, democratic, and open spirit.

References

Bauman, Z. (2017). *Retrotopia*. Cambridge: Polity Press.

Doron, S. (2011). Learning to accept the angel of death with equanimity: Tagore and Korczak in the Warsaw ghetto. In *Rabindranath Tagore: A timeless mind. Commemorating the 150th Birth Anniversary of Rabindranath Tagore*. London: Tagore Center, pp. 74–84.

Irvin-Erickson, D. (2017). *Raphaël Lemkin and the concept of genocide*. Philadelphia: University of Pennsylvania Press.

Korczak, J. (1994). *Dzieła Tom 3. Wolumin 2. Publicystyka społeczna (1898–1912)*. (Works Volume 3, Articles on social issues (1898–1912). Warsaw: Latona.

Korczak, J. (1996). *Dzieła Tom 6. Sława. Opowiadania (1898–1914)*. (Works, Volume 6, Fame. Stories (1898–1914). Warsaw: Latona.

Korczak, J. (2003). *Ghetto diary*. New Haven, CT: Yale University Press.

Korczak J. (2008). *Pisma rozproszone. Listy 1913–39*, Tom 14, *Z listu do Mieczysława Zylbertala* (Collected writings. Letters 1913–39, Volume 14. Letter to Mieczysław Zylbertal), May 23, 1937, p. 222 (author's translation).

Korczak, J. (2018a). *How to love a child and other selected works*, Vol. 1. London and Chicago: Vallentine Mitchell.

Korczak J. (2018b). *How to love a child and other selected works*, Vol. 2. London and Chicago: Vallentine Mitchell.

Korey, W. (2001). *An epitaph for Raphael Lemkin.* New York: The Jacob Blaustein Institute.

League of Nations. (1924). *Geneva Declaration of the Rights of the Child,* September 26.

Lemkin, E. (2013). *Totally unofficial: The autobiography of Raphael Lemkin.* Frieze, D.-L. (Ed.). New Haven and London: Yale University Press.

Levitsky, S., & Ziblatt, D. (2018). *How democracies die.* New York: Crown.

Nagorski, A. (Interviewee), Margaret Warner (PBS book conversation interviewer). (2012). Hitlerland: American Eyewitnesses to the Nazi Rise to Power (PBS series episode). In *PBS News Hour.* Retrieved from https://www.pbs.org/newshour/show/americans-with-a-front-row-seat-to-the-rise-of-hitler

Olczak-Ronikier, J. (2011). *Korczak: Próba biografii.* Warszawa: Wydawnictwo W.A.B.

Riemen, R. (2018). *To fight against this age: On fascism and humanism.* New York: W.W. Norton & Company.

Snyder, T. (2017). *On tyranny: Twenty lessons from the twentieth century.* New York: Tim Duggan Books.

Endnotes

1 Mainly vast pedagogical literature by Korczak, legal writings and an autobiography by Lemkin, as well as biographical, pedagogical, legal and human rights studies.

2 Lemkin spent the rest of his life trying to make this document part of the international law. For this work he was several times nominated for the Nobel Peace Prize. In the recommending letter to the Nobel Prize Committee in 1951 Harvard professor Paul A. Freund wrote: "The entire campaign [for the Genocide Convention] was carried by Dr. Lemkin on a voluntary basis in the pattern of personal crusade." In Freund's opinion, the Convention "is a very important milestone in the development of International Law and a vital step in securing International Peace" (*An Epitaph for Raphael Lemkin,* The Jacob Blaustein Institute, p. 57).

3 Similar to Socrates, Lemkin was convinced that to be able to understand something, you need to call it by its proper name. Before Lemkin invented the word "genocide," Churchill called mass murder a "crime without a name."

CHAPTER NINE

Echoes from Korczak: Children's Participation Today

Ewa Jarosz

DURING THE LAST decade the number of children participating in social actions and making decisions concerning themselves has dramatically increased and become the subject of different studies. While some authors still use the phrase "children's participation" (Lansdowne, 2010; Thomas, 2002), others prefer the term "active citizenship of children" (Cockburn, 2013). However, the underlying concept remains unchanged: testifying to the importance of the child's subjectivity.

From the moment of its approval in 1989, The Convention on the Rights of the Child (United Nations, 1989) has been actively promoting the view of a child as a social actor entitled to have his/her voice and the right to decision making, social activities, and political participation (Cockburn, 2013; Lansdowne, 2010). Today, children are more widely recognized and respected as social activists, reviewers of social and political decisions, equal partners with adults, and researchers of their own reality (Coleman, 2010; Dahl, 2014; Wyness, 2012).

Tracing the Roots Back to Janusz Korczak

The idea of children's citizenship was raised at least as far back as the 18th century in the works of Kant, Hegel, and Rousseau, who were all protagonists of the view of a child as an equally valid citizen. Later on, Montessori and Dewey also reiterated the importance of children's rights (Milne, 2013). Some modern researchers concentrate on indicators of children's activities as clear signs of their participation, for example, in such social acts as strikes for shorter school hours or for banning corporal punishment in schools (Tisdall, 2015).

This chapter (in its longer version) has been originally published in *Polish Journal of Educational Studies*, 2018, vol. I, pp. 33-50.

Apart from the above notable thinkers and practitioners, I argue that Janusz Korczak remains the founder of the modern concept of children's participation. He was indeed the first who provided an overall description of the child's right to participate in social life. He also emphasized the value of children's freedom, subjectivity, and potential to have one's own voice and to make reasonable choices. Korczak was among the first who recognized a child to be a full-fledged citizen regardless of age (Cockburn, 2013; Krappmann, 2013; Milne, 2013).

In this latter sense, Korczak's approach influenced the development of a contemporary concept of children's citizenship, and serves as a reminder that every child receives an undeniable right for citizenship at birth confirmed by many years of Korczak's practice (Krappmann, 2013; Milne, 2013; Mitchell, 2015). To this day his work with children is considered the first experiment of social participation by children and the implementation of genuine democracy in an educational context (Milne, 2013).

From Korczak to Modern Children's Participation

In this chapter I discuss well-documented, but less well-known, views held by Korczak regarding children's participation and show their place and meaning in our modern understanding of children's rights.

Respect child's subjectivity and his/her voice. For Korczak, the foundation of building relationships with children was to respect their subjectivity, which meant listening to the child and acknowledging his or her point of view. He believed in a child's ability to present reasonable opinions, and make constructive choices and responsible decisions. Korczak (1984) wrote: "The child is a rational being. He appreciates the needs, difficulties and impediments in his life" (vol I, p. 76), and he continues, "...the child...is able to consider the serious problems of adults" (vol. I, p. 128). Korczak demanded the recognition of a child's point of view.

This thought is clearly expressed in the most fundamental way in Article 12 of the CRC (United Nations Convention on the Rights of the Child, 1989) (with regard to children's participation):

> States Parties shall assure to the child who is capable of forming
> his or her own views the right to express those views freely in all

matters affecting the child, the views of the child being given due weight in accordance with the age and maturity of the child.

For Korczak, respecting a child's voice was equal to providing the child's need for recognition. He emphasized that every "child wants to be treated seriously..." (1984, vol. I, p. 191). Modern research supports the necessity of recognition as a crucial developmental experience for children, the lack of which causes negative individual and social consequences in the future (Graham, Fitzgerald, Smith, & Taylor, 2010).

Children as advisers and reporters of their lives. Korczak (1984) was indeed a pioneer in understanding the importance of recognizing children's own voices in solving their problems. He considered children to be the best experts on their lives. On behalf of the children he commented: "If grown-ups asked us, we could often advise well. We know better, what we suffer from, ... we do know ourselves better" (vol. III, p. 417).

There is strong research evidence today that supports the necessity to involve children themselves in exploring different problems that affect them and—even more—to encourage children's participation as co-researchers or leading researchers (Dahl, 2014; Hart, 1992). One example is child journalism using diverse media formats, including cyberspace. But originally it started with Korczak and his *Little Review*, a popular publication from 1926 until 1939, with a circulation of about 50,000, being probably the first children's newspaper in the world where children posted their stories, described existing problems, and reported various events. Such and similar activities represent the sphere of informal and natural children's participation in developing their social lives, sharing stories, and creating their own culture.

Children are capable of self-governance. Korczak (1984) was a true believer in self-governance and tried to provide his charges with every opportunity to practice it on a daily basis (vol. III, pp. 223–228). He went even further by calling for self-determination. His orphans had the power and space where they could decide on their own and govern themselves. And they really did it, organizing various activities and participating in them without being controlled or censored by adults.

Today, self-governance initiated and led by children, remains the core of our understanding of children's participation. Comparing Korczak's vision with modern taxonomies of children's participation we find a number of similarities, and self-governance is often placed at the top. Among examples is the classic Hart's Ladder of Participation entitled "Child initiated, shared decisions with adult" (Hart, 1992, p. 4), Treseder's (1997) model "Child initiated and directed," Lansdowne's (2005) model "Child-led participation," Davis's Matrix (2009), and Wong and Zimmerman (2010), to name just a few. However, the children's activity in autonomous child-led organizations at local, national, and international levels stands out as the most efficient (Johnson, 2009). And again, it was Korczak who called for children to unite and form their own international associations that would provide all young people in the world with equal rights.

Participation and self-governance as ways to develop citizenship skills. Korczak believed that a child is able to develop his or her social competencies, citizenship skills, and social engagement through practice. To familiarize children with citizenship activities and to practice social participation without direct control from adults, Korczak created such special tools as the Children's Parliament, Court of Peers, and the newspaper along with a number of others less known. These tools helped children to acquire self-discipline, and self-control, and to foster cooperation. These activities were also instrumental in developing children's skills of predicting the consequences of their decisions and actions.

Modern educational practice is hardly different from Korczak's ideals. To this day we consider children's active participation an important goal and a valuable result of any successful citizenship education (Cockburn, 2013). It is also recognized as a strategy and a method to develop children's skills for citizenship and social maturity. The research shows that practicing participation remains the most effective way for children to reach the highest possible level of citizenship as an adult (Levy, 2016).

A child is already a citizen. "Children are not the people of tomorrow, but people of today" (Korczak, 1994, p. 226). As stated earlier in this chapter, Korczak considered every child a full-fledged member of society, and as such s/he should possess social entitlements similar to adults. Thus, in Korczak's view, a child not only had the right to be heard and make decisions, but also the right to participate in different social actions—providing critical opinions, composing and sharing information, etc. The miniature democratic society created by Korczak in his orphanages allowed its members full access to multiple "citizenship means" and institutions.

Comparing this practice with the children's rights described in Articles 12–17 of the CRC, we find a number of similarities among the social activities offered to children by Korczak nearly a hundred years ago. For example, in Article 17, "the child has access to information and material from a diversity of national and international sources, especially those aimed at the promotion of his or her social, spiritual and moral well-being and physical and mental health."

But what is particularly important, Korczak (1928) actually proclaimed a child as "already a resident, citizen . . . . Not will he be, but already is" (p. 2). While the terms "citizen" and "citizenship" were not central categories in Korczak's philosophy of education, he is still considered to be the first who recognized this particular social status of a child. This approach echoes modern discourse on children's participation where the terms "children's citizenship" and/or "active citizenship of children" remain quite popular (Cockburn, 2013; Lister, 2007; Milne, 2008).

Child's participation and/or children's participation: individual and collective. Korczak presents us with a dual understanding of children's participation in social life. He used to write of an *individual* child as a citizen and a community member, underlining his or her right to make decisions and to be respected in the sphere of dreaming of and creating his or her individual world. At the same time Korczak comments on the relationships between adults and children, which provide a deeper understanding of how he treated a collective sense of children's participation. Korczak suggests describing children as a social group. In his orphanages, Korczak managed to create a community of children as a group co-working with adults. In this situation, children, being a group and a community, were treated as a social subject and a partner to the community of grown-ups.

The same two dimensions of participation—individual and collective—are expressed in the contemporary idea of children's citizenship (Cockburn, 2013; Hart, 2009; Lansdowne, 2010; Milne, 2013). What is more, a collective aspect of children's participation presides today, being celebrated in both theory and political documents (Liebel, 2008). Children are mostly seen as a social group that has the right to participate in social life and civil activities, and in all social and political decision-making processes.

Children are an excluded social group. While analyzing the children's status known at his time, Korczak labeled it as "social exclusion." That was, in fact, his main critique of intergenerational relations (Liebel, 2014). Comparing the social situation of children with other socially discriminated groups familiar to him, Korczak (1919) stated, "Being centered on our own struggles, our own troubles, we fail to see the child, just as at one time we were unable to see the woman, the peasant, the oppressed strata and oppressed peoples" (p. 71). Considering the social exclusion of children unacceptable, Korczak did everything in his power to revert it to "social inclusion," which translated into providing children full access to information and involving them in making decisions and participating in different social actions.

Today we witness real-life situations that demonstrate children as still being a socially excluded group, and a growing number of publications that present children's situation in the light of social inequalities and discrimination. Gradually, this approach with its background in the ideology of democracy is becoming a new theoretical, but also political, paradigm in considering children's participation with an often-used term, "adultism" (see, e.g., Liebel, 2014).

Equality, partnership and cooperation of children and adults. The relationships of children and adults should be based on mutual respect and equality in accordance with Korczak (1984). "Unintelligently, we divide years into less or more mature ones. There is no such thing as present immaturity, no hierarchy of age" (vol I, p. 79). Children are equal partners; "they are entitled to be taken seriously. They have a right to be treated by adults with tenderness and respect, as equals" (vol. I, p. 77). Korczak (1984) kept saying that a child "in the matter of intellect is at least equal to an adult but has no experience" (vol. I, p. 151). He also described the life of adults and children as *an equivalent text* (vol. II, p. 284). The above are just a few examples from Korczak's works that present his demand for equality among children and adults.

In all his years of working with young people, Korczak discovered how much adults could actually learn from them if they speak not "to the children but with the children" (1984, vol. I, p. 281). Korczak (1984) was a strong advocate of a certain type of adult-child collaboration, described in his well-known phrase: "Not a despotic order, stern discipline and distrustful control, but tactful understanding, faith in experience, collaboration and coexistence" (vol. I, p. 76). Korczak recognized the relationships between children and adults (as groups), as an exchange between partners where the authority is not pre-assigned but gained. The acknowledgment of children and adults as equal partners led Korczak to run his orphanages as places of their co-existence and cooperation, and a community co-managed by both groups.

Equality, collaboration, and partnership remain the pillars of the children's participation concept today as shown in multiple studies (Hart, 1992; Mereoiu, Abercrombie, & Murray, 2016) and in political documents that explain and recommend the implementation of children's participation across all social levels (e.g., Rec, 1864). Today, we are fully convinced that children's participation also means, as stated by Hart (2009), "all those instances where children collaborate with other children or with adults, to make decisions or plan activities together" (p. 7). We recognize the increase of children's participation as facilitation of a dialogue and social learning between groups and an encouragement of intergenerational projects that engage children and adults (Percy-Smith & Thomas, 2010, pp. 3–4).

Children can retrieve the society. Janusz Korczak was convinced himself and tried to convince his contemporaries that the world would be a better place if children were respected and well treated as the "future landholders of the world" (p. 341). He believed that children could radically improve the situation because "the unknown person inside each of them is the hope for the future" (Korczak, 1984, vol. I, p. 76). At the same time Korczak (1984) was aware of the necessity not to rush the results and to wait until the children grow up and "take the wheel": "The child is the tomorrow.... He will be a worker, a citizen, an employer" (p. 75). He viewed children as the better part of the society, as genuine, full of energy and creative human beings with a natural sense of democracy and justice. That is why the renovation of the society might start through children's participation. Korczak considered children's input into social life as a positive boost or some sort of a social transfusion; it was not a romantic dream but rather a result of realistic observations of the children's world and their feelings.

We share the same faith today while witnessing numerous examples when children manage to change local environments, become leaders and educators in their neighborhoods, and, as a result, transform the entire community (Hart, 1992; Shier, 2010). Similar to Korczak, we believe that the quality of social life can be improved by implementing the rights of children's regular participation in it on a global level (Milne, 2013). More so, this participation will help to establish justice in the world where children are treated as "full holders of the right today" with the understanding that "they will be the guardians of human rights tomorrow" (Santos Pais, 2016).

Public and political participation of children. Some authors claim that Korczak did not support the idea of broader children's participation—at local or national levels. For example, Krappmann (2013) states that Korczak limited this participation to the institutional level, protecting his charges from the negative influence of the wider society while trying to raise them as social innovators in a closed environment—athough Krappmann (2013) admits that Korczak presumably would not have objected to the public acceptance of children's participation at all.

My own research leads to the conclusion that Korczak (1984) possibly thought about the *political engagement* of children. In *How to Love a Child* he mentions, "from children's self-government to parliaments of the world" (vol. I, p. 211), while in "Child's Right to Respect" (1984) he is even more explicit: "Politicians and lawgivers make tentative efforts, and time and again they blunder. They deliberate and decide on a child, too. But who asks the child for his opinion and consent? What can a child possibly have to say?" (vol. I, p. 65).

Today, the participation of children is promoted at different social levels (Lansdowne, 2011)—from local collaboration to continental and even global scales, and in different forms—councils of youth, children's parliaments, youth conferences, youth commissions, etc. There is strong evidence of the necessity to develop children's participation in public arenas (e.g., Thomas, 2002) through varying forms of representation creating children's decision-making institutions as co-existing and cooperating with those of adults. Such sort of cooperation could serve as proof of the social inclusion of children and the acknowledgment of them as social subjects, social actors, and agents of their own civil rights.

Along with the above ideas, we should also consider public protests and strikes as areas of political participation for children (Hart, 1992; Thomas, 2010), together with their activities in cyberspace, etc. In the modern world, young people are provided with opportunities to be engaged in politics as autonomous actors (e.g., in voting, volunteering in civic organizations, political protests, graffiti, and so on) (Toots, Worley, & Skosireva, 2014). Milne (2013) states that any children's activities that express their political views should be seen as their political participation, no matter whether this activity is consistent with adult rules or not, and regardless of its real impact on the society.

Conclusion

As I have argued in this chapter, a modern concept of children's participation grew out of Korczak's understanding of children, their social position, and their ability to engage in different social activities. Some of Korczak's ideas remain pillars of our understanding of the concept of children's participation, and after a hundred years, they are still alive and timely.

Indeed, there is much to do if we want to follow his philosophy of cooperation and partnerships between children and adults, pursue his dream to renovate society providing children with equal rights, rebuild social awareness to guarantee participation of children by law, and recognize children as political actors. But there is one thing in particular that could be implemented quickly—that is, to initiate and sustain an ongoing dialogue with children about their participation in schools, other institutions, local communities, and nations. This dialogue should help to answer important questions about children's participation and address them in collaboration with children themselves. I am deeply convinced that Korczak would recommend it to us without hesitation.

References

Cockburn, T. (2013). *Rethinking children's citizenship.* New York: Palgrave Macmillan.

Coleman, J. (2010). *The nature of adolescence* (4th edition). London: Routledge.

Dahl, T. (2014). Children as researchers: We have a lot to learn. In G. Melton, A. Ben-Arieh, J. Cashmore, G.S. Goodman, N. Worley (Eds.). *The SAGE handbook of child research* (pp. 593–618). Los Angeles: SAGE.

Davis, T. (2009). *Can social networks bridge the participation gap?* Retrieved from http://www.timdavies.org.uk/2009/05/18/can-social-networks-bridge-the-participation-gap

Graham, A., Fitzgerald, R., Smith, A., & Taylor, N. (2010). Children's participation as a struggle over recognition. Exploring the promise of dialogue. In B. Percy-Smith & N. Thomas (Eds.). *A handbook of children and young people's participation: Perspectives from theory and practice* (pp. 293–305). London: Routledge.

Hart, R. (1992). Children's participation: From tokenism to citizenship. *Innocenti Essays, 4,* Florence, Italy: UNICEF International Child Development Centre.

Hart, R. (2009). Charting change in the participatory settings of childhood. In N. Thomas (Ed.), *Children, politics and communication: Participation at the margins* (pp. 7–30). Bristol, England: Policy Press.

Johnson, V. (2009). Children's autonomous organizations: Reflections from the ground. In N. Thomas (Ed.), *Children, politics, and communication. Participation at the margins* (pp. 31–48). Bristol, England: Policy Press.

Korczak, J. (1919). *How to love a child.* Warsaw-Krakow, Poland: Publishing Society in Warsaw.

Korczak, J. (1928). An informative outline with a preface. In M.Rogowska-Falska (Ed.), *Zaklad Wychowawczy "Nasz Dom."* Warczawa: Nakladem Towarzystwa "Nasz Dom."

Korczak, J. (1984). *Pisma wybrane [Selected letters].* Transl. by Aleksander Lewin. Warsaw: Nasza Księgarnia.

Korczak, J.(1994). *Dzieła [Works]. Vol. 3.* Warsaw: Oficyna Wydawnicza Latona.

Krappmann, L. (2013). *The child as a citizen.* In B. Smolińska-Theiss (Ed.), *The year of Janusz Korczak 2012. There are no children, there are people* (pp. 333–354). Warsaw: Office of the Ombudsman on Children's Rights.

Lansdowne, G. (2005). *The evolving capacities of the child.* Florence: UNICEF.

Lansdowne, G. (2010). *Addressing the balance of power.* In M. Shurman (Ed.), *Valuing children's potentials* (pp. 45–46). Brussels: Eurochild.

Lansdowne, G. (2011). *Every child's right to be heard. A resource guide on the UN Committee on the Rights of the Child General Comment No. 12,* Save the Children UK, London.

Levy, J. (2016). Democracy begins with children's rights. *Pedagogika Społeczna, 60*(2), pp. 61–66.

Liebel, M. (2008). Citizenship from below: Children's rights and social movements. In A. Invernizzi & J. Wiliams (Eds.), *Children and citizenship* (pp. 32–43). Los Angeles: SAGE.

Liebel, M. (2014). Adultism and age-based discrimination: A challenge for children's rights research and practice. In CREAN (Ed.), *Children and nondiscrimination: Interdisciplinary textbook* (pp. 119–143). Tallinn: University Press of Estonia.

Lister, R. (2007). Unpacking children's citizenship. In A. Invernizzi & J. Williams (Eds.), *Children and citizenship* (pp. 9–19). London: SAGE.

Mereoiu, M., Abercrombie, S., and Murray, M. (2016). One step closer: Connecting parents and teachers for improved student outcomes, *Cogent Education, 3,* pp. 1-19.

Milne, B. (2008). From chattels to citizens? Eighty years of Eglantyne Jebb's legacy to children and beyond. In A. Invernizzi & J. Wiliams (Eds.), *Children and citizenship* (pp. 44–54). London: SAGE.

Milne, B. (2013). *The history and theory of children's citizenship in contemporary societies.* New York: Springer.

Mitchell, R. (2015). Children's rights and citizenship studies: Re-theorizing child citizenship through transdiciplinarity from the local to the global. In W. Vandenhole, E. Desmet, D. Reynaert, & S. Lembrechts (Eds.), *Routledge International handbook of children's rights studies* (pp. 164–182). London and New York: Routledge International.

Percy-Smith, B., & Thomas, N. (2010). Emerging themes and new directions. In B. Percy-Smith & N. Thomas (Eds.), *Handbook of children and young people's participation. Perspectives from theory and practice* (pp. 356–366). New York: Routledge.

Santos Pais, M. (2016). *Special Representative of the UN Secretary General speech during the high level conference on a new European strategy on the rights of the child*, Sofia 5.04. Retrieved from http://www.coe.int/en/web/children/sofia2016

Shier, H. (2010). Pathways to participation revisited. Learning from Nicaragua's child coffee workers. In B. Percy-Smith & N. Thomas (Eds.), *Handbook of children and young people's participation: Perspectives from theory and practice* (pp. 215–229). New York: Routledge.

Thomas, N. (2002). *Children, family, and the state: Decision making and child participation.* Bristol, England: Policy Press.

Thomas, N. (2010). Conclusion: Autonomy, dialogue and recognition. In N. Thomas (Ed.), *Children, politics, and communication. Participation at the margins* (pp. 185–198). Bristol, England: Policy Press.

Thomas, N. (2012). Love, rights and solidarity: Studying children's participation using Honneth's theory of recognition. *Childhood, 19*(4), 453–466.

Tisdall, E.K. (2015). Children and young people's participation. A critical consideration of Article 12. In W. Vandenhole, E. Desmet, D. Reynaert, & S. Lembrechts, *Routledge international handbook of children's rights studies* (pp. 185–200). London and New York: Routledge International.

Toots, A., Worley, N., and Skosireva, A. (2014). Children as political actors. In G. Melton, A. Ben-Arieh, J. Cashmore, G.S. Goodman, & N. Worley (Eds.), *The SAGE handbook of child research* (pp. 54–80). Los Angeles: SAGE.

Treseder, P. (1997). *Empowering children and young people: Promoting involvement in decision-making.* London: Save the Children and Children's Rights Office.

United Nations. (1989). Convention on the Rights of the Child. *Treaty Series, 1577* (3).

United Nations Committee on the Rights of the Child (CRC) (2009, July 20). *General comment No. 12: The right of the child to be heard*, CRC/C/GC/12, available at https://www.refworld.org/docid/4ae562c52.html [accessed 14 April 2019].

Wong, N.T., & Zimmerman, M. (2010). A typology of youth participation and empowerment for child and adolescent health promotion. *American Journal of Community Psychology, 46*(1–2). Retrieved from https://doi.org/10.1007/s10464-010-9330-0

Wyness, M. (2012). *Childhood and society* (2nd ed.). London: Palgrave Macmillan.

CHAPTER TEN

Human Rights Library:
An Interview with Jonathan Levy

Interviewers: Tatyana Tsyrlina-Spady, Peter C. Renn,
and Amy Spangler

1. When and how did you learn about Korczak? Why did you decide to use his ideas?

I was educated to become a teacher trainer and also a trainer of early childhood educators. I did my master's in philosophy of education at the London Institute of Education, and over there one of my professors R.S. Peters, briefly touched on Korczak in one of his lectures. But my real appreciation of Korczak came much later in life.

Early in my career I decided to spend the time on the ground in humanitarian services—mainly training educators who worked for Save the Children and for UNICEF. Because of that I traveled and worked in the field in Afghanistan, India, and Darfur. And it struck me very clearly as a young man that in everything I knew about children's lives and the ways they were taught, there always remained one most important question: How would you expect the child to learn mathematics or geography or anything else when the child is hungry and/or frightened, or a victim of all sorts of abuse, or a witness to different atrocities?

So it became obvious to me that the basis of what we now call *the rights of a child* or later on, the United Nations Convention on the Rights of the Child and a direct link to what we call "freedom to learn," meant being freed but not being worried. Practically, children's basic rights turned into the most fundamental thing for me. I remember often thinking about a huge gap between a discourse that was very political and legal in regard to these issues and the pedagogy I learned, unknown to many educators and not used in practice. This became an obsession that led to more research and publishing some manuals about teacher training.

At this point I relooked at the great pedagogues, particularly those of the early 20th century, like Celestin Freinet, Ovide Decroly, Maria Montessori, John Dewey, and so on. As a student learning about them originally, I did not really understand the depth of what they were talking about. Then I discovered Korczak, and I realized that what he was doing and what he did was the topical problem and the way we should have been doing it. That's when I became inspired with his work and realized that as we were no longer living in the 1920s–1930s, we were still in need to carry on this inspiration. As a matter of fact, Korczak introduced pedagogy or educational thinking based on the rights of the child and made them come alive in a real way for children and adults. Realizing the importance of it grew into a strong passion and with it came an understanding of the necessity to help professionals learn about Korczak. In cooperation with UNICEF I started the work of developing training modules on what could be practically called "the pedagogy of children's rights."

I am not a purist, and I don't want Korczak to become a museum piece. I would rather develop his ideas and bring them to today's educators. I can imagine that Korczak himself would love to see his ideas being used in the work with children of all ages. So my work is mainly about how to make his pedagogy relevant to the children today and much less about Korczak himself and what he did in his time.

2. Was there any specific moment that inspired you to begin practicing the Human Library, and what it means in practice?

It was mostly due to the development of the CATS[1] program (Children as Actors for Transforming Society). What we wanted to do and what we realized was that professionals were experiencing difficulties with children's participation; we were in fact missing an active model of doing it. We developed CATS with an idea in mind to create *an active laboratory* where children and adults could experiment with participation. We felt it was something that people did not know and did not see in practice—actual children's participation. While in principle we agreed that children would become active participants, we were still missing the actual model of doing it. We were looking for different situations and ways. In small groups we found a lot of stuff which was influential and could enable children and adults to co-construct, design, and work together, but in large group activities, like 300 people, there remained a lack of activities that would allow the same results. We searched for different techniques, and the "Human Library" was among others that we decided to experiment with. It really worked as it allowed both—children at a very young age and adults of any age as well—to disclose and tell their stories. Practically everybody was able to participate because everybody was interested in people's stories. I think Korczak gave storytelling a great deal of time through theatre performances and other media that enabled an interesting relationship between adults and children.

In a nutshell, the Human Library is a place where books are people who have stories to tell, and reading becomes a conversation. The room is set up like a library with "live" books and "librarians" help readers to find the stories that interest them most. "Books" talk to a small group of "readers" who are interested in their stories during 10 minutes and then there is a question/discussion time for about 15 minutes. It is very important to set a time limit for people to be able to "read" different books and circulate around the room. We aim to focus on people as factors for creating change. Through the use of the Human Library approach, participants receive an opportunity to learn rich examples of experiences from the world of children's rights and democratic participation.

3. Did you invent the Human Library yourself or did you get it from some source?

I did not invent this method; I just adapted it to the area of children's rights. I believe the actual method was created either in Scandinavia or in Canada. Originally it was designed for intercultural relationships and was done in libraries over a week or two-week periods. So it looked exactly the way we were doing it. The method was intended to attract people who had interesting stories to share coming from different cultures, the stories that you would not discover otherwise. Essentially, you could read a book, which was a person. When I learned about this method, I started thinking of whether we could adapt it to the context where we were working and emphasize the element of an intergenerational communication specifically within the sphere of children's rights and check if this process is for us. So my contribution is mainly the adaptation of this method to fitting what we were doing. The Human Library is just one method that we used among many others.

4. What steps do you recommend a teacher should follow to integrate this activity in his or her classroom?

To help teachers to put it into practice, I think it is very important that children have time to reflect and to feel confident. I think it is a question of self-esteem and confidence for children to explore what stories they wish to share with people. I mean that teachers or other adults should not tell them which stories to share or orient them in the direction they would prefer but rather let children have an opportunity to volunteer. This is one of the principles: if you are going to be a book, you have to be a volunteer. So you don't ask children to participate, you ask them: "Who would like to participate in it?" Not everyone wants to be a book, not everyone is comfortable with disclosing personal stories. So you need to deal with volunteers and provide children with time to develop their stories.

It is very important to let children understand that during the process adults would neither correct them nor put words into their mouths. Stories should be authentic, and adults should be guiding the process and help the children to prepare to do that. It is not difficult at all. There is also a necessity to prepare the readers and ask them to listen as well. This technique works when the children are really listened to without being interrupted, which allows them to explain their story in full. There are some ground rules to tell everybody, but on the whole it is not a complicated preparation process.

It could be a class activity, or a whole school activity, or an open day when parents are involved as well. The technique could take very different forms depending on the scale you want to do it on. We did it with 300 people, for example, and had books everywhere in a huge room with roughly 15 to 20 books and people just moved around and circulated. We had dedicated librarians and a lot of different materials prepared by adults. By the way, we also had little children, 6 to 7 years old, who were books; they presented more visual books, which had mostly drawings and paintings and not so much written materials.

Ideally, you might think of having different sections of the library, choosing books on different topics, children of different ages presenting them. So you have different books, different problems, and different experiences, exactly like in a real library.

When we were using it at CATS conferences, we had a different theme each year, so we were asking people to produce books around the conference theme. In schools, it could be about child advocacy, and the questions could be around the following questions: Are you involved in a project? Are there things that you want to change in the society? This will allow involving children with different experiences in this activity. At the very start we circulate the following flyer, where topics could be, of course, different (see Figure 10.1):

FIGURE 10.1

BOOKS HAVE THE POWER TO INSPIRE US, NOW IMAGINE BOOKS THAT COME TO LIFE!

There are many stories to tell of children, youth, and adults contributing to build a sustainable planet and making a more fair, safe, and just world for everyone.

DO YOU HAVE A STORY TO TELL?

Please consider being a "Human Book" in
THE HUMAN LIBRARY

As a "Human Book" you will be "checked out" by "Readers" who are interested in hearing your story of children and adults making a change for a better and more sustainable world:
You will go with your "Readers" to a section where you can share your story, and the "Readers" will ask you questions.

Different "shelves" are available:

- PEOPLE: We are committed to promote human rights and equality.

- PLANET: We stand up to save our planet.

- PARTNERSHIP: We believe in solidarity and support between people.

- PEACE: We are active to promote and implement peace.

- PROSPERITY: We take action to develop our communities.

**Your group is welcome to propose
more than one "Human Book."**
Please read the attached documents for more information on book themes and how it will work.

5. What age range should the children be in order to participate in the Human Library? If these are children of all ages, then how do you recommend to keep the information "developmentally appropriate"?

Just to repeat as I have already touched upon it, we had children as young as 5 to 6 years old. We also had teenagers and adults. This technique allows a very wide range of ages. I have said that young children narrated their stories via pictures. As for other modes, we start with structuring the approach at different age levels.

As for the framework for children, we ask children to share something which comes from their own experience. It is not an abstract thing. It is something where they were involved or they want to be involved in, or they feel hungry about. It is about the nature of the book. There should be an element which says what you want to do, so that they can share things they like to engage in or want to change. For example, children choose the topic of bullying, and they talk about their own experience of bullying or being bullied and discuss what could be done about it. This would be a typical topic or subject.

6. When others ask questions during the Human Library, how does the person with the story say that he or she is not comfortable answering a question? Are the people telling the stories prepared for this? How? Are there or should there be guidelines for participants?

To tell you the truth, we never actually had a problem with it. We never did it in isolation, and the context of CATS conferences is very favorable in this regard; adults are involved in the protection of children's rights, and children are already engaged and active in this process as well. But it is probably wise to explain, in general terms, what the child protection policy is. It mostly means not to hurt children, not to criticize, and not to put down any experience shared with us but instead to accept it. I think it should be done following the principles of child safekeeping. It is not so much about the Human Library as it is about child's safekeeping policy in general.

7. Did you notice any difference using your Human Library with American teenagers in comparison with your prior practice? If yes, please clarify.

This is an interesting question. At our CATS conferences in Switzerland we had American teenagers along with other children from 50 nationalities. Last year there were a few members of the anti-gun movement. One of those American students was actually a book in the Human Library, and she was brilliant. I think she was very confident because she got used to speaking and disclosing in her movement. In general, I feel that American teenagers possess a higher level of openness and readiness for disclosure in comparison with us Europeans. If to mention African, Asian, or Latin American kids, their stories tend to be, by definition, more dramatic; they are talking about child marriage and child labor, some of them are street kids, and something like that. So their stories are very difficult and very powerful with a lot of violent backgrounds.

The experience with the Seattle 2018 Korczak conference version of Human Library was very interesting as we had a transgender person and a young man who came out for the first time to announce that he was gay, which again proves that the technique is very powerful. The American teenagers were wonderful, and I enjoyed working with them. I noticed they tend to be more personal about their own experiences and they talk a little less about global campaigns or looking at societies in a more macro way, concentrating more on their individual experience.

8. How has leading this activity changed your life?

I don't think it has, and I don't want anyone to assume that a technique is so powerful that it could change one's life. But there were some changes in my life and work with children: I let go of control, allowing children to have spaces where they can fully express themselves; I am also risk-taking with children, letting them have their freedom. It is probably a variation of using different things.

9. What are other interventions based on Korczak's ideas which you have developed and which could be useful for American teachers?

I have worked over time on developing an instructional design basis, which is very varied and has two aspects inspired by Korczak. First, every child needs a coherent story, and second, we need a more holistic approach as our secondary education has developed into some sort of a patchwork-type teaching. I believe it is the same in the United States.

What I have been always trying to develop is a story with chapters that goes through and links all things together. At the same time the actual experiences that we are providing through such a story are very varied.

Today, I think the biggest problem we face in education is boredom and the reduced attention level, so the more varied the experiences are, the more interest we create in children. I wouldn't say it could be just Korczak, probably Dewey as well, but these educators really inspire. I believe in moving from large groups to small groups, to individual exercises, to very playful and crazy moments, and also to very serious moments. Gaming, simulations, role play, and so on are also very important.

The children's play is always innovative. For example, if you want to explore children's lives, and you have 300 children and adults, it is better to do it if you design a *timeline* because you have so many different countries and cultures. For example, you choose the topic of children's rights. We had different children on the floor for each presentation, but beforehand they did a lot of research on the history of how a children's rights approach developed in the United States, in India, in Zimbabwe, and many other places in the world. So you can unite them by continent and design a timeline describing when things moved and put specific dates. And then we looked up what children's rights mean today. This is just one example. Rather than standing on a stage and explaining these things, you want children to be involved and doing active research. This is the key element for me.

There are also other moments that are most spontaneous. Actually the combination of these different moments for children is most important as Korczak did in his Orphans' Home—from the theater to playing games, and so on. And we don't do anything much more different than that. We are just bringing all these things together.

10. As a principal [Amy Spangler], the idea got me thinking about the entire school being engaged in this process, on an ongoing basis. I thought that any topic could be posted within the community for students, staff, and families to participate both as storytellers and listeners. I am wondering what the largest scale is that you have done for this project? If you have not yet done this with a large school community, would you be interested in trying it?

Yes, definitely, not necessarily storytelling. What would be really exciting is to have teachers and parents listen to children, and this is the key point of a Human Library. Afterwards, many parents told me that was for the first time they understood their child very deeply in comparison with what they normally do and discovered something about their child they did not know before. Traditionally, in routine family life we don't normally listen to our children or give them the opportunity to share with us. Also, concerning teachers, they are not always able to see what's going on in the heads of their students and/or realize their full potential. So this technique is very revealing for teachers, which often ends up with comments like, "Wow, I've discovered I have such amazing kids in my class [or in my school]."

In general, I think there are a lot of advantages that make it so important to consider the Human Library more as a wider school process or a community activity than just a one-class activity. It could be done in the actual library, creating a real library atmosphere, and it is a lot of fun.

As for repeating this technique during the school year, it should not be very frequent, as anything else, because then it will lose its dynamic and novel nature. I would say it could be done no more frequently than once a term or maybe even once a year.

11. What other aspects of Korczak's life and his approach in the orphanage/ school would you recommend that a public school endeavor do? For example, the bets or something else?

To be honest, I think there are many things that Korczak did because of a particular time, place, and context. For example, I would not do the children's court the way he did in his orphanage. I would rather think of how he brought, in a systemic way, all the children's rights together; how he really reflected on the issue of children's protection, which lines up with emancipation and liberation; how he explored the conditions that liberate children; how he made them feel safe so they could fully participate, and when they actually participate; how they could be involved in improving protection for everyone, including adults; and finally, what they could suggest to make it a better environment.

Along with participation, there is another important issue—that of provision. I mean the necessity to provide children with space, time, materials, and activities: everything which allows them to not be worried or feel overprotected or under-protected, and be able to fully participate.

When children participate, they experience all the different rights brought together in the Convention. I believe that Korczak actually did it in his experience, which allows us to say that he developed all the necessary conditions for this. We keep finding them in his heritage and adapt them to any school environment and today's reality. This, by itself, is working for the development of real democracy, which also creates the pleasure of learning.

Endnotes

1 More details at https://www.caux.ch

Part II: Assignments

1. What is Korczak's attitude towards child-centered pedagogy? Could he be called a follower of the progressive reform movement?

2. Make a list of children's rights composed by Korczak (as cited in Lifton, 2018, pp. 336–337).

3. Compare children's rights as suggested by Korczak with the rights proposed in the Convention on the Rights of the Child (1989).

4. State your opinion on Korczak's (*How to Love a Child*, 1919) notion of children's social exclusion: "Being centered on our own struggles, our own troubles, we fail to see the child, just as at one time we were unable to see the woman, the peasant, the oppressed strata and oppressed peoples" (p. 71).

5. After studying an interview with Jonathan Levy, choose a topic for a possible Human Rights Library session and compose a plan for how to use it with high school students.

PART III
Nurture and Care:
Early Childhood Support as a Basis
for a Happy and Successful Life

CHAPTER ELEVEN

Meeting Basic Needs and Getting Children on Track to Fulfill Their Potential

Angela M. Kurth, Darcia Narvaez, and Mary S. Tarsha

EVERYTHING ALIVE HAS basic needs that must be fulfilled in order to live and thrive. Basic needs fulfillment is an area of research that is burgeoning (e.g., Ciarrochi, Kashdan, & Harris, 2013). Although a great deal of attention is given to economic well-being (Evans, 2017), psychological and social well-being are even more fundamental. Among adults, basic needs fulfillment is related to well-being. Noble and colleagues noted that although thwarting of basic psychosocial needs was predictive of poor mental health outcomes in adults, positive fulfillment of needs was necessary for a feeling of well-being (Noble, Kurth, & Narvaez, 2018a). This finding aligns with the World Health Organization's (1948) definition of overall health as not merely the absence of disease but as encompassing physical, mental, and social well-being (Vansteenkiste & Ryan, 2013).

Children have many basic needs that must be met for them to grow into thriving people and lifelong learners. Recognizing the importance of children's needs is repeatedly emphasized in Korczak's (1967b) teachings:

> It is not a question of how and what to demand from a child, not of bidding and forbidding, but of what he lacks, what he has in excess, what he desires, and how much he can afford to give of himself. (p. 33)

Korczak encouraged educators to pay attention to every detail of a child's behavior because even small gestures could be the important symptoms that reflect his/her inner world. "What a fever, a cough, or nausea is for a physician, so a smile, a tear, or a blush should be for an educator. Not a single symptom lacks significance" (1967b, p. 33).

As Korczak pointed out, at times, adults fail to take children and their needs seriously because they think children have a long life ahead of them, many years to find fulfillment, success, and well-being—later (Korczak, 1967a). In essence, what Korczak is describing is how some adults minimize the importance of childhood, thinking that unmet needs early in life have little to no consequences—"children are resilient" (Lancy, 2014). However, failing to meet children's basic needs is not only disrespectful but creates sometimes insurmountable challenges for children in subsequent years (Shonkoff & Phillips, 2000). Consequently, a greater awareness is necessary regarding children's needs and how these relate to their flourishing, both in the home and in the classroom. Korczak understood the gap in the educational community's awareness of children's needs and when he stated, "It is a fact—the teacher has not been taught" about children's needs (Korczak, 1967b, p. 34). The purpose of this chapter is to introduce educators to children's basic needs.

Child Flourishing

Korczak's overarching aim was child flourishing, a sorely needed emphasis today. Flourishing is holistic and inclusive of physiological, emotional, psychological, social, and moral health (Gleason & Narvaez, 2014). Flourishing involves the presence of good outcomes, rather than merely the absence or avoidance of poor outcomes or survival alone. Flourishing children show empathy and concern towards others and, with cognitive maturation, the overall community. A flourishing person develops moral sensitivity and learns to prioritize their moral values over other values by being proactive in situations that demand this. Korczak demonstrates what a spiritually flourishing adult looks like. A flourishing adult is autonomous, yet has a strong social connection that reaches beyond the individual's own community as a boundary for concern, to all of humanity and all living beings. How do we help children reach such heights of development?

Basic needs fulfillment during childhood may be particularly important. For example, adults whose needs are fulfilled during childhood have better outcomes; those who feel that their needs were not met in childhood are more likely to report poorer health, less well-being, and more depression as adults (Noble, Kurth, & Narvaez, 2018b).

Educators are often faced with children whose needs are not being met adequately outside the classroom. Here we discuss two models of basic needs and how teachers can meet children's needs within the classroom: neurobiological needs and core social motives.

Neurobiological Needs

In the current cultural climate, many children come to school having suffered unmet neurobiological needs. Educators are sometimes at a loss for how to help these children, needing specific practical frameworks and methods for offsetting the consequences and the burden of unmet needs.

Humans evolved more primary, neurobiological needs represented by the evolved nest, a developmental system for the highly immature human child who takes decades to develop fully (Konner, 2005; Narvaez, 2019). The common care practices of the evolved nest are listed in Table 11.1. Because many children today are not immersed in a supportive nest of care, they come to educational and community settings stressed, anxious, and not ready to learn.[1] Young children entering school without their needs met require additional nurturing. Their neurobiological systems are dysfunctional due to an absence of nurturing. Being frequently and/or intensely stressed can be toxic in the early years when the stress response and other physiological systems are setting their parameters for lifelong function (e.g., Lupien, McEwen, Gunnar, & Heim, 2009). Too much stress during sensitive growth periods leads to dysregulation, threat reactivity, and a disposition towards social distrust and self-protection (Narvaez, 2008; 2014). Threat reactivity impairs openness and higher-order thinking, making getting along with others challenging and learning difficult. This means educational institutions and community-based organizations must attend to children's basic needs in order to *prepare* them to suitably cooperate and learn (Narvaez, 2018).

---

1   As Tatyana Tsyrlina-Spady points out, "Being a trained medical doctor, Korczak understood really well how stresses impact children and their ability to develop and learn. Korczak's way of teaching future teachers is well documented and some strategies became really well known, for example, the one when he brought a young elementary school student to the seminar which he conducted in the X-ray room, actually showing on the screen the rhythm of the heart of the stressed and nervous child (movie *Korczak* by A. Wajda, roughly minutes 10–12)."

We describe how educators can meet these needs. Obviously, the birth experience and breastfeeding are not part of an educator's portfolio. However, the rest of the nest's components are valuable contributions educators can make throughout childhood (and into adulthood!). We include examples of educational approaches that emphasize each component.

Responsivity. Classroom components outlined by the National Association for the Education of Young Children (NAEYC, 2009) conform with Korczak's principles for educating children. NAEYC too emphasizes observation and knowledge about the child, which is a form of responsivity which in family settings supports prosocial and cooperative capacities (Eisenberg, 1995; Kochanska, 2002). Another way to provide responsive care in the classroom is to respect the changes and seeming regressions of learning and development in children. Korczak (1967a) described this well when he passionately articulated, "Respect for the mysteries and fluctuations of the toil of growth!" (p. 370). Educators can practice responsivity by first acknowledging that learning and development are in fact mysteries which require fluctuations, waxing and waning, progressing and regressing. With this in mind, the educator can better respect the child's developmental track, providing helpful and effective guidance in a responsive manner.

Touch. Affectionate touch (e.g., hugs, cuddles, holding, carrying) is an integral component of the development of secure attachment in young children (Feldman & Eidelman, 2004). Affectionate touch also facilitates the development of social capacities (Narvaez, Panksepp, 2013). What can teachers do to meet children's needs for affection while respecting appropriate boundaries? For young children, group affection activities can be used to help students practice appropriate activities with peers, such as friendly ways to say hello (McEvoy, Twardosz, & Bishop, 1990). In classrooms with older students, teachers can implement appropriate touch by allowing for personalized greetings at the door. These activities allow the children to guide interactions in a consensual and appropriate manner.

Social Climate. McMullen and McCormick (2016) believe that fostering self-respect can be achieved through a culture that honors who the child is, what the child believes, and what the child feels. By communicating respect to the child, she develops a sense that she is worthy of respect. Montessori classrooms echo this emphasis on respect (Montessori, 1966). Teachers can help promote relational well-being in the classroom by focusing on affinity, which can be encouraged through affectionate touch and nurturance within a positive social climate (McMullen & McCormick, 2016). Another way to promote a positive climate in the classroom is for educators to practice a key philosophy of Korczak's pedagogy, which is to first strive to understand the child, enter into their world, and then demonstrate respect towards him/her (Lewowicki, 1994). In this way, the teacher can set the tone for the classroom and teach other students how to respectfully engage one another and, consequently, catalyze an environment of rich social support.

Play. Play is a normal part of childhood but has been shortchanged by schooling and continues to diminish. The Reggio Emilia approach emphasizes play, creativity, and discovery for young children in a way that engages with the local community, such as exploring the neighborhood to observe particular phenomenon like rainstorms (Gandini, 2012). Other teachers effectively create a space for children to safely engage in rough-and-tumble play by setting clear expectations and boundaries about protecting and caring for one another in the play setting (Huber, 2016). Social play contributes to the development of emotional self-regulation and mitigates social aggression (Flanders & Herman, 2013). Regular and multiple recesses in primary school increase focus during schooling tasks (Rhea & Rivchun, 2018).

Village. Teachers focus on promoting respectful communication among all members of the caregiving community: caregivers, children, and families. The goal of communication is mutual understanding, which contributes to the well-being of all involved. The children themselves are part of the village. As Korczak (1967a) proclaimed, "Children account for a considerable portion of mankind, of the population, of nationals, residents, citizens, and constant companions. They were, they will be and they are" (p. 336). Supporting children sets the trajectory for their developmental track and the future course of the community. By supporting each child, the teacher is helping not only that individual but the community as a whole.

Basic needs. Several basic needs have been associated with school achievement. These needs must be met in order for an individual to commit to learning and socialization or else misbehavior and inattention can ensue. Social determination theory (Deci & Ryan, 1985) comprises three key basic needs: a sense of *belonging* in the group, feeling *competent* enough to complete the tasks assigned, feeling *autonomous*, like one's life is one's own. Additional needs have been identified by others, including having the self-control needed for a task (Zimmerman, 2000), having a sense of meaning or purpose (Damon et al., 2003; Staub, 2003), and opportunities for self-development (Fiske, 2004). Often, educators can trace a student's uncooperative behavior to a missing basic need in that moment of misbehavior (Watson & Ecken, 2018).

One model for describing basic needs is called "core social motives," the types of aims individuals have that are correlated with happiness and well-being. These include what is known as the BUCET list: Belonging, Understanding, Control, Enhancing self, and a sense of Trust (Fiske, 2004). Each of the BUCET list components are related generally to well-being, physical and mental health irrespective of socioeconomic status, indicating that psychosocial resources alone contribute to health outcomes (Matthews, Gallo, & Taylor, 2010; Noble, Kurth, & Narvaez, 2018a). We further examine each aspect of basic needs using the BUCET framework, and how teachers can help students meet those needs. *Belonging* involves the need to form long-term, supportive relationships with others, and contributes to a person's sense of well-being as well as physical and mental health (Baumeister, 1991; Moak & Agrawal, 2010). When teachers care for and support students, helping them feel welcome and "known" by the teacher and respected by peers, students develop a greater sense of belonging, which fosters higher motivation and achievement (Klem & Connell, 2004; McNeely, Nonnemaker, & Blum, 2002). Educators in every classroom can seek to establish a secure relationship with each child. Individuals like to *understand* their lives and to have a sense of purpose, meaning, and life coherence, all of which are associated with well-being and longevity (Fiske, 2004; Hill & Turiano, 2014). An example of communities that regularly practice awareness of their sense of purpose is found in several sustainable indigenous societies. Within these communities, understanding of oneself and the world around you means developing one's heart-mindedness, an integration of emotional intelligence and intuition (Narvaez, 2019).

Several of the BUCET features cohere in classrooms. For example, the Child Development Project developed and studied caring school and classroom communities which support student development in multiple ways. One key aspect included control and autonomy. *Control* reflects the ability to influence the outcomes of life events, which is closely related to the psychological concepts of autonomy (freedom over one's own behavior) and competence (sense of efficacy in interactions with others; Deci & Ryan, 1985), and is also related to better health and happiness (Taylor & Brown, 1988). Those who lack control in home and work settings have an increased risk for depression and anxiety (Griffin, Fuhrer, Stansfeld, & Marmot, 2002). Too many children arrive at school without having experienced a sense of control in their lives, but teachers can rectify this by providing opportunities where students have authentic control over activities and practices in the school environment. Korczak implemented this by providing each child with a sacred space for their own things.

In caring classroom communities, there are multiple opportunities to grow one's self through coached social skills and opportunities for students to help and collaborate with one another. Such practices enhance the self. *Enhancing self* refers to the desire to feel confident in one's self-worth (self-esteem) and motivation for self-enhancement (Fiske, 2004). Self-esteem is related to physical and mental health: lack of self-esteem leads to adolescents' risky health behaviors such as problem eating and suicidal ideation (McGee & Williams, 2000). Feeling embedded in and skillful in sociality with one's community builds an experience and sense of *trust*. Trust involves the overall perception of the world as benevolent, a key aspect of healthy development and a variable that is related to better health, longevity, and lack of depression (Kim, Chung, Perry, Kawachi, & Subramaniam, 2012).

Conclusion

How can teachers support meeting children's basic needs and thereby foster their well-being? Narvaez (2010) contrasted three kinds of classroom focus: mastery learning, caring community, and sustaining climate (see extensive discussion of the latter in chapter 23). *Mastery learning classrooms*, which promote high achievement, help students self-regulate their learning, foster deep learning, maintain student interest, and exhibit flexible learning procedures. These approaches are considered best practices in teacher education. *Caring community classrooms* give students voice in classroom decisions and share responsibility for classroom tasks; teachers guide conflict resolution openly and justly, encouraging peer interaction and interpersonal sensitivity. Caring community classrooms provide the support students need for achievement and prosocial behavior (Battistich, 2008). A *sustaining classroom* adds to these by attending to basic needs, enhancing individual self-actualization and human potential. Ethical capacities and leadership skills are emphasized with global awareness and community partnerships to address a larger purpose for the group: Who should we be?

The sustaining classroom and school employ effective practices for student self-development, beginning with meeting basic needs. For a student to be open to ongoing experiences, their needs and individuality should be acknowledged and considered by a responsive and nurturing educator. In such a relationship, the child can thrive as a person and as a student. Discipline becomes coached character development rather than punishment (Narvaez, 2008). Educators trust the students' own inner compass towards reaching their potential and assist them on the path to a good life.

Children's community potential is shaped by intentional guidance for purposeful, democratic participation (Narvaez, 2011) where students care for one another's welfare (Power & Higgins-D'Alessandro, 2008). Development occurs in a context of supportive relations that include not only the child's family and classroom but also the wider community. Reinvigorating and coordinating the child's network of support among family, community, and neighborhood institutions means that educators align goals to build assets and foster flourishing both in the child and in the neighborhood. In this way, educators contribute to humanity's ideal ecological system of support, one that aligns with Korczak's ideals.

Table 11.1. Components of Humanity's Evolved Nest (Evolved Developmental Niche)

Humanity's Evolved Nest
Soothing perinatal experiences (e.g., no separation of mother and baby or imposed distress)
Extensive breastfeeding
Positive social **climate**
Responsivity to needs, keeping distress to a minimum
Positive affectionate **touch**
Allomothers, a "**village**" of multiple responsive adult caregivers
Self-directed **play**
- with multi-aged playmates
- in the natural world

References

Battistich, V. A. (2008). The Child Development Project: Creating caring school communities. In L. Nucci & D. Narvaez (Eds.), *Handbook of moral and character education (1st ed.)*. Mahwah, NJ: Erlbaum.

Baumeister, R. (1991). *Meanings of life*. London and New York: Guilford.

Ciarrochi, J., Kashdan, T.B., & Harris, R. (2013). The foundations of flourishing. In T.B. Kashdan & J. Ciarrochi (Eds.), *Mindfulness, acceptance, and positive psychology: The seven foundations of well-being* (pp. 1–29). Oakland, CA: Harbinger Press.

Damon, W., Menon, J., & Bronk, K. C. (2003). The development of purpose during adolescence. *Applied Developmental Science, 7*(3), 119–128. https://doi.org/10.1207/s1532480xads0703_2

Deci, E. L., & Ryan, R. M. (1985). The general causality orientations scale: Self-determination in personality. *Journal of Research in Personality, 19*, 109–134. https://doi.org/10.1016/0092-6566(85)90023-6

Eisenberg, L. (1995). The social construction of the human brain. *American Journal of Psychiatry, 152*, 1563–1575. https://doi.org/10.1176/ajp.152.11.1563b

Evans, G.W. (2017). Childhood poverty and adult psychological well-being. *Proceedings of the National Academy of Sciences, 113*, 14949–14952

Feldman, R., & Eidelman, A. I. (2004). Parent-infant synchrony and the social-emotional development of triplets. *Developmental Psychology, 40*, 1133–1147

Fiske, S. T. (2004). *Social beings: A core motives approach to social psychology*. New York: Wiley.

Flanders, J.L., Herman, K.N., & Paquette, D. (2013). Rough-and-tumble play and the cooperation-competition dilemma: Evolutionary. In D. Narvaez, J. Panksepp, A.N. Schore, & T. Gleason (Eds.), *Evolution, early experience and human development: From research to practice and policy* (pp. 371–387). New York: Oxford University Press.

Gandini, L. (2012b). Connecting through caring and learning spaces. In C. Edwards, L. Gandini, and G. Forman (Eds.), *The hundred languages of children: The Reggio Emilia experiences in transformation*, 3rd ed. (pp. 317–342). New York: Praeger.

Gleason, T. R., & Narvaez, D. (2014). Childhood environments and flourishing. In Narváez, D., Valentino, K., & Fuentes, A. (Eds.), *Ancestral landscapes in human evolution: Culture, childrearing and social wellbeing*. Oxford University Press, USA.

Gottlieb, G. (2002). On the epigenetic evolution of species-specific perception: The developmental manifold concept. *Cognitive Development, 17*, 1287–1300. https://doi.org/10.1016/s0885-2014(02)00120-x

Griffin, J. M., Fuhrer, R., Stansfeld, S. A., & Marmot, M. (2002). The importance of low control at work and home on depression and anxiety: Do these effects vary by gender and social class? *Social Science & Medicine, 54*, 783–798. https://doi.org/10.1016/s0277-9536(01)00109-5

Hill, P. L., & Turiano, N. A. (2014). Purpose in life as a predictor of mortality across adulthood. *Psychological Science, 25*, 1482–1486. https://doi.org/10.1177/0956797614531799

Huber, M. (2016). *Embracing rough-and-tumble play: Teaching with the body in mind.* St. Paul, MN: Redleaf Press.

Kim, S. S., Chung, Y., Perry, M. J., Kawachi, I., & Subramanian, S. V. (2012). Association between interpersonal trust, reciprocity, and depression in South Korea: A prospective analysis. *PLoS ONE, 7*, e30602. https://doi.org/10.1371/journal.pone.0030602

Klem, A. M, & Connell, J. P. (2004). Relationships matter: Linking teacher support to student engagement and achievement. *Journal of School Health, 74*(7), 262–273.

Kochanska, G. (2002). Mutually responsive orientation between mothers and their young children: A context for the early development of conscience. *Current Directions in Psychological Science, 11*(6), 191–195.

Konner, M. (2005). Hunter-gatherer infancy and childhood: The Kung and others. In B. Hewlett & M. Lamb (Eds.), *Hunter-gatherer childhoods: Evolutionary, developmental and cultural perspectives* (pp. 19–64). New Brunswick, NJ: Transaction.

Korczak, J. (1967a). The child's right to respect. *Selected works of Janusz Korczak, 355–377.* Retrieved on December 13, 2018, from http://www.januszkorczak.ca/publications

Korczak, J. (1967b). Educational factors. *Selected works of Janusz Korczak, 33–92.* Retrieved on December 13, 2018, from http://www.januszkorczak.ca/publications

Lancy, D.F. (2015). *The anthropology of childhood: Cherubs, chattel, changelings.* 2nd ed. New York: Cambridge University Press.

Lewowicki, T. (1994). Janusz Korczak. *Prospects, 24*(1–2), 37–48.

Lupien, S. J., McEwen, B.S., Gunnar, M. R. and Heim, C. (2009). Effects of stress throughout the lifespan on the brain, behavior, and cognition. *Nature Reviews Neuroscience, 10,* 434–445.

Matthews, K. A., Gallo, L. C., & Taylor, S. E. (2010). Are psychosocial factors mediators of socioeconomic status and health connections? *Annals of the New York Academy of Sciences, 1186,* 146–173.

McEvoy, M., Twardosz, S., & Bishop, N. (1990). Affection activities: Procedures for encouraging young children with handicaps to interact with their peers. *Education and Treatment of Children, 13,* 159–167.

McGee, R. O. B., & Williams, S. (2000). Does low self-esteem predict health compromising behaviors among adolescents? *Journal of Adolescence, 23,* 569–582. https://doi.org/10.1006/jado.2000.0344

McMullen, M.B. and McCormick, K. (2016). Flourishing in transactional care systems: Caring with infant toddler caregivers about well-being. In D. Narvaez, J. Braungart-Rieker, L. Miller, L. Gettler, and P. Hastings (Eds.), *Contexts for young child flourishing: Evolution, family and society.* New York: Oxford University Press.

McNeely, C. A., Nonnemaker, J. M., & Blum, R. W. (2002). Promoting school connectedness: Evidence from the national longitudinal study of adolescent health. *Journal of School Health, 72,* 138–146.

Moak, Z. B., & Agrawal, A. (2010). The association between perceived interpersonal social support and physical and mental health: Results from the National Epidemiological Survey on Alcohol and Related Conditions. *Journal of Public Health, 32,* 191–201. https://doi.org/10.1093/pubmed/fdp093

Montessori, M. (1966). *The secret of childhood.* New York: Ballantine Books.

Narvaez, D. (2008). Human flourishing and moral development: Cognitive science and neurobiological perspectives on virtue development. In L. Nucci & D. Narvaez (Eds.), *Handbook of moral and character education* (pp. 310–327). Mahwah, NJ: Erlbaum.

Narvaez, D. (2010). Building a sustaining classroom climate for purposeful ethical citizenship. In T. Lovat and R. Toomey (Eds.), *International research handbook of values education and student well-being* (pp. 659–674). New York: Springer.

Narvaez, D. (2011). Neurobiology, moral education and moral self-authorship. In. D. de Ruyter & S. Miedema (Eds.), *Moral education and development: A lifetime commitment* (pp. 31–44). Rotterdam: Sense Publishers.

Narvaez, D. (2014). *Neurobiology and the development of human morality: Evolution, culture and wisdom.* New York: W. W. Norton.

Narvaez, D. (2018). *Basic needs, wellbeing and morality: Fulfilling human potential.* New York: Palgrave-MacMillan.

Narvaez, D. (2019). Original practices for becoming and being human. In Narvaez, D., Four Arrows, Halton, E., Collier, B., & Enderle, G. (Eds.), *Indigenous sustainable wisdom: First-Nation know-how for global flourishing.* New York: Peter Lang.

Narvaez, D., & Bock, T. (2014). Developing ethical expertise and moral personalities. In L. Nucci & D. Narvaez (Eds.), *Handbook of moral and character education* (2nd ed.) (pp. 140–158). New York: Routledge.

Narvaez, D., Panksepp, J., Schore, A., & Gleason, T. (Eds.). (2013). *Evolution, early experience and human development: From research to practice and policy.* New York: Oxford University Press.

National Association for the Education of Young Children (2009). Developmentally appropriate practice in early childhood programs serving children from birth through age 8. Retrieved March 12, 2018, from https://www.naeyc.org/positionstatements/dap

Noble, R., Kurth, A., & Narvaez, D. (2018a). Measuring basic needs satisfaction and its relation to health and well-being. In Narvaez, D. (Ed.), *Getting to human potential: Basic needs, well-being, and morality.* New York: Palgrave-Macmillan.

Noble, R., Kurth, A., & Narvaez, D. (2018b). Basic needs satisfaction and its relation to childhood experience. In Narvaez, D. (Ed.), *Getting to human potential: Basic needs, well-being, and morality.* New York: Palgrave-Macmillan.

Oyama, S., Griffiths, P. E., & Gray, R. D. (2001). *Cycles of contingency: Developmental systems and evolution.* Cambridge, MA: MIT Press.

Power, F.C. & Higgins – D'Alessandro, A. (2008). The just community approach to moral education and the moral atmosphere of the school. In L. Nucci & D. Narvaez (Eds.), Handbook of moral and character education (1st ed.). Mahwah, NJ: Erlbaum.

Rhea, D.J., & Rivchun, A.P. (February, 2018). The LiiNK Project®: Year 2. Effects of multiple recesses and character curriculum on classroom behaviors and listening skills. *Frontiers in Education.* https://doi.org/10.3389/feduc.2018.00009

Taylor, S. E., & Brown, J. D. (1988). Illusion and well-being: A social psychological perspective on mental health. *Psychological Bulletin, 103,* 193–210. http://humancond.org/_media/papers/taylor_brown_88_illusion_and_well_being.pdf

Vansteenkiste, M., & Ryan, R. M. (2013). On psychological growth and vulnerability: Basic psychological need satisfaction and need frustration as a unifying principle. *Journal of Psychotherapy Integration, 23,* 263–280. https://doi.org/10.1037/a0032359

Watson, M., & Eckert, L. (2018). *Learning to trust.* New York: Oxford University Press.

World Health Organization. (1948). Preamble to the Constitution of the World Health Organization as adopted by the International Health Conference, New York, June 19–22, 1946; signed on July 22, 1946, by the representatives of 61 States (Official Records of the World Health Organization, no. 2, p. 100) and entered into force on April 7, 1948.

CHAPTER TWELVE

The Canadian Model of Community Social Pediatrics: Respecting Children's Right to Quality Education through Integrated Healthcare

Gilles Julien and Hélène (Sioui) Trudel

Introduction

Our experience shows that even children living in disadvantaged households have the potential to be successful at school although the development of such potential is dependent on a number of factors.[1] At the same time, teachers who have to address the needs of children with learning difficulties and disruptive behaviors also face multiple challenges, particularly when specialists and resources at school are insufficient. All of this adds to teachers' stress and causes a higher risk of burnout. Consequently, students would have to adapt to new teachers and their methods and styles, sometimes, in a single school year.

However, there exists a direct link between a student's school failure and poor economic status of his/her family. The latter could lead to poor stimulation, social exclusion, toxic environments, exposure to violence, lack of support, loss of motivation, and delinquency (Center on the Developing Child at Harvard University, 2011; Diamond, 2002). These obstacles often correspond to a breach of the child's fundamental rights as enunciated in the Convention on the Rights of the Child (1989) (henceforth, CRC).

The violation of children's rights, as expressed in school failure, also comes from the lack of tools that are required to provide the best possible learning environment within the school building. In fact, such tools are not available for a large population of vulnerable children when they reach pre-kindergarten age.

These children end up waiting and failing, progressively losing motivation until they drop out of school. There is also a lack of specialized resources and services to support such children, which also serves as more evidence of disrespect of children's rights to receive education adapted to their needs.

In Quebec, and no doubt throughout Canada and elsewhere, there is a deep concern over high rates of children dropping out of school, especially in the most troubled neighborhoods. Not surprisingly, graduation rates are also disastrously low in these communities: 30% of Quebec youth celebrate their 20th birthday without having completed high school or professional training. The percentage is even higher for young people from low-income families (Institut de la statistique du Québec, 2014).

This reality is also shared by teachers in Montreal, Canada, where a new approach, called Community Social Pediatrics (CSP), was introduced in the early 1990s in close partnership with medical workers, elementary schools, and community groups. It is an integrated health care initiative that brings together professionals working closely with children whose global health status is compromised by the existence of toxic stress arising from austere living conditions. As these children often suffer from complex trauma disorder, a different kind of care is required to help them gain a positive experience in school.

In the Canadian model of CSP, rooted in Montreal, children are considered as having the capacity to fully participate in the decision-making process that may have a direct impact on their lives. Regardless of their age, children are given the primary role, along with their parents and immediate family, when it comes to understanding their difficulties, behavior, and global health status. They are also included in the discussion to find long-lasting solutions to their problems. As such, this model carries values that are closely related to those promulgated by Janusz Korczak: children are human beings, not preparing to become such in the future. Their dignity must be respected in every action taken in their superior interest. These core values lay at the heart of the CSP model.

Health care providers, social workers, lawyers, and some other professionals are trained to read the Convention on the Rights of the Child (1989) as a whole document, and to collaborate as a team with teachers, which consequently favors the emergence of a shared responsibility that respects the rights of children and allows them to flourish. This strategy also ensures comprehensive, integrated access to quality education for the most vulnerable children.

In this chapter we describe how the CSP model helps in accumulating strength and synergy within the community to empower children and their parents while assisting teachers, health care providers, and the like. We start by discussing the situation of a child who was referred to our CSP Center by a teacher because of her disruptive behavior in class. Then we examine the importance of the teacher's role in CSP, and end by explaining the process of our work with schools and other institutions that share a common understanding of children's difficulties and the necessity to respect their rights to a global health status.

The Desperate Situation of Melina

Far too many children from disadvantaged neighborhoods suffer from the consequences of cumulative toxic stresses or post-traumatic experiences. The growth of toxic stress that often results from poor living conditions can be diminished by adopting a collaborative model based on a coherent action plan prepared in a consensual manner. The latter means we need to share information which will help us to understand possible behavioral problems and better address and adapt our support to meet the child's needs.

As an example, let us examine the situation of Melina, a 10-year-old child, referred to our CSP Center by her teacher because of disruptive behavior in class.

The girl arrived together with both parents, which is quite rare in this neighborhood. Her teacher and counselor joined them, along with the social worker from the local health clinic who was already involved with the family. Once everyone arrived, we invited Melina and others to the room that serves for physical medical examinations and for discussions usually around a kitchen table with fresh fruit, paper, and crayons on it. The room also has a special place for children, where they can play, if they so wish, while still being able to listen to and respond to comments during the meeting. Melina chose to sit at the table with everyone else.[2]

After welcoming the girl, I introduced the people working with me, including the social worker, and asked Melina whether she could introduce us to the people who accompanied her. She was pleased to do so. We also asked her whether she could tell us the reason why she paid us a visit. She responded that she had some problems at school, and that she had no friends. Looking at the crayons, she requested some paper and immediately started drawing. Then she raised her head and said, "I love going to school but I have problems."

I explained that we were all interested in helping her. Then I approached Melina, curious to see what she was drawing. She had drawn beautiful dresses, and Melina explained that she wanted to become a fashion designer in the future. I encouraged her to continue, and asked if it was alright to invite the adults to tell me why they had come to the Center. She nodded in approval.

The schoolteacher explained that Melina had been transferred to a specialized class to address her learning difficulties and behavioral problems. Formally in the third grade, Melina's school performance was evaluated at the first-grade level. It sounded like she lacked motivation but Melina interjected saying that she loved school.

Despite being in a specialized class to better suit her needs, Melina had started developing behavioral problems in the form of passive resistance. She was also frequently absent from school. When present, she would often bring reassuring objects, such as stuffed animals, with her from home. Unable to adequately socialize with other children, even pushing them away when they became insistent, Melina was always seeking the presence of adults. Her problems emerged when she was transferred to a regular class. Since then she had continued to fall behind but was not allowed to repeat a year to catch up.

The school personnel attributed Melina's difficulties to the trauma associated with the family's immigration to Canada and her chronic exposure to violence back in a war-torn native country and an inability to study regularly prior to moving to Quebec. Still, no one in her family could understand how such a brilliant child would fail at school. Melina's mother explained that the family immigrated to Canada when Melina was six years old. She had been enrolled in a special integration class to help her adapt to the culture while learning French. She made good progress with acquiring her language skills, and it was determined she was ready to be integrated into a regular Grade 1 level class the following year. She produced the impression of a happy child, known to be sociable and not afraid to speak out. Melina was also helpful at home and was lovingly taking care of her little sister.

However, at some point the mother noticed that her daughter started acting in opposition to family members. She had also experienced sleeping difficulties and gloomy, even suicidal, thoughts. We asked Melina if she would agree for us to continue discussing this matter, and Melina nodded her head in agreement with what her mother was saying. The woman continued, looking for Melina's approval—as if Melina knew what her mother was going to say. The girl stopped drawing, slowly raised her head, and looked at her mother. She was indeed listening, but at the same time she was gazing at the stained-glass window, depicting children playing with kites.

During the meeting we also learned that shortly after their arrival in the country, the family had suffered a traumatic event—Melina had been the victim of violence at the hands of a neighbor. She might have been sexually assaulted, but she had remained silent about that possibility. She started seeing a psychologist.

I asked for permission to do Melina's physical examination, which she agreed to and then inquired about my medical instruments, so I proceeded while we continued to talk. I told her that she was in good health, but Melina complained, whispering, that she had frequent headaches after school. It felt like she had more to say and wanted to stay for longer. I helped the girl to gently climb down from the examination table while telling her she had done a good job. She smiled and seemed satisfied. With no other questions Melina returned to drawing.

During the examination, her father shared with the social worker that he had been trained as an engineer in his country of origin, and could easily make ends meet. But in Canada his diploma was not recognized. The family was struggling financially and had difficulties in adapting to the local culture. He himself had no energy to go back to school but needed to support his family, so he ended up working in the black market economy, earning very little and receiving no social benefits. Moreover, his employer was recently exposed by the government, and the family was threatened with deportation!

After the physical examination, Melina and I went back to the table where I sat beside the girl. I offered Melina a book and invited her to read a few lines. She quickly finished a part of her drawing and examined the book before selecting a page. It was obvious that she experienced difficulties in following the sequence of words and syllables. The teacher intervened stating that we had to take into account that Melina was actually at the Grade 1 level, not Grade 3. She also added that Melina was easily distracted in her tasks, which was confirmed during her examination: when asked, Melina had not been fully attentive. Clearly, she could not understand parts of the question, and tried to hide this by focusing her attention on other elements, painfully searching for answers which she never found.

Throughout this first meeting, Melina had demonstrated an interest in trying to take part in the discussion. Sometimes she even spoke up, commenting, agreeing or disagreeing with a suggestion that directly concerned her. She was willing to receive a helping hand.

It became obvious to everyone present at the meeting that Melina had a history of complex traumas: an exposure to extreme violence at a very young age, a forced and difficult immigration to Canada, another exposure to a number of toxic stresses such as difficult living conditions, poverty and isolation, as well as a violent assault on her physical integrity. Above all, she was experiencing the unjust and untenable situation of possible expulsion from her new homeland. After 45 minutes, we all shared the same story, the same understanding that Melina's complex traumas were affecting her language and comprehension, and that emotional difficulties could be a significant factor. Melina seemed to have rather good potential, but she was reacting by manifesting great anguish. She was simply unable to learn under such circumstances.

The common action plan was to be centered on Melina's needs. In CSP, every action that is taken will be directed at ensuring the respect of the Convention, read as a whole, and even going further as you will see.

We agreed that we had to:

- First, support Melina's potential: her drawing and an interest in fashion and music (she is a very good singer according to her mother).
- Encourage her desire to succeed despite all the difficulties she has encountered.
- Integrate Melina into a support group to adapt to her new environment.
- Find a volunteer, a "Big Friend," who can help her better integrate into the neighborhood and the city, and also serve as her guide and mentor.
- Sign her up for a self-esteem workshop for girls offered at our Center, and for other upcoming activities provided by our partners.
- Find a local family who can be paired with and support Melina's family in their struggle.
- Check for any physical disorders.
- Arrange for Melina to have an eye exam to exclude vision problems that could be causing her frequent headaches at school and difficulty reading.

- Also check for attention deficit disorder without hyperactivity (ADD), and for possible learning disorders like dyslexia.
- Strengthen Melina's psychological and emotional health through sessions with our music therapist, who will ensure a follow-up with the psychologist and the psycho-educator.
- Promote Melina's motivation and perseverance at school by adapting methods both inside and outside the classroom.
- Refer the case to our certified lawyer-mediator to ensure that the family receives all possible assistance to improve their living conditions and mitigate the risk of deportation.
- Make sure that Melina experiences some success through a follow-up of the integrated action plan with regular communication between all participants in this joint project.

Thus, one of the important keys to practicing CSP is to ensure the continued presence and mobilization of the child and his or her parents, starting from the initial contact. This results in sharing sensitive information for understanding the child's needs while working together on the best plan of action to assure the child's global health status and success. Furthermore, this approach is also based on the meaningful participation of the child, regardless of his/her age, thereby ensuring that the children's interests are considered and that their rights are respected.

This concerted plan becomes particularly relevant to teachers whose role is essential in achieving equity for children.

Respecting Children's Rights to Quality Education and Global Health

In the CSP model, teachers are considered active members of the "village" interested in the well-being of children. This acknowledgment of the village is essential in any action designed to support the child's global development and to respect the Convention read as a whole document.

While an impressive number of countries have ratified the Convention—Canada being among those first countries (in 1991)—we continue to witness numerous societal problems that highlight ongoing violations of children's rights. These violations even occur in the fields of education, without anybody being aware of it. Here are three examples.

First, the Convention acknowledges that parents, extended family, and others where appropriate and in the respect of local custom, are the first to have responsibilities, rights, and duties to ensure that their children's rights are respected (Article 5). Indeed, most societies attribute this role to parents and families. Although they play an important societal role for their children's development, they need appropriate assistance (Preamble). It implies that parents must never be left to struggle on their own and must be assisted when required and not judged as being incompetent.

Yet, in our educational system parents are far too often excluded from discussions, while children are mostly ignored. Rather than being allowed to participate as key stakeholders, parents often receive a ready-made intervention plan, regardless of the fact that their informed approval is a premise to ensure adherence. Even worse, not identifying the source of children's learning difficulties often leads to a misunderstanding of their global health status, possibly resulting in giving children services and medications they do not need.

The second example is bullying in schools. Although children have the right to their physical integrity and dignity, at least half of children in the low-income communities where we work have reported to our CSP team being victims of hurtful words, threats, or physical aggression by one or more other children. Victims also indicated they had sought the help of an adult in the school system but were not heard or helped.

Children must feel safe when attending school, and when this is not the case their rights are being breached. Because bullying often takes place at school or on the way to or from school, serious actions must be taken by teachers and principals to address a child's complaint in this regard. This issue concerns all of us because such violence and intimidation may have serious consequences for the child (e.g., being unmotivated or socially withdrawn, or even entertaining suicidal thoughts).

Our last example relates to budget cuts in the field of education, and especially to the lack of focus on building maintenance leading to environmental concerns for children and school staff. A few years ago, the CSP team was treating children with asthma due to substandard housing. We had different ways of doing it, including engaging in mediation with landlords to fix the family's living environment. If this avenue was not efficient in producing rapid change, then we paired with litigators. However, we observed that a significant number of children attending the three primary schools close to our CSP Center were also being affected. We learned that the schools had not been properly maintained and that teachers were falling ill. After several meetings with the school administrators over almost a year, they finally agreed to address this serious health problem.

Several hundred children were moved to another neighborhood during the day, as a temporary solution. They returned home tired and stressed. Some were absent quite often after missing their bus. Parents could not afford to take them to a distant school. Most children could not participate in afterschool programs, as they arrived home too late. Teachers could not attend the CSP clinic. In the end, children had no services. It took seven years before one of the schools opened its doors again; the other two schools still remain closed as this chapter is being written.

Before these elementary schools closed their doors, the CSP Center had succeeded in setting up a thriving community of practice around the children and their families. Children passed by the CSP Center two or three times a day on their way to and from school. Some would stop by to say hello—others to eat or seek refuge. Teachers, the school administration, and specialists regularly got together with the Center staff to discuss the children's well-being. In this friendly environment, parents were comfortable sharing their worries and their successes. But when children were moved away, it was difficult to attend to their needs.

The parents lost touch with teachers, who no longer passed through the neighborhood on a daily basis. Regular and informative contacts between school staff and parents became complicated, school absenteeism increased. For the CSP team, it was catastrophic in terms of not being able to act in prevention and protection of these children. Society had virtually forgotten that all children deserve a quality education. The suggested solution is disrespectful to children's rights and dignity.

The best way to ensure the implementation of the Convention as a whole is to rebuild our "village" based on trusting relationships around the child. This is what the CSP model aims to do, ensuring that any child left behind gets all the tools they need to succeed. The model is unique in its integrative approach combining law and social medicine, and allowing an effective liaison with the educational, environmental, cultural, and social spheres. Above all, it favors a shared responsibility and an optimal healthy and successful outcome for each child.

The right to quality education for all children implies a number of different steps. To succeed, quality stimulation in early childhood is essential, adequate preparation for school entry is critical, and access to a supportive environment must be universal. It is absolutely imperative that all schools provide easy access to high-quality educational resources and effective learning tools for all children in order to respect and promote their right to succeed.

A good example is the *school readiness program* initiated by a school principal with a CSP team. It was implemented in two different low-income communities in Montreal. The goal was to screen children who seemed unprepared for school. We identified all children who were registered at four years old for the first time in the school system. These children were invited to participate for free in the so-called *school readiness summer camp,* within the walls of the school the child would attend in September. There, a team offered different services to meet their needs: language, socialization, behavior, secure attachment, motricity, motivation, and reassurance. A joint assessment to determine the child's difficulties and needs was carried out. A specific action plan was drafted for those children with a low readiness score and an implementation strategy was designed for them before the new school year started.

On the first day of school, the child's teacher was informed and invited as a partner in the team. Throughout the school year, the child's progress was evaluated periodically, and the plan was adjusted as needed to ensure the child's success. It proved to have a positive impact on the lives of many children and at a minimal cost.

In the end, gathering the "village" for the child is a more natural and powerful way for caring for our children before the government gets involved. In our understanding this is how we can build a just society for all children.

Conclusion

Over the last 30 years, our experience working with the Community Social Pediatrics (CSP) model has proven to serve both children and teachers well. This Canadian model, closely related to Korczak's strategies, is an innovative approach in health care to ensure the educational success of the most vulnerable children. It demonstrates how children's rights can be respected through the collaboration of all important stakeholders, including teachers, health care providers, youth protection workers, social workers, lawyers, and accredited mediators, but also parents, members of the extended family, the child's social network, and, of course, children themselves.

At the CSP clinic, children participate as equal partners along with professionals from the school, health care, social services, community groups, and others. Together they work at understanding and integrating all the information they have—to share and collaborate on an action plan "with" and "for" the child, to improve his or her global health status, and to make sure that all needs are addressed and all rights respected. Every member of the group works towards a consensus to prioritize actions. Children thus receive comprehensive diagnostics and necessary services with the help of teachers and others.

Finally, the CSP approach shows that it is vital for all actors in the educational system—with children foremost in mind—to make sure that all children they serve have access to all the tools and support measures to assure their success. We need to become familiar with the Convention, as it serves as a strategy to help all children to maintain a global health status. We need to remember that every child comes into the world with his or her own gifts. Surrounded by a "village" children have a better chance to develop their gifts and to flourish in a just society.

References

Center on the Developing Child at Harvard University. (2011). *Building the brain's "air traffic control" system: How early experiences shape the development of executive function.* Working Paper 11. Retrieved from http://www.developingchild.net

Diamond, A. (2002). Normal development of prefrontal cortex from birth to young adulthood: Cognitive functions, anatomy, and biochemistry. In D.T. Stuss & R.T. Knight (Eds.), *Principles of frontal lobe function* (pp. 466–503). New York: Oxford University Press.

Institut de la statistique du Québec. (2014). *Faible revenu et inégalité de revenu.* (Low income and income inequality). Quebec: Gouvernement du Québec, 1–124.

Endnotes

1 This chapter is based on papers by Dr. Gilles Julien and Helene (Sioui) Trudel published in the Special Issue (2017) of the online journal *Russian-American Education Forum* (rus-ameeduforum.com), 9(3).
2 Melina's story is described by Dr. Julien.

CHAPTER THIRTEEN

Janusz Korczak and Developmentally Appropriate Practice

Hillel Goelman

THIS CHAPTER EXPLORES how Korczak's ideals and practices made their way into the mainstream of childhood education and care many years after his death. The National Association for the Education of Young Children (NAEYC) established an approach to child development called Developmentally Appropriate Practice (DAP) (NAEYC, 2009) that echoed much of Korczak's call for child-centered policies and practices which took into account the whole child.

It is important to point out both the similarities and differences between Korczak's work and the teaching strategies recommended in DAP. To start with, Korczak and DAP drew upon the principles of progressive education articulated by such luminaries as Comenius, Pestalozzi, Froebel, Dewey, Steiner, and Montessori. These pioneers were responsible for emphasizing the basic humanity of children and the importance of their autonomy, the unique developmental characteristics of each child, and the role of adults in facilitating the child's development in all areas of the curriculum. Both Korczak and DAP argued that it should become the first priority to understand the child now, at his/her current level of development, current characteristics, behaviors, likes, and dislikes.

The differences include the fact that Korczak was writing based on his observations, insights, programs, and activities in his Warsaw orphanage for children ages seven to 15. In contrast, DAP focuses primarily on educational practices in preschools and the primary grades for children ages three to eight. DAP is geared exclusively to children's participation in part-day or full-day early childhood education programs. Korczak provided the children in his care with an all-encompassing 24-hour environment which nurtured their health, safety, nutrition, welfare, and inherent rights. Korczak's concerns went far beyond the child's school-focused activities and behaviors and included attention to children's health and well-being from morning to night. To Korczak, the orphanage was an approximation of what a "children's republic" might one day look like.

While there are areas where clear parallels can be drawn between Korczak's work and DAP, much of the similarity between the two can be discerned through a more careful analysis of both. In many cases the ideas that Korczak emphasized explicitly are alluded to more implicitly in the corresponding statements in DAP. The argument here is that many of Korczak's values and practices are strongly echoed—if not directly stated—in DAP'S recommended practices.

For the purposes of this chapter, we begin with a list of five educational values derived from Korczak's works and later on identified by the Yad Vashem, the World Holocaust Education Centre in Jerusalem (Yad Vashem, n.d.). In our analysis we consider these values in both Korczak's policies and practices and in the corresponding components found in DAP. The Yad Vashem list of educational values includes (1) respect for the child, (2) independence, (3) democracy and self-government, (4) freedom to create, and (5) games and play. While this taxonomy can be a helpful outline of the different ways in which Korczak's principles of pedagogy were translated into practice, it has its limitations. For example, missing from this list is Korczak's emphasis on the observation of children's physical, social, and emotional development in the orphanage. Also, a number of these values are, in Korczak's work, redundant. Korczak's value of "independence," for example, overlaps with "democracy and self-government," given Korczak's emphasis on the requirements of citizenship in the orphanage and the forms of self-regulation used in the orphanage.

For ease of comparison of Korczak's work and DAP, this list has been modified in the following way:

1. Respect for the child
2. The importance of observation
3. Democracy, self-government, and self-regulation
4. Games, play, and the freedom to create

The primary methodology used in this study is close textual analysis of the writings of Korczak and the NAEYC position statement on Developmentally Appropriate Practice.

Respect

There are numerous references to the importance of respect for the child throughout Korczak's writings. Some examples:

> [Adults must have] Respect for the mysteries and the ups and downs of that difficult task of growing up. Respect for the here and now, for the present. How will she be able to get on in life tomorrow if we are not allowing her to live a conscious, responsible life today? We must respect every moment, because each will pass and never return. (Korczak, 2007, p. 30)

> Years of work have made it ever more clear that children deserve respect; that they enjoy a sunny atmosphere of gentle feelings, cheerful laughter, lively first efforts and surprises; of pure, bright loving joy; where work is dynamic, fruitful and beneficial. (Korczak, 2018a, p. 317)

It is important to point out that this plea for respect for the child was not an unattainable goal or platitude. Korczak instituted programs and activities in the orphanage that manifested the many different ways in which he created an environment of respect for all of the children, their feelings, expressions, ideas, fantasies, and their sense of justice. There were many vehicles that demonstrated his respect for children. The orphanage gave voice to the children through the democratically elected Children's Parliament and the elected Children's Court in which all children and staff (including Korczak) could be confronted with challenging behaviors and incidents in which children or staff would have to justify their actions that might appear to be in violation of the rules and expectations of the orphanage.

While Korczak wrote extensively about the importance of respect, he was not embarrassed to also express the importance of love. Love was not a commodity to be shared with children on a conditional basis or in reward for certain actions or behaviors. Love was a key element of all interpersonal interactions in the orphanage. Current educational philosophies and practices make little reference to the importance of love. This becomes apparent as we look to the ways in which the principles of Developmentally Appropriate Practice interpret "respect" in the latter part of the 20th century.

When DAP discusses the importance of respect for the child, it is referring to the importance of a respectful environment in the classroom where children can rely upon their safety and security. DAP states,

> What is known about the social and cultural contexts in which children live—referring to the values, expectations, and behavioral and linguistic conventions that shape children's lives at home and in their communities that practitioners must strive to understand in order to ensure that learning experiences in the program or school are meaningful, relevant, and *respectful* (author's emphasis) for each child and family . . . Among these understandings, we absorb "rules" about behaviors—such as *how to show respect*, how to interact with people we know well and those we have just met, how to regard time and personal space, how to dress, and countless other attitudes and actions. (NAEYC, 2009, p. 10)

Respect in DAP is part of a social contract among the teachers, students, and their families. This can be seen in the DAP statement that,

> Children learn to respect and acknowledge differences of all kinds and to value each person . . . . Each member of the community respects and is accountable to the others to behave in a way that is conducive to the learning and well-being of all. (NAEYC, 2009, p. 17)

DAP is to be commended for identifying respect for the child as a key component of Developmentally Appropriate Practice (NAEYC, 2009). This is consistent with DAP's perspective on the "whole child," that is, his/her value as a human being transcends the specific curricular areas which DAP goes into in great detail. Implicitly and explicitly, DAP gives examples of respecting the child's autonomy and individuality in classroom life.

Observation

Efron (2005) has written extensively on Korczak's considerable use of observation as a means of learning about the children in the orphanage. She and others have pointed out that Korczak drew on his training as a physician in order to carefully observe all aspects of youngsters' growth, health, nutrition, and social

and emotional development. He made careful observations and compiled extensive notes in individual sessions with each child but was also an astute observer
of child-child and child-adult interactions in all aspects of life in the orphanage.
He was able to describe children's growth and behavior over time and in many
different situations. He took notes on children's changing problem-solving skills
in real-life interactions: mealtime, chores, bedtime, in the Children's Court, in the
Children's Parliament, in their articles in the children's newspapers and their participation in group play and especially in dramatic play. Efron (2005) commends
him on the nature and style of his observations:

> Another salient characteristic of his observation notes is the reflec-
> tive, honest, and self-critical retrospective on the inquiry process.
> He reveals his doubts, mistakes, and frustrations with himself as
> he reacts to his own notes. (p. 151)

Hammarberg (2009) summarized Korczak's use of observation with an
emphasis on its importance and timely nature:

> The parts of his research that still hold good today are probably his
> observations of children, particularly his way of reporting what
> he had noted. Here his interdisciplinary perspective and his lit-
> erary talent come into their own. He gives the results of careful
> and patient observations of children in a language not normally
> associated with science and research reports. In an almost impres-
> sionistic literary style he conveys exact and sensitive pictures of
> children's situations and their way of being. (p. 16)

The NAEYC Position Statement on Developmentally Appropriate Practice
also places great emphasis on teacher observation and recordkeeping. Observation is seen as the most authentic and helpful form of determining a child's
strengths and challenges in all curricular areas and behavior management. Observation is described as a critical activity in the cycle of teacher decision making
on the best ways to match children's developmental status with curricular goals
in the classroom. Observation assists the teacher in designing and implementing
appropriate classroom activities and opportunities for learning.

In this way, observation is considered to be highly preferable among one-time assessments of discrete areas of knowledge, skill, or performance. DAP (NAEYC, 2009) states that,

> This general knowledge [of a child's development], along with what
> the teacher learns from close observation and probing of the in-
> dividual child's thinking, is critical to matching curriculum and
> teaching experiences to that child's emerging competencies so as
> to be challenging but not frustrating. (p. 15)

Democracy, Independence, Self-Governance, and Self-Regulation

Korczak often wrote about the orphanage serving as a model of a "children's republic" in which children's rights and voices would help to guide the democracy and judicial aspects of community life. As noted, he implemented a system where all children could participate in the creation of a Children's Parliament, Children's Court, and children's newspapers. Hartman (2009) quotes Korczak on the purpose and functioning of the Children's Court:

> Different people live together ... The courts keep watch to ensure
> that big people do not hurt small, and that little persons do not dis-
> turb their elders; that the clever do not exploit or laugh at the less
> clever; that the quarrelsome do not pester others and do not tease
> them; that the cheerful do not play foolish tricks on the down-
> hearted ... The court may forgive but may also rule that somebody
> has acted unjustly and very, very badly. (p. 17)

When Korczak spoke of the importance of self-regulation in children, it was less a call for modifying individual behavior but rather a statement of one of the governing principles of the Children's Republic. Korczak believed—and acted on these beliefs—that the children's lives in the orphanage had to be governed by a commitment to a community in which children had to recognize the expectations, opportunities, and limitations of individual actions. For Korczak, self-regulation was an essential part of a child learning to become a contributing and participating member of the community of children in the orphanage. When a new child entered the orphanage, he/she was appointed a mentor who would help the child recognize the function of the community and the children's roles and responsibilities there. This mentoring then was a key part of children's learning of the skills of self-regulation and how those skills would contribute to a just and fair community experience. Self-regulation in the orphanage was a critical component of understanding the children's current level of social responsibility and expectations.

To a certain extent DAP echoes Korczak on self-regulation when it states that, "Each member of the community respects and is accountable to the others to behave in a way that is conducive to the learning and well-being of all" (NAEYC, 2009, p. 17). While DAP also makes reference to the importance of children learning the social skills of self-regulation, this term took on a different perspective in the preschool and primary school settings in which DAP was applied compared to Korczak's orphanage. In these settings, self-regulation was seen as more of an individual task and characteristic than a social commitment to the welfare of the entire classroom of which he/she was a part. Further, in the DAP statement self-regulation was seen as a key developmental step that would benefit the child later on in his/her academic experiences. For example, it says that,

> A number of factors in the emotional and social domain, such as independence, responsibility, self-regulation, and cooperation, predict how well children make the transition to school and how they fare in the early grades . . . . Moreover, helping children from difficult life circumstances to develop strong self-regulation has proven to be both feasible and influential in preparing them to succeed in school. (NAEYC, 2009, p. 7)

The DAP statement goes on to discuss the importance of educating children to be aware of and become active participants in a democratic society at an adult stage of their lives:

> Teachers and administrators in early childhood education play a critical role in shaping the future of our citizenry and our democracy. Minute to minute, day to day, month to month, they provide the consistent, compassionate, respectful relationships that our children need to establish strong foundations of early learning. By attending to the

multiple domains of development and the individual needs of those in their care, early childhood professionals who employ developmentally appropriate practices engage young children in rich out-of-home early learning experiences that prepare them for future learning and success in life. (NAEYC, 2009, p. 23)

Games, Play, and the Freedom to Create

Korczak saw that the freedom to create and to play—games with rules, dramatic play, and unstructured play—were all essential parts of a child's being and expression. He saw these expressions as especially important given the children's backgrounds of deprivation, poverty, and hunger. He pointed out that children have the right to play, to be independent, and to initiate and maintain their play according to their own hopes, dreams, fantasies, and creativity.

The respect for children's voices mentioned above was also manifested in Korczak's encouragement for children to write articles for the children's newspaper. Dramatic play (as discussed in detail below) was another way in which children were encouraged to voice their fears, sadness, anger, happiness, excitement, and anticipation. Korczak applied the ideal of respect into practical activities and programs. Children, quite simply, had the right to respect, and Korczak and the staff created a safe and supportive environment based on the assumption of respect for each and every child.

Korczak himself modeled the importance of creativity in many ways. The orphanage provided the children with opportunities to explore and express their dreams, fantasies, and hopes for a better world in which children were free to be children. Korczak created stories, novels, and plays which the children listened to attentively and read on their own and in small groups. His children's novels included *King Matt the First* (1923, 1986) and *King Matt on a Desert Island* (1923, 2009). He gave them the opportunity and encouragement to write articles for the children's newspaper, *The Little Review*.

Korczak and DAP are in strong agreement that play should be seen as the child's first language. It is through play that children explore and experiment with the real world and express their own personal fantasies and wishes. Play is seen as the most basic representational activity that children engage in. Through their play a block can represent a truck, a doll can represent a baby, and a stick can represent a hammer. DAP also points out that play can serve a vital function in children's learning self-regulation. This, in fact, is seen as one of the major functions of games with rules where children are expected to act in accordance with the possibilities and limitations of the games' rules.

Play is an important vehicle for developing self-regulation as well as for promoting language, cognition, and social competence, roles, interacting with one another in their roles, and planning how the play will go. Children engage in various kinds of play, such as physical play, object play, pretend or dramatic play, constructive play, and games with rules. Observed in all young animals, play apparently serves important physical, mental, emotional, and social functions for humans and other species, and each kind of play has its own benefits and characteristics. (NAEYC, 2009, p. 14)

DAP makes an explicit reference to another aspect of play that Korczak emphasized—dramatic play. The DAP statement points out that dramatic play presents opportunities for creativity and also establishes boundaries and generates expectations within which children must act out roles that are consistent with character, plot development, and meaning. Dramatic play is seen in DAP as an essential element of children's lives which facilitates their linguistic, cognitive, social, emotional, and moral development. In this way, the DAP statement on dramatic play very closely mirrors Korczak's approach to it as well.

Conclusions

Both Korczak and DAP place great importance on all forms of play. Play gives children the opportunity to enact the principles of the first three educational values identified by Yad Vashem at the beginning of the chapter. In both approaches children's play is to be treated with great respect as it represents expressions of their own dreams, fantasies, imaginations, and creative desires. Both Korczak and DAP stress the importance of observing children's spontaneous play, games with rules, and dramatic play as strong indicators of children's language, social knowledge of others, and their developmental skills in participating with others in order to maintain and advance the content of the play. Play also provides children with opportunities for learning the importance of self-regulation as a means of children understanding the limits of the boundaries in their play and the importance of recognizing the rights of their playmates.

While the DAP statement does not explicitly cite Korczak's work, this chapter argues that many of the basic principles and practices articulated by Korczak also find expression in DAP. In some cases, comparisons of Korczak and DAP reveal striking similarities. In many other cases, as our study shows, DAP offers very strong echoes of Korczak's approaches to childhood education, child welfare, and advocacy. We may see Korczak's work as planting the seeds of child-centered progressive education which bore fruit in DAP. Perhaps the most important similarity between Korczak and DAP is their focus on all aspects of the health, education, development, and welfare of the whole child. It is clear that Korczak and DAP share a strong belief in the importance of respecting children, carefully observing their development, granting them decision-making rights, and supporting their different forms of play. Despite their very different timeframes and great geographical distances, it is remarkable to find these shared beliefs in children and childhood.

References

Efron, S. (2005, March/April). Janusz Korczak: Legacy of a practitioner-researcher. *Journal of Teacher Education, 56*(2), 145–156.

Hammarberg, T. (Ed.). (2009). *The child's right to respect: The Korczak lectures.* Strasbourg: Council of Europe.

Hartman, S. (2009). Janusz Korczak's legacy: An inestimable source of inspiration. In T. Hammarberg (Ed.), *The Legacy of Janusz Korczak* (pp. 13–23). Strasbourg: Council of Europe.

Korczak, J. (1923, 1986). *King Matt the first.* (R. Lourie, Trans). New York: Farrar, Straus and Giroux.

Korczak, J. (1923, 2009). *King Matt on a desert island.* London: JPE Publications.

Korczak, J. (2007). *Loving every child: Wisdom for parents.* (S. Joseph, Ed.). Chapel Hill, NC: Algonquin Books of Chapel Hill.

Korczak, J. (2018a). *How to love a child and other selected works,* Volume 1. London: Vallentine Mitchell.

Korczak, J. (2018b). *How to love a child and other selected works,* Volume 2. London: Vallentine Mitchell.

NAEYC. (2009). *Position statement on developmentally appropriate practice.* Washington, DC: Author. Retrieved May 5, 2019, from https://www.naeyc.org/resources/topics/dap

Yad Vashem. (n.d.). Educational values from the Korczak legacy. Retrieved November 5, 2018, from https://www.yadvashem.org/education/educational-materials/learning-environment/janusz-korczak/korczack-values.html

CHAPTER FOURTEEN

Preschoolers as Explorers: How to Ensure Respect for Their Rights

Ljubov M. Klarina

NEARLY A CENTURY ago Janusz Korczak (2009) observed, "The features of the world have changed.... Muscles have lost their exclusive status and value. Knowledge and the intellect have increased in respect" (pp. 23–24). What was true then is even more true today. The rapid transformation of technology and professions makes it almost impossible to predict what kind of knowledge and skills present-day children will need in their adult lives. Thus, one of the primary objectives of modern education is the development not only of a child's intellect but also their curiosity and critical thinking. Among the most important are such skills as formulating problem situations and analyzing them, offering and validating hypotheses, and reflecting upon actions and their possible consequences. When properly shaped, these skills constitute a solid basis for making conscientious decisions, acting upon them, and overcoming fear of the unknown.

Exploring one's surroundings is a natural process for humans, but it is particularly pronounced in young children who are just learning to interpret and make sense of the world. It is imperative to equip children with all necessary tools for their exploration as soon as possible. When entering an unknown world, a child encounters a great number of puzzles and uncertainties. Practically from birth, he or she will exhibit a drive to explore them, which allows for their survival into adulthood. Adults, however, are not always supportive of this behavior. Korczak (2009) weighed in on the phenomenon as follows: "We grow weary of the active, bustling, fascinating life and its mysteries; we tire of questions and expressions of wonder; discoveries and experiments that frequently end with unfortunate results lose their appeal" (p. 30). Worried about their children's lives and health, as well as their own property, teachers and parents often cut short children's attempts at exploration, thus robbing them of the joy of discovery. As a result, cognitive risk taking and independence are greatly diminished.

The desire to learn something new encourages self-understanding while promoting understanding of the surrounding world. As a result, the child gains a greater sense of the impact of his or her actions and the limits of possibility for future action. This further enables children to live full lives and to celebrate their personal freedom and creativity. Support of preschoolers' innate yearning to understand and learn sets the stage for positive development and educational experiences, which are of course extremely important.

How can adults help children to grow and sustain their drive to learn? What conditions must be present to activate and prolong children's exploratory behavior so that they develop their cognitive abilities? My research identifies such conditions and also proposes methods for their implementation, while identifying the most effective modes of interaction between adults and children in preschool and kindergarten. I have devised several pedagogical interventions and techniques that help stimulate children's cognitive activity (ages three to seven). They have been implemented in seven Moscow preschools and kindergartens in a joint educational complex with over 750 children and 40 teachers since the 2017–2018 school year.

Methodological and Theoretical Foundations

From the very first step, the practical implementation of this project posed certain challenges. Most notably, many preschool teachers are used to treating their students as "obedient performers" who possess no interests or intentions of their own, but instead only the ability to follow adults' instructions. My hypothesis was that studying Korczak's legacy would change participating teachers' attitudes.

The current research is based on Korczak's argument that every child deserves respect, including the "respect for his lack of knowledge" and "for the effort of learning" (Korczak, 2009, p. 36). Emmi Pikler (1902–1984), a Hungarian pediatrician and pedagogue, founder of the Lóczy orphanage in Budapest for young children under five years old, agreed.

The guiding principles of her comprehensive educational system for preschoolers are the twin concepts of care and respect: Pikler found that friendly interactions of adults with children during their rearing and the adult's behavior adapted to the child's expressed needs are essential for children's healthy development. She strongly objected to adults deciding everything for children as if the latter had no wishes or desires of their own (Pikler & Tardos, 2001). It is widely acknowledged and further confirmed by Canadian researcher Enid Elliot (2007) that Pikler's ideas were greatly esteemed, not only by her fellow citizens, but also by modern Western scholars and practitioners.

Research Categories in Use

The theoretical foundations of the suggested interventions are informed by Lev Vygotsky's cultural historical theory of psychological development and Sergey Rubinshteyn's idea of agent-based activity. According to the latter, agency is an essential human characteristic revealed in people's ability to alter the environment and themselves, whereby they become agents of their own activity—in other words, authors and masters of their own lives (Rubinshteyn, 1997, pp. 83–86). Unlike those who execute somebody's will, agents determine their own values and meanings, and set goals depending on their appraisal of a given situation and the available resources (including resources related to a given personality).

I identified the following structural components of "agency" as a research category: first, an agent's own *point of view* and, second, the resultant *activity*. The agent's *point of view* is marked by its self-determination, which, in turn, is based on the agent's key values and perspectives. The *agent sees the activity* as a holistic structure that encompasses the entire process of realizing an identified goal. (For more, see Klarina, 2016.)

Research shows that a preschooler is not yet able to be the agent of his or her own activity; thus, in accordance with Vygotsky's theory, the agent of preschoolers' education and development is an *event-related fellowship*. I propose that this fellowship of children and adults implies mutual assistance, joint creative activities, empathy, understanding, and respect for one's partners' interests, inclinations, and features, including their rights and obligations. Korczak was a master of creating such fellowship in his orphanages. It is especially important during preschool, when every child needs a trusted adult, a member of the child-adult fellowship, who is truly interested in all spheres of the child's life, related events, and in his or her inner world and future.

Pedagogically speaking, it is important that the suggested methods be aimed at designing conditions for preschoolers to become agents of their cognitive activities, and it is vital that the "child-adult event-related fellowship" have a pronounced cognitive-exploratory orientation. In such fellowships, people respect children's right to both their "lack of knowledge" and their yearning for knowledge, as well as the right to ask questions about any objects, phenomena, or aspect of reality. Educators need to carefully analyze children's questions in order to understand children's concerns. Questions of a cognitive nature are always the result of a preschooler's hard work and self-determination; they are motivated by a drive to understand—*What do I want to know? What interests me?*—and framed by a search for the appropriate structure and wording for said questions.

Guiding Ideas Related to the Proposed Educational Interventions

Traditional methods of instruction in Russian preschools and kindergartens are often limited to the transfer of information from adults to their charges; in contrast, our approach centers on the teacher's need to identify and create conditions that encourage the development of a child's cognitive-directed agency. As theory and practice show, the formation of a preschoolers' cognitive-directed agency is the result of his or her expanding interests; in contrast, the development of a preschooler's cognitive abilities is informed by mastery of the means and ways of cognition, among them, exploratory procedures.

After analyzing children's questions, teachers select those that help structure cognitive tasks that, apart from being interesting to children, are also developmental in nature. Having become immersed in such activity, preschoolers—assisted by adults—are able to build new concepts of reality, master the structure of exploratory activity and its corresponding actions, and obtain all necessary means and ways for cognition.[1]

Basic ideas of how to create conditions for children's cognitive development were introduced by Vygotsky (1935) in his speech at the all-Russian conference on preschool education, where he said: "While infants learn in accordance with their own program, school-age children use the teacher's program; preschoolers

---

1 Use of the term "cognitive means" intends to capture standards, concepts, speech, the "language" of games, fairy tales, etc. This stands in contrast to "ways of empirical cognition," which refers to observation, examination of objects, experimentation, development and application of models, etc., logical reasoning (analysis of objects, their comparison, classification, etc.), and work with information (information collection, data validation, analysis, interpretation, etc.). Of course, teachers should also take into consideration the preschoolers' age, their unique interests, as well as their level of development.

are able to learn only as much as they adopt the teacher's program and it becomes their own" (p. 26).

Many people questioned the first part of this statement wondering whether infants were really capable of learning "in accordance with their own program" and whether their development would still happen in this situation. Responding to these doubts, Vygotsky (1935) described a situation of teaching a child under three years old how to speak. He emphasized the fact that "the succession of developmental stages that the child is going through and their duration is determined not by his mother's program, but by what the child is getting from the immediate environment" (p. 21).

These aspects of how preschoolers investigate their surroundings are further supported by Pikler's observations and practice. For example, she explained that to develop cognitive initiative and independence in infants and preschoolers, one needed to provide them with the conditions to move freely. Why? Because bumping into new objects sparks the child's innate curiosity, which he or she is eager to satisfy. Educators and parents provide children with the ability to explore their *immediate* environment while enriching it with various objects (of course, provided that they are safe). When the child is given the opportunity to move around, he or she follows his/her own "program" and explores the world outside. In addition, children also receive an opportunity to study their own bodies and spatial location together with exploring their own ability to overcome multiple obstacles. In other words, young children have their own insight into their developmental process, which should help determine what conditions, provided by adults, can maximize their development.

I find these ideas extremely important in designing the program aimed at preschoolers' cognitive development, as they effectively solve the problem of continuity. Furthermore, they support Vygotsky's argument that a three- to seven-year-old child is unable to master anything new or experience any associated inner changes before the act of seeking "novelty" becomes integrated into the child's own intentions. Put differently, a child's ability to master new material hinges on the child's desire to do so. As a rule, such yearning appears if the preschooler is interested in the adult's proposal. In this case the adult's "program"—its goals, objectives, and content—may become the child's "program." Otherwise, the child will just imitate (and often reluctantly) the educational activity he/she is expected to demonstrate, and as a result, no genuine learning or development will happen.

In other words, if the teacher introduces the cognitive problem, it is important to make it particularly interesting and inviting for preschoolers. That is why we pay so much attention to the conditions of organizing an educational process. The first, essential step is to endow this process with positive emotions that transform children's puzzlement into cognitive interest and risk taking to find the right answer, filling them with the genuine joy of discovery.

An educational process is a system of educational situations (ES) which can either be planned in advance or occur spontaneously. As a rule, the process is triggered by the introductory ES in which the teacher sparks children's cognitive interest in a subject and then works alongside them to make its meaning more apparent. In this way, the ES has the potential to become really interesting, and the cognitive objectives that will be achieved come into focus. The children, assisted by the adult, discover what they already know about the subject in question, what they are interested to learn, and share their suggestions about possible solutions and ways to validate them. During the discussion, the teacher clarifies children's perceptions and the ways they will be used to solve the problem. Then the teacher plans further action that will yield the development of cognitive-directed agency and their cognitive activity. Finally, the teacher specifies all the necessary conditions provided in the given situation.

Later on, the teacher creates another ES in which children (either independently or with his or her help) validate their assumptions, analyze the results, draw conclusions, and develop follow-up plans about further exploring their surroundings. The distinguishing characteristic of these educational situations is the established partnership between children and educators, which is the meaningful result of their working together. Children are provided with an opportunity to act as independently as possible—to express their ideas, take exploratory actions, generalize, make conclusions, etc.

To help the children construct and develop a wholesome worldview, teachers design for an integrated exploration of various spheres of life. A resource for children in their quest for the information needed to solve cognitive tasks, teachers often involve (and expand upon) games, movements, productive activities, socialization, introduction to fiction and cognitive reading, book illustrations, theater performances, cartoons, video, visual and auditory materials, etc.

While children acquire new concepts about the real world, exploratory procedures, ways and means of cognition, their teachers organize creative and revision-oriented ESs. They motivate children to apply the acquired cognitive "tools" in similar and novel conditions created during didactic games, role-playing, etc. Lastly, children are offered a series of reflexive ESs including their consideration of successful (or unsuccessful) ways and means applied in solving the problem as well as their emotional reflections on the cognitive process and its results (by answering questions like, "What has especially interested/puzzled/made you think or pleased you?"). During the reflection period, children often come up with new questions, and then the reflection turns into a discussion of new plans and ways to find solutions.

One of the most significant conditions of achieving adequate child development is to apply the same requirements and approaches to all children. Equally important is to establish partnership communication with the children's parents and to share with them the values and meanings used in the work with their children. Special attention should be paid to the concept of every "child having the right to be respected." Based on jointly agreed values, teachers and parents together work out goals, objectives, methods, and actions that would contribute to their children's cognitive development. Parents are involved in supporting the educational process, first started at the preschool or kindergarten, and continued at home. In this way, parents take into consideration teachers' recommendations and their children's wishes.

Conclusion

This chapter provided a brief description of a pedagogical intervention aimed at developing preschoolers' cognitive abilities. Our work has not yet been completed and is still in progress. However, even at this early stage, one sees that many preschoolers have expanded their cognitive interests. This is especially evident by the number and content of their questions. The children have become more enthusiastic and independent in solving their own problems, and also more successful in engaging in exploratory procedures. The growing number of participants and the quality of their projects during our annual Festival of Young Learners and Explorers ("Uznayki and Umeyki") testify to the positive results of our efforts.

So far, the results of all participating educators demonstrate the efficiency of the suggested pedagogical interventions. They also show that Korczak's call to respect children's "lack of knowledge" and their right to make mistakes have been integrated into daily preschool and kindergarten activities. My practical experience of partnering with Moscow educators affirms the need to further implement the legacies of Janusz Korczak and Emmi Pikler today.

References

Elliot, E. (2007). *We are not robots: The voices of daycare providers.* Albany: State University of New York Press.

Klarina, L.M. (2016). The problem of preschool children's subjectness development: Can it be solved if teachers lack professional subjectness? *Russian-American Education Forum: An Online Journal, 8*(1). Retrieved from http://www.rus-ameeduforum. com/content/en/?task=art&article=1001176&iid=24

Korczak, J. (2009). The child's right to respect. In *Janusz Korczak's legacy. Lectures on today's challenges for children.* Strasbourg: Council of Europe Publishing. Available at https://www.coe.int/t/commissioner/source/prems/PublicationKorczak_ en.pdf

Pikler, E., & Tardos, A. (2001). *Laßt mir Zeit. Die selbständige Bewegungsentwicklung des Kindes bis zum freien Gehen* [Give me time. The development of an independent movement of the child before she starts walking freely]. Munich: Pflaum.

Rubinshteyn, S.L. (1997). *Chelovek i mir* [Man and the World]. Moscow: Nauka.

Vygotsky, L.S. (1935). *Obuchenie i razvitie v doshkol'nom vozraste / Umstvennoe razvitie v protsesse obucheniya. Sb. statej.* [Teaching and development at preschool age]. In *Mental development in the process of teaching. Collected papers* (pp. 20–32). Moscow, Leningrad: Gosudarstvennoe Uchebno-Pedagogicheskoe Izdatel'stvo.

CHAPTER FIFTEEN

Why Children Should Learn to Take Risks

Helma Brouwers

> *As a child I used to play outside a lot, with friends. We built huts in the woods, called ourselves The Hawks, our leader was Prince Nee-O-O, and we were constantly in war with another group called The Dare Devils. One day we set fire in their hut, one girl got hurt, only a little. But her mom was furious. So were our parents. We needed to apologize, which we did, reluctantly. Even though we understood we went too far. The next game now became to negotiate for peace with our opponents which was not too difficult, because we were just playing and in play everything is possible.*
> —A FORMER STUDENT'S PERSONAL STORY SHARED IN HER JOURNAL

> *I used to play with friends in the lumber yard in our street, a few blocks away from where we lived. We could climb the tree trunks, ride the carts over the rails, and when the owner arrived (attracted by all the noise we made) we hid ourselves behind the piles of wood. He never found us!*
> —A FORMER STUDENT'S PERSONAL STORY SHARED IN HER JOURNAL

STORIES LIKE THESE you might hear often when you ask adults to share their most intense play experiences as children. It turns out those intense and exciting experiences have some common characteristics:

- There were no adults around to warn children of any possible danger.
- There were no conventional toys involved.
- In their play situations children sensed excitement, fear, and danger.

Obviously, children like to look for the kind of excitement adults easily call dangerous, forgetting about how they felt when they were younger. Most children, by the way, survive almost all of those so-called too dangerous situations. Particularly parents, but also professional educators, are so very afraid that something might happen to their children, they constantly watch them, forbid them to go somewhere by themselves, and immediately take them away from anything that presents the slightest risk.

Based on my experience as an educator and teacher's instructor, here is how I see the reality for children, the reality which leaves them overprotected:

- Parents constantly supervise their children, never letting them explore and experience for themselves.

- Children are often overloaded with conventional toys that leave little room, if any, for developing their own imagination.

- Adults (parents and educators) make every attempt to eliminate any possible risks from their children's or students' lives, and from their own as well.

Parents, who always try to clear the path for their children's lives, are often called Lawnmower or Snowplow parents. Interestingly, many of us consider this as good and responsible parenting. But in reality, such overprotected children miss many opportunities to see how the world reacts to their actions and to experience how to deal with risks in a safe way. Overprotected children become anxious, fearful, and depressed while children instead should be adventurous and engaged in risky and exciting playful situations. After all, children who are less protected seem to have fewer accidents than overprotected children (Brussoni, Brunelle, Pike, Sandseter, Herrington, Turner, Belair, Logan, Fuselli, & Bell, 2014).

The Right To Their Own Death

Janusz Korczak was the first to formulate basic children's rights. As stated in his renowned *Magna Carta* (Korczak, 2018) we read:

Children have the right to be who they are
Parents expect their children to be what they want them to be, without taking into consideration the child's own nature. In schools we standardize

development and learning instead of allowing all students to follow their own interests and aspirations.

Children have the right to the present day

Today is what counts for children; today has to be lived fully. Childhood is not a waiting room for adulthood. Nevertheless, adults often tell children that what they have to do might be uninteresting, dull and boring, but . . . it will become important in the future.

Children have the right to their own death

Korczak himself was brought up as a child who was supposed to always behave properly, to stay clean, and not play with children who are dirty from the street. And he really suffered in this "golden cage." He longed for adventure like most children do. This experience must have been his inspiration to advocate for this radical, uncompromising right (Lifton, 1988, pp. 13–19).

The child's right to his or her (henceforth, her) own death is certainly troublesome. We could easily blame Korczak for not having children of his own and therefore not understanding how valuable a child is to her parents. But nowadays many educators seem to realize that this parental fear can turn into unnecessary overprotection, which comes at the cost of sacrificing their children's well-being and, ultimately, their safety.

I think Korczak would have fulminated against the situation when children are not allowed to run on the school playground because they might fall and hurt themselves, or against city councils which forbid children to sleigh down a snowy hill because the community cannot guarantee their safety.

As we can see from this last example, it is not only parental fear that prohibits children from doing what they like most, but also the fear of the consequences in case something goes wrong. Compared to Korczak's time, this risk-avoiding attitude has certainly become much worse today.

The Danger of Overprotection and the Need for Risk Competence

Parents who want their children to grow up safely should not try to avoid all possible dangers, but instead help them cope with risky situations, so that they will be able to develop *risk competence, the ability* to estimate where possible danger can come from and how to deal with it in a safe and responsible way. Recent research proves that children with risk competence remain in charge of their behavior in dangerous situations in comparison with children who are kept away from all possible risks (Brussoni et al., 2014). A few years ago Tully and Spiegler (2011) published a book arguing that children should do at least 50 dangerous things, not because they should get hurt, but because they should learn how to handle fire, knives, scissors, etc. without getting hurt. If we don't provide our children with the opportunity to experience risky situations, they will hurt themselves much more easily when confronted with this same fire, knives, scissors, etc. (Tully & Spiegler, 2011).

A growing number of studies show that risky games are important for children's physical development, their sense of autonomy, their cognitive and social development, as well as for their mental health. They also prevent misbehavior and learning problems (Eichsteller & Holthoff, 2015).

FIG. 15.1 THE LEARNING ZONE MODEL, SENNINGER 2000

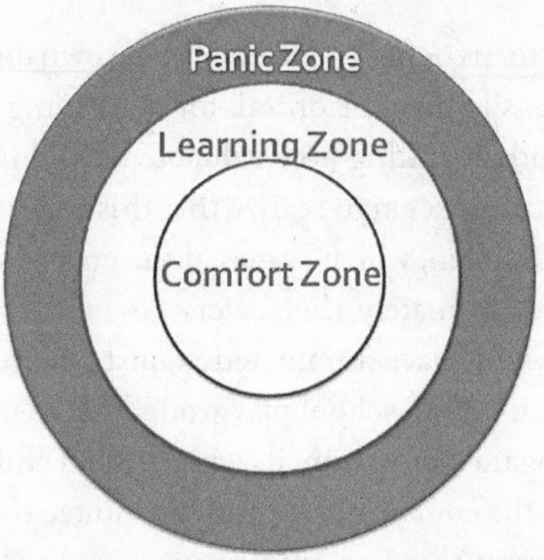

According to Senninger (2000), learning takes place when we leave our comfort zone in which everything is familiar and well known, and enter the learning zone without overstepping into our panic zone, where fear hinders any learning from happening (see Figure 15.1). Every learning process has elements of leaving the comfort zone, and entering and exploring the unknown and the unpredictable. According to Eichsteller and Holthoff (2015), risk competence develops gradually and naturally when children are able to explore their learning zone and avoid entering their panic zone, where the risks are too great to actually cause trauma, serious harm, or even death.

Eichsteller and Holthoff (2015) state that all our adventures, actions, and experiences have a profound impact on the development of children:

> The risks we have taken, the challenges we have overcome enrich our inner world, affect us emotionally and shape our identity. They give us a sense of mastery, of taking responsibility for our actions, the thrilling feeling that we can control what happens to us. (p. 12)

Spending their childhood safely in buggies, behind screens, or in the backseat of a car won't provide our children with these critically important experiences, and won't shape their identity in a positive and competent way. The feeling that your life is happening to you instead of you having some sort of control over it is the very cause of depressive feelings in children and adults (Chorpita & Barlow, 1998).

This presents one more reason why we should refrain from putting too many restrictions on our children's sense of adventure. American researcher Peter Gray (2015) reports a severe decline in free play time for children in the last five decennia which coincides with an equally severe increase of depression and anxiety in children at a very young age. Gray postulates a possible causal effect between those two phenomena. The lack of playtime, in his opinion, can trigger all kinds of mental disorders. If we don't change this, we will end up with a generation of people who have not developed the necessary competencies to live, to behave in a socially appropriate way, or to cope with difficult situations.

Children who play seek out the limits of their physical competence, and the limits of their actions. They try again, and maybe fail sometimes and hurt themselves, or even break their bones, but that's how they learn. Even when they get hurt more seriously, Korczak would still say . . . they have the right, even if it causes their death . . . . Because, as Korczak puts it: "Children are not your possession" (1986, p. 22).

Gray (2015), while considering playing from an evolutionary perspective, states that it is a natural way "of ensuring that children . . . will learn what they must to survive and do well" (p. 139). Gray (2015) refers to imaginative play that is self-chosen and self-directed and "that is motivated by means, more than ends" (p. 142). Obviously, games and other adult-directed plays or sports cannot claim to have the same benefits for children's development and learning as free play.

How to Develop Risk Competence?

So do we have to expose our children to challenging situations and just witness who survives? Of course not. Especially very young children need adults to learn how to think in terms of cause and effect, and to predict the consequences of certain actions. But there is a considerable difference between the attitude of an adult who says, "Stay here because out there is dangerous," and "High tide is coming very soon; the water is rising quickly, so you need to pay attention and stay away from this sandy island because it will disappear underwater soon." In other words, you either display your own adult fear, or you help your children to understand how to deal with a particularly dangerous situation. Learning to reflect on risky situations or mistakes is certainly better than avoiding them.

FIG. 15.2 ELEMENTS OF RISK COMPETENCE (EICHSTELLER & HOLTHOFF, 2015, P. 19)

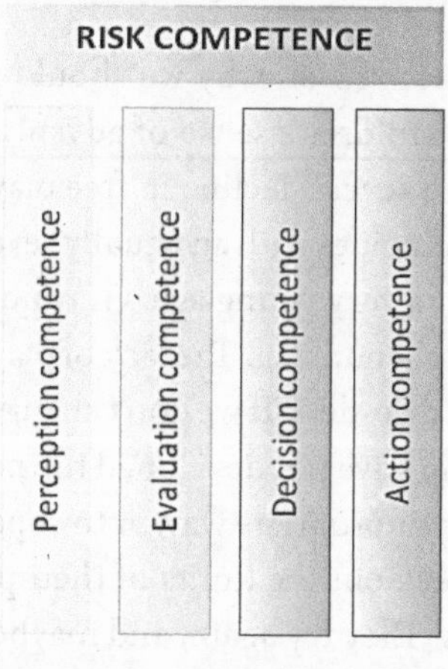

Developing one's risk competence means, "refining the ability to recognize and correctly assess potential hazards." It also includes "the ability to make decisions that enhance safety and realize those through focused actions" (Eichsteller & Holthoff, 2015, p. 18). These authors (2015) identify four elements that play an essential role (see Figure 15.2):

a. *Perception competence:* recognizing potential hazard (e.g., identifying the potential danger of a rotten tree branch or the slippery rock you are climbing).

b. *Evaluation competence*: assessing the level of risk involved (e.g., estimating whether the current might be too strong to swim in without being dragged away).

c. *Decision competence*: making decisions based on safety considerations instead of peer pressure, for instance, when jumping off a high cliff.

d. *Action competence*: acting successfully in risky situations, for example, biking down a difficult track, requiring both physical skills and mental strength to master the challenge (pp. 18–19).

This model offers educators guidelines to assess children's levels of competence and to learn how to support and further develop them.

The educator's role in stimulating risk competence. Guiding the process of developing a child's risk competence can only be done when we refrain from our own perspective and start thinking from her perspective. It is not a feeling of fear that should determine our actions but care about the child and her capacity to deal with current and future risks.

For instance, we see a 10-year-old boy putting a thin plank over a ditch with shallow water. He wants to use it as a bridge to cross the ditch. How should we react? It largely depends on the child's level of risk competence, his prior experience with the materials, and other characteristics of this particular situation.

We need to know if the boy has some understanding of thin planks that can break under his weight (*perception competence*). Can he make an estimate of the danger he might face if the plank breaks? How deep is the water in the ditch he might fall in (*evaluation competence*)? Does he generally pay attention to the safety of himself and others with the decisions he makes (*decision competence*)? Will he panic or stay calm when the plank bends, and finally, is he agile enough to walk on this narrow plank (*action competence*)?

All this knowledge about the child, his competence, and the situation will inform us if and how to react. We should also realize that our mere presence can take away the child's own sense of responsibility; he might stop thinking for himself and rely only on our judgment. So when a child has sufficient risk competence, it is better to withdraw and not intervene at all, not even with wise remarks and warnings.

We need to consider both external risks and the child's internal risk to know what the best pedagogical action should be. The child's risk competence will only improve if the child is fully involved, and takes an active part in evaluating and assessing the situation and her own competence. The hardest thing for adults is to trust children while research constantly shows us that children seldom take unnecessary risks.

Adventure playgrounds. Most European towns and cities nowadays lack the places for children to play freely and independently. The stories at the beginning of this chapter come from my former college students who grew up in rural areas where one could play without adult supervision.

The good news is that many parents and professional educators realize that we should offer children adventure playgrounds, particularly in cities where traffic has taken over. This means creating situations that allow children to experience the right amount of risk and the right level of challenge.

We can find such playgrounds in big cities all over the world—in Berlin, New York, and Amsterdam, to name just a few. There are playgrounds where children can build rafts for the pond, bridges to cross the ditches, and entire wooden houses. They can also climb trees and swing on ropes, make bonfires, and cut branches from trees to build huts. For children, it is a real joy to play with unconventional, natural materials: this free and dangerous play fulfills the most basic needs of young humans. Children who do not have the opportunity to play adventurous games because their parents are afraid they might get dirty or something might happen to them have their childhood taken away from them. And that won't go unpunished!

References

Brussoni, M., Brunelle, S., Pike, I., Sandseter, E., Herrington, S., Turner, H., Belair, S., Logan, L., Fuselli, P., & Bell, D. (2014). Can child injury prevention include healthy risk promotion? *Injury Prevention, 21*(5), 1–4.

Chorpita, B., & Barlow, D. (1998). The development of anxiety: The role of control in the early environment. *Psychological Bulletin, 124*, 3–21.

Eichsteller, G., & Holthoff, S. (2015). Waarom kinderen risico's moeten leren nemen [Why children should learn to take risks]. In *Het recht van het kind op leven en dood* [The child's right to life and death]. In *Janusz Korczak Yearbook*. Gorinchem, The Netherlands: Narratio.

Gray, P. (2015). *Free to learn.* New York: Basic Books.

Korczak, J. (1986). *Hoe houd je van een kind* [How to love a child]. Utrecht, The Netherlands: Bijleveld.

Korczak, J. (2018). *How to love a child and other selected works.* Portland, OR: Vallentine Mitchell.

Lifton, B. (1988). *The king of children.* New York: Farrar, Straus & Giroux.

Senninger, T. (2000). *Abenteuer leiten—in Abenteuern lernen* [To guide adventure: Learning by adventure]. Münster, Germany: Ökotopia.

Tulley, G., & Spiegler, J. (2011). *50 dangerous things (you should let your child do).* New York: New American Library.

Part III: Assignments

1. Comment on the following excerpt from Korczak's *Educational Factors* (1967): "It is not a question of how and what to demand from a child, not of bidding and forbidding, but of what he lacks, what he has in excess, what he desires, and how much he can afford to give of himself" (p. 33).

2. How could children's basic needs be met through creating caring communities? Give examples from Korczak's practice at his Home for Orphans.

3. Briefly describe *community social pediatrics* and explain the reasons why and how it is relevant to Korczak's concept of children's rights.

4. After comparing *Developmentally Appropriate Practice* (National Association for the Education of Young Children, 2009) and Korczak's approach to children's development, show (with examples) whether the former is based on the ideas of Korczak.

PART IV
Respect and Inspire:
From School Years to College

CHAPTER SIXTEEN

Responsibility for Self, Others, and the Community: Practical Implications of Korczak's Educational Vision

Sara Efrat Efron

HANNAH ARENDT (1993) compares diving into the treasures from the past to the act of a "pearl diver who descends to the bottom of the sea . . . to pry loose the rich and the strange, the pearls and the coral in the depths and to carry them to the surface" (p. 205) as "thought fragments" (p. 206) that enable viewing the present with new and fresh eyes. Such a "pearl" is Janusz Korczak, whose death, as well as his life, remains a moral declaration, which shines through the fog of history. The focus of this chapter is on interrogating Korczak's far-sighted educational vision, examining its relevancy to the current discourse, and being a transformative call for a paradigm change that "inspires educators to regenerate and rejuvenate their current practice" (Alexander, 2003, p. 386). More precisely, I explore his perspective, thoughts, and actions through the lens of responsibility: an educator's responsibility for the child and the child's responsibility for herself, others, and the community.

Educator's Responsibility for the Child

The word *responsibility,* according to the Cambridge Dictionary and the way it is usually used, means having a duty to fulfill or being in a position of authority over someone. The emphasis is on the obligation *I* am supposed to take upon *myself.* The etymological root of the word, however, is different; it comes from the Latin verb *respodere*—response; the ability to respond, which moves the center of attention from oneself to the person one responds to. The change of focus requires an ability to push aside one's own interests and goals, and concentrate on the other, attending to his or her (henceforth, her) needs, struggles, dreams, and hopes. Such a response-ability is a reminiscence of Buber's (1965) I-thou relationship, Noddings's (2014) works or what Iris Murdoch (1970) described as "unselfing" to be completely open to the other.

For Korczak, the educator's ability to respond to the child begins with the recognition that every child is complex, unique, and full of contradictions and mystery. "A hundred different hearts beat beneath exactly the same uniform and in each case a different difficulty, different work, different cares, and concerns" (Korczak, 1967a, p. 208).

Although far from perfection, every child deserves the right to be what she is, and their unique personalities, beliefs, and interests should be valued. Only fools, Korczak (1962) declared, "who dislike thought will be disappointed by differences and angered with variety" (p. 41). It is the responsibility of the educator to respect and respond to the differences among individuals in all their qualitative richness.

This child-centered response-ability does not imply a romantic or naïve perception of the child. Korczak (1967a) differentiated between a teacher's *sentimental love*, which sees the child in a glorifying way, and an educator's *pedagogical love*, which recognizes that the child's world "is not trifling, but significant, not innocent, but human" (p. 254). The teacher needs to find a balance between the acceptance of the child's right to be herself and the establishment of a disciplined setting that allows her to become what she can be.

Moreover, response-ability and pedagogical love are not necessarily permissive. They acknowledge that for an educational work to be successful, order and lawfulness must be preserved. Giving a student a free hand, without any guiding expectations, "would ... turn a bored slave into a bored tyrant and will either weaken [the child's] willpower or poison it" (Korczak, 1967a, p. 135). From Korczak's perspective, rules and regulations are there to support the child, and not to strengthen the teacher's authority (Efron, 2008). If an educator loses sight of the child's authentic needs and wants, a disciplinary system that initially was designated to protect the child may create a barrier between the teacher and the students and become ineffective (Korczak, 1967a).

Furthermore, pedagogical love does not mean imposing the teacher's goals on the learner but requires the educator to be open to the child's perspective on the future. In Korczak's view, teachers are making a big mistake when they try to mold the children and coax them into conforming to their system of values (as cited in Shner, 2012). Such an attempt, insisted Korczak, is either ineffective or damaging. Children's efforts to behave in a way that pleases authoritarian adults, rather than out of their own volition, typically lead to hypocrisy or distress. When the child's "true character shows itself, not only the teacher but the child as well, will surely be hurt" (Korczak, 1992, p. 172). Rather than turning to the young and declaring unwaveringly: "I will make a man out of you!" the response-able educator addresses the child and patiently asks, "What are you going to make of yourself?" (Korczak, 1967a, p. 154).

Korczak (2001) presented an educational approach where children are being perceived as agents of their own growth, and educators are not imposing their will on students letting them make their own choices. With such choice, insisted Korczak, comes responsibility. The teachers may steer, but in the end, it is up to the learner to face the challenges that life presents, and take response-ability for whom they become. Children should be encouraged to act sensibly and ethically not out of fear of punishment, but out of choice (Lewin, 1997). Such an educator, remarked Korczak (1967a), "does not enforce but sets free, does not drag but uplifts, does not crush but shapes, does not dictate but instructs, does not demand but requests" (p. 196).

In the Children's Republic, Korczak created a social and educational environment that facilitated self-actualization of students as individuals and as members of a democratic community. The response-ability of the educators was to facilitate the educational experiences that enhance children's ability to take responsibility for themselves, for others, and for their community. In the following sections, I will describe the frameworks, processes, and strategies practiced in the orphanages that were directed toward achieving these goals.

Responsibility for Self

For Korczak (1992), children have the right to plan and take control of their struggles to overcome their weaknesses, and to try, and at times fail, to better themselves. Children deserve respect for their efforts, their successful ones as well as their "setbacks and tears" (p. 176). His goal was to instill within the orphanage's students an understanding that their ethical and unethical decisions and actions lay with them. At the same time, he wanted the children to know that he and the other educators were always there to support and provide help. For Korczak, developing a self-directed and autonomous child required knowledge of the child, a trusting relationship, strategies that enhance self-improvement, and a forgiving and patient environment.

Knowledge of the Child

Children develop their social, emotional, and ethical identity out of their own life experiences, and their particular familial, social, and cultural background. Being able to assist children in becoming responsible for themselves begins with knowing who the child is, and who she might become. Three questions, stated Korczak, guide the educator's quest for understanding the uniqueness and complexity that each child presents: What is the child's past? Who is the child now? And how does the child view her future?

> I kiss the children with a glance, a thought, a question. Who are you, who are such a wonderful secret to me, and what shall you bring with you? I kiss you with an effort of will: How can I help you? I kiss the child as the astronomer kisses the star, which is, who has been, and which will be. (Korczak, 1992, pp. 183–184)

Building a Trusting Relationship through Dialogue

Knowledge of the children offers opportunities to assist them with helping themselves. From Korczak's perspective, there was no better way of gaining such knowledge than through listening. The adults may be better informed and far more experienced than the children, but the child is much more knowledgeable when it comes to herself. The children know what they think, feel, or fear much better than the teacher will ever be able to grasp (Korczak, 1967a).

Access to such knowledge is achieved by building trusting relationships through dialogue. Similar to Buber's assertion (1965) that "relation in education is one of pure dialogue" (p. 98), Korczak (1992) believed in the power of dialoguing with children. When educators converse with the children in a way that reassures them that they are listened to, new opportunities for guidance and support are opened. In such conversations there is "no hierarchy of age, no higher or lower grades of pain or joy, hopes or disappointments" (p. 179).

In the orphanage, Korczak and the staff encouraged the children to speak with them in private without constraint. Once a week, Korczak's door was opened for any child who wanted to go in and converse. In those conversations, Korczak (1992) maintained, "two equally mature moments, mine and the child's intertwine" (p. 179). Additionally, a mailbox was set up in the institutions in which the children inserted notes and letters describing their problems, complaints, fears, and wishes. Korczak read these notes and answered in writing or invited the child in for a face-to-face talk (Cohen, 1994; Eden, 2000).

The contribution of such dialogues, stated Korczak (1967a), was invaluable: "When we gain the child's respect and trust, once he can confide in us out of his own free will, and tell us what he has the right to do—there will be less puzzling moments, less mistakes" (p. 129). In the eyes of Korczak (1967a), building trust "is more important than love" (p. 399).

With that, Korczak recognized that trust could not be expected to come quickly and teachers were advised not to press children to express their feelings or to reveal their secrets if they were unwilling to do so. Gaining students' trust can come into existence only when the educator relinquishes the control due to her authoritative status, meets the child at the same level, and "does not speak *to* the child but *with* the child" (Korczak, 1967a, p. 345). In such dialogues, the children sense that the teacher respects their individuality and listens to their thoughts, feelings, wishes, worries, frustrations, and doubts.

Children's Self-Improvement

For Korczak, a trusting relationship with an educator was the cornerstone of the child's moral, social, and emotional development, but in the end, the success of such growth depends on the child's willingness to take responsibility for her actions. Such willingness, Korczak believed, is derived from self-awareness and from a sense of agency. Two main strategies, ballots and wagers, were implemented in the institution to help children become conscious of their difficulties, realize the impact their actions produce on their social surroundings, and heighten the sense of agency while improving their behavior.

Ballots. Through ballots children gained an acute awareness of any social problems and of how their peers perceived their behavior and actions. Every year, in secret surveys based on given criteria, children were asked to express how each of the members of the Children's Republic had contributed to the community. Those votes enabled each child to recognize how the surrounding community recognized their good and bad attributes as a "citizen" of the youth community. While some researchers (e.g., Dror, 1998) criticize the pressure caused by the surveys, others maintain that the results of the ballots fostered children's will to change and overcome some of their antisocial tendencies (e.g., Eden, 2000).

Wagers. Regulating one's behavior through self-imposed wagers was another effective strategy for helping children become responsible for their self-improvement. The wagers were bets taken by individual children, in the presence of Korczak, as stimuli for overcoming some of their problems. In private meetings, requested by the children themselves, they would voluntarily bet on overcoming any identified faults. Their choice of overcoming a dysfunctional behavior or developing a desired skill involved reflections on who they were, and the kind of person they wanted to become. Korczak recorded the bets, the number of violations, and the success of achieving the desired goals. These bets were on a variety of issues, such as fights, abusive language, cheating, and thefts. Korczak allowed children, who preferred to keep their privacy, not to reveal the nature of the behavior they wanted to overcome, and the subject of the bet.

Not always were the children able to fulfill their promises. In such cases, they honestly shared their inner struggles: "I desired but I couldn't. I knew I ought to, but I wasn't able to manage" (Korczak, 1967a, p. 196). After admitting failure, a child could undertake a new bet. These moments of setbacks and inner struggles helped to bring children and teachers closer together—the adults' trust and lack of judgment remained critically important in maintaining children's motivation for improvement. (See more details in the chapter by Lasota.)

Atmosphere of Patience and Forgiveness

The self-improvement process was never rushed, as Korczak (1967b) explained that the child will inevitably "struggle, suffer disappointments and shocks. Let him seek his own ways and means. Let him experience the joy of small and isolated victories. I help them with the sweet atmosphere of my boarding schools" (p. 532).

Korczak's attitude toward his students, who were struggling with their inner demons, was distinguished by its acceptance, patience, and forgiveness. The children in his institution knew that they were accepted as they were, but there was also a mutual expectation that they would keep trying and take advantage of future opportunities for improvement (Silverman, 2017). Korczak (1967a) related a conversation he had with a child that captured the essence of this attitude:

> "You are quick-tempered,"—I tell a boy—"All right if you must hit someone, hit but not too hard; lose your temper if you must, but only once a day." And, he added, "You have my word for it, in that single sentence, I have summarized the educational method I employ." (p. 148)

Thus, through knowing and respecting who each student was and through a continued dialogue Korczak helped the children overcome their difficulties, personal problems, and behavioral challenges. Empathizing with the child's struggles, Korczak also recognized the challenge the teachers faced as they followed the children through their uphill battle with patience. Constantly encouraging the child, even in times of regression, and avoiding critical or accusing responses, required trust in the child and in the process.

Responsibility for Others

Helped by Korczak's program to develop a sense of responsibility for their actions through trusting relationships, a forgiving environment, and a systematic process for self-improvement, most of the children were able to regulate their own behavior and overcome their social or emotional difficulties. However, some continued to struggle, demonstrating an inability to adjust to the institution's social demands on their own. For such children Korczak introduced a powerful educational innovation—a cross-age peer-mentoring program.

Cross-age peer mentoring. This program aimed to develop, among the children, a sense of responsibility for each other. That responsibility meant that the children-mentors took it upon themselves to respond to their peers' social challenges and to help overcome them.

The basis of the cross-age peer-mentoring program was Korczak's belief that children understand each other better than anyone else can. Adults, Korczak (1992) sadly asserts, often misunderstand, misjudge, and underestimate the child. "You don't understand our ways and have no insight into our affairs" (p. 83). Shlomo Nadel recalls that the Old Doctor believed "the only way to penetrate the barrier that these children built around themselves" was to connect them with "a close companion, a sort of an older brother or sister" (as cited in Lipiner, 2015, p. 14). Once the children trusted their "older brothers or sisters," they opened up, shared their inner worlds, and confided in them. The influence of the guardians was based on personal trust, and often remained stronger and more meaningful than that of the teachers (Eden, 2000).

In the Children's Republic the mentors or guardians (as they were referred to in the institution) offered assistance and support to the peers who faced challenges in adapting to the orphanage's routines and rules (Cohen, 1994; Eden, 2000). The mentors were veteran residents of the Children's Home and were familiar and comfortable with the institutional culture and routines. They volunteered for this role, but their appointment had to be approved by other children during the Children's Parliament meetings. The mentorship lasted for three months but could be extended for another three months if both parties asked for it (Lipiner, 2015). The mentors and the mentees met regularly and engaged in conversations, play, or other structured activities that forged a close relationship between the two (Eden, 2000).

In the journals, the mentors recorded their experiences and reflected on the activities they shared with the mentored peers, noted conflicts and unexpected incidents or their uncertainties, shared moments of insights, and raised relevant questions. At the end of the three-month period, they were expected to put together a report to summarize the mentoring experience and to comment on any achieved progress. Korczak and Stefania Wilczyńska read the diaries and responded to the issues raised by the mentors (Dror, 1998). The educators themselves also benefited from the peer-mentoring program, as it allowed them to follow the progress of the socialization for the most vulnerable children (Eden, 2000).

Cross-age peer mentoring for new children. Most of the children in Korczak's care came from low-income families and, prior to the orphanage, experienced severely neglected conditions. Many had behavior difficulties (Dror, 1998; Lipiner, 2015), lack of social skills, and trust in others, which presented a significant barrier to their effective integration into the Children's Home.

The appointed mentors introduced the new children to the educational environment and its rules, routines, and regulations. They also protected the newcomers from other children's verbal or physical assaults and served as their liaisons. In other words, the veteran children eased the transition period and helped newcomers establish connections with peers and teachers. Here is how Nadel remembered his meeting with Felek, his orphanage guardian:

> Felek managed to gain my trust from our first meeting.... Here I was, a newly arrived seven-year-old that had already had his fill of hardships. Felek led me to my assigned place in the dining room, showed me my bed in the immense hall in which the children slept, gave me a tour of the many rooms in the orphanage, and explained my new duties. (Lipiner, 2015, pp. 2–3)

Cross-age peer mentoring for children with social problems. Another group of students that required help from their older "brothers and sisters" were youngsters who lacked the social skills necessary for belonging to the children's community. They "erected invisible walls" (Lipiner, 2015, p. 9) between themselves and their environment, had difficulties being accepted by their peers, or were unable to adjust to the community's rules. As a result, these children received a low social evaluation by their peers in the yearly ballot or were sentenced by the Children's Court for breaking the rules, which put them at risk of being expelled from the institution (Dror, 1998).

The explicit disapproval of their behavior and the "court sentences" increased these children's feelings of alienation, aggression, and estrangement, and contributed to a negative emotional and social cycle. But even in those lonely days, the vulnerable children felt they had at least one person on their side—the peer-mentor who engaged them in scaffolding the acquisition of the desired social skills. With this help, most of these children were able to improve their behavior and raise their social status.

Ada Hageri-Poznansky (1982) interviewed students who were educated in Korczak's orphanage, and reflected on the level of support, guidance, and protection given to them by their guardians. For example, Israel Zyngman was constantly misbehaving and finally faced being expelled from the orphanage. Luckily, he recalls, he found a guardian who "agreed to take me under his wing. During all the three months of protection, I withstood the test" (Zyngman, 1976, as cited in Eden, 2000, p. 222, translated from Hebrew by me).

The students and educators of the Children's Republic felt that the cross-age mentoring contributed to the social life of the institution (Eden,

2000). The mentorship program emphasized the children's responsibility for each other's well-being. They could not ignore the challenges faced by new students or remain indifferent to children with underdeveloped social skills. The peer-mentoring program reinforced the sense of the community as a family, where the older siblings helped foster their little brothers' or sisters' self-confidence, intrinsic strengths, and trust in others. At the same time, the younger, struggling mentees gained strong motivation for self-improvement, realizing that the community cared about them.

Responsibility for the Community

The third dimension of responsibility that Korczak developed at the orphanage was the children's responsibility for the internal organization of their community. The required skills and motivation were obtained through daily experiences of self-governing. Korczak (1967a) developed it out of a conviction that "children have every right to live in groups... arranged by their own efforts and suited to their own conceptions" (p. 403).

The children's self-rule was expressed in mediating a whole array of organizational responsibilities that shaped community life—participating in governing and running the Children's Republic, finding solutions to numerous challenges, and judging their peers. The experience of active involvement in the construction of their lives "arranged by their own efforts... to suit their conceptions" (1967a, p. 402), taught the children the complexities and the possibility of living together in harmony while acknowledging and respecting individuality and differences.

Responsibility for Self-Government

The purpose of self-government was not to provide the orphanage's children with unrestrained freedom that might turn into chaos. However, Korczak (1967a) was convinced that children have the right to participate in discussions and make decisions on issues concerning them directly. It is a "child's irrefutable right," he proclaimed, "to voice his thoughts, to actively participate in considerations and verdicts concerning him" (p. 129). What is needed, he asserted, is a thoughtful balance between the teacher's knowledge, skills, and experience, and the children's right to participate in leading their own collective lives. In the Children's

Republic, the responsibility for operating the community's affairs was shared between the adults and the students. Clear regulations and rules, determined jointly through democratic discourse, obligated both groups equally and served as the basis for the community's social and moral norms (Efron, 2008; Silverman, 2017). The shared responsibility, Korczak (1992) explained, was also a practical strategy, since "without the participation of experts we will not be successful. And the expert is the child" (p. 174).

There were several self-governing organizational structures in the Children's Home that were created by Korczak *with* the children rather than *for* the children. The students had their own Children's Court, Children's Parliament, Children's Council, and their own newspaper. To each of these organizations, an educator was attached as an adviser without voting rights.

Children's Court. Korczak (2018), who saw himself as a "constitutional" educator (p. 244), perceived the Children's Court as a pillar of the school's self-governing infrastructure, which provided the children with a forum to serve as judges of their peers (Engel, 2008). The primary goal was to protect each child.

> But the court must defend the quiet children so that they're not harmed by the aggressive and the impudent ones; the court must defend the weak so that they're not tormented by the strong; the court must protect the conscientious and the diligent so that they're not held back by the careless and the lazy; the court must see that there's order, for disarray is most harmful to good, quiet, and conscientious people. (Korczak, 2018, p. 208)

The court embodied the values that Korczak (2018) wanted the children to learn: "The court is not justice, but it should strive for justice; the court is not truth, but it desires the truth" (p. 208). The court's verdicts aimed to teach the children how to settle conflicts in a humanistic, just, and thoughtful way that fostered sensitivity for both—the child who was hurt and the one who did the hurting. Remembering his own experience in Korczak's institution, Nadel proposed that the establishment of the court was based on Korczak's belief in children being "able to bear social judgment, grasp the concept of their own welfare versus the general welfare, and conduct themselves according to social laws" (Lipiner, 2015, p. 11).

The Children's Court was made up of five students elected democratically by their peers. Stefa Wilczyńska was present at every trial, and although she had no right to vote, she provided her advice to the children, but they were not obligated to accept it. According to Nadel, the rotation of the judges was very important for Korczak, since he didn't want to create an everlasting group but rather have every child experience the perspectives of a judge, a plaintiff, and a defendant (Lipiner, 2015).

The court's verdicts were based on a clear and detailed legal code, a "codex," written by Korczak (2018) and grounded in its principled declaration, "If some-one does something bad, it's best to forgive him" (p. 208). From the rules of law published in the orphanage chapter in *How to Love a Child* (2018, pp. 214–238), it is clear that the court's goal was to educate rather than to punish. Most of the verdicts "were formulated in terms of self-awareness and self-betterment" (Berding, 2018, p. 434), and were summarized and publicly posted. The court warned, advised, explained, and helped the child to recognize the conditions that caused the transgression and patiently advised how they could improve once they had the trial experience (Efron, 2008; Silverman, 2017).

Korczak believed that the experience of serving as judges in the Children's Court taught the institution's inhabitants to appreciate the values of orderly, just, and ethical community life. The children-judges became mindful of the respon-sibility that the role of a judge entailed and learned to reason and make informed and ethical decisions. This role also helped them to grasp the importance of for-giveness. The accusers, as well as the defendants, became aware that there is a due process of fairness that guarded and maintained the idea of justice and respect for the rights of others. Nadel relates that the court significantly decreased incidents of violence and disorder inside the orphanage (Lipiner, 2015).

Children's Parliament

The Children's Parliament was the highest body of self-government and formed the legislative power within the Children's Republic. Once a year the children elected among themselves 20 delegates for the parliament (Korczak, 1967a). All children could vote, but, the delegates were chosen among students who had not been tried for dishonesty. The latter could still be elected after they, through wagers and mentoring, had rehabilitated themselves. Thus, becoming a parliamentarian served as a motivational technique for modifying and improving the social behavior of problematic children (Korczak, 1967a).

The parliament was presided over by Korczak and was convened in the Grand Hall before the whole community. The general assembly's discussions revolved around the educational, social, and ethical issues of the institution, and its delegates passed, rejected, or amended proposals for laws established by the Children's Court (Cohen, 1994). The parliamentarians fixed the community's calendar and set up the holidays as well as other events in orphanage life. The parliament was also involved in the admission of new children and examining resolutions with regard to the expulsion of students. Additionally, as shown above, experienced children were elected during the general assembly to serve as cross-age peer mentors of children with social challenges (Cohen, 1994; Dror, 1998; Eichsteller, 2009; Engel, 2008).

Korczak (1967a) expected the members of the Children's Parliament to run fair, effective, and productive meetings. He saw the meetings' value in the ability "to steer the collective conscience of a community, enhance the sense of joint responsibility, and leave their marks" (p. 403). Due to his early disappointment by the quality of the general assembly's meetings, he warned against unavailing discussions made up of "surplus of words" (p. 403) that led to meaningless and insignificant decisions. Korczak (1967a) emphasized, "There is no more useless comedy than to stage an election and voting to secure a result . . . . A meeting should be business-like. The children's remarks should attentively and honestly be heard, with no misrepresentation or pressure" (pp. 401–403).

To prevent such ineffective meetings, members of the Children's Parliament were encouraged to think independently and to express their opinions on what needed to be done. Criticism was not stifled, and children's probing questions were not swept under the rug. On the contrary, their autonomy, critical thinking, and initiatives were encouraged and reinforced.

The Parliament's public meetings taught Korczak's charges to appreciate the value of a democratic debate and decision-making regarding real issues and their consequences. The children gained confidence in their own ability to assume the responsibility for assuring social cohesion within their community. They also recognized the importance of being active participants in building a fair, democratic, and just society.

The commitment to the three forms of responsibility encouraged the children to aim at self-improvement on personal, interpersonal, and collective levels. Taking responsibility for self fostered the children's awareness of the consequences of their actions and strengthened their ability to overcome problems and to set and achieve desirable goals. Taking responsibility for each other taught them to listen to and enhance their sensitive response-ability to the needs of the individuals around them. Taking responsibility for their community obliged them to consider the welfare of the group as a whole and to be actively involved in constructing a democratic and ethical common life.

Insights and Reflections

Korczak exemplifies a unique phenomenon in the authoritarian educational climate in Poland in the first part of the last century. His institutions serve as exceptional organizations that demonstrate the commitment to love and respect at a time when children were mostly silenced and oppressed. For over 30 years, Korczak advanced an alternative vision of education, implementing his ideas in an orderly and pragmatic environment.

Korczak accepted the children as they were, respected their struggles with their inner demons, and patiently, respectfully, forgivingly (but relentlessly) helped them to grow and take charge of their own lives. Despite the harsh political and social reality of racial hatred and ever-spreading violence, the Children's Home graduates developed a strong sense of identity, a secure emotional and social base, a sense of efficacy, and an unbroken quest for a life oriented towards truth, equity, and justice.

Korczak presented his pioneering ideas and practices not as a dogmatic schema but rather as a personal knowledge of practice (Clandinin & Connelly, 1996) gained through years of experience (Efron, 2005; 2008). For him, his praxis was to serve as a starting point for teachers' own continued theorizing in the context of their "own knowledge, passion, beliefs and in accordance with the specific contextual circumstances in which one has to act" (Korczak, 1978, p. 305).

For these reasons, Korczak neither composed an organized theory, nor claimed his practice to be a roadmap for future educators. In my view, he tried to show that the emphasis should be placed on the pedagogical love with the orientation towards planting, within the learners, the responsibility for themselves, others, and a just and democratic community. Korczak's educational praxis may serve as a mobilizing model for a school and classroom life in which student's autonomy, self-improvement, caring relations, and active involvement are of no less importance than gaining knowledge.

Many of the programs, methods, and strategies pioneered by Korczak were considered by the educational community of his time as revolutionary, impractical, utopian, and even "futuristic." Some of these methods, like self-regulation strategies, cross-age peer mentoring, the trusting relationship between students and teachers, and the emphasis on children's social and emotional well-being have been "discovered" lately by educators and are presented as promising and original innovations. Others, like students' participation in governing the school and children as judges of their peers, are still regarded as impractical and too "futuristic."

Korczak, a visionary pioneer who was ahead of his time—and in many ways ahead of our time—can be perceived as the "rich and . . . strange" pearl that we draw from the depth of the past (Arendt, 1993, p. 205) to look at the present with fresh and brave eyes. His deep understanding of the "child's soul" and his sense of moral justice may inspire us to develop within our students the willingness to take upon themselves the responsibility for self-improvement as individuals, peers, and active members of their community.

References

Alexander, H. A. (2003). Moral education and liberal democracy: Spirituality, community, and character in an open society. *Educational Theory, 53*(4), 367–387.

Arendt, H. (1993). Walter Benjamin: 1892-1940 (trans. H. Zohn). In H. Arendt, *Men in dark times* (pp. 153–206). New York: Harcourt Brace & Company.

Berding, J. W. A. (2018). Janusz Korczak and Hannah Arendt on what it means to become a subject: Humanity, appearance and education. In M. Michalak (Ed.), *The rights of the child yesterday, today and tomorrow: The Korczak perspective* (pp. 432–449). Warsaw: Rzecznik Praw Dziecka.

Buber, M. (1965). *I and thou* (R.G. Smith, Trans.). New York: Routledge.

Carver, C. S., & Scheier, M. F. (1999). Issues in the self-regulation of behavior. In R.S. Wyer (Ed.), *Perspectives on behavioral self-regulation* (pp. 1–101). Mahwah, NJ: Erlbaum.

Clandinin, D. J., & Connelly, F. M. (1996). Teachers' professional knowledge landscapes: Teacher stories, stories of teachers, school stories, stories of school. *Educational Researcher, 25*(3), 24–30.

Cohen, A. (1994). *The gate of light: Janusz Korczak, the educator and writer who overcame the Holocaust*. Cranbury, NJ: Associated University Press.

Dror, Y. (1998). Educational activities in Janusz Korczak's orphans' home in Warsaw: A historical case study and its implications for current child-care and youth care practice. *Child & Youth Care Forum, 27*(4), 281–298.

Eden, S. (2000). *Henryk Goldszmit–Janusz Korczak: The man, the educator, the writer*. Jerusalem: Janusz Korczak Association in Israel.

Efron, S. (2005). Janusz Korczak: Legacy of a practitioner-researcher. *Journal of Teacher Education, 56*(2), 145–156.

Efron, S. (2008). Moral education between hope and hopelessness: The legacy of Janusz Korczak. *Curriculum Inquiry, 38*(1), 39–62.

Eichsteller, G. (2009). Janusz Korczak: His legacy and its relevance for children's rights today. *The International Journal of Children's Rights, 17*(3), 377–391. DOI: 10.1163/157181808X334038

Engel, L. H. (2008). Experiments in democratic education: Dewey's lab school and Korczak's Children's Republic. *Social Studies, 99*(3), 117–121.

Hageri-Poznansky, A. (1982). *Haish ah-akshan, Janusz Korczak mikarov* [The stubborn man: Janusz Korczak closely]. Tel Aviv: Hakibbutz Hameuchad.

Korczak, J. (1962). Rules of life in J. Korczak. *Pedagogical writings* (Trans. D. Sadan & S. Metzer). Tel Aviv: Hakibbutz Hameuchad.

Korczak, J. (1967a). How to love a child (J. Bachrach, Trans.). In M. Wolins (Ed.), *Selected works of Janusz Korczak* (pp. 81–462). Washington, DC: The National Science Foundation.

Korczak, J. (1967b). The little brigand. (J. Bachrach, Trans.). In M. Wolins (Ed.), *Selected works of Janusz Korczak* (pp. 530–533). Washington, DC: The National Science Foundation.

Korczak, J. (1978). *Dat Ha-Yeled* [The child's religion] (D. Sadan & Z. Arad, Trans.). Tel Aviv: The Yitzchak Katzenelson, Beit Locahmei Haggetato & Hakibbutz Hameuchad.

Korczak, J. (1992). *When I am little again and The child's right to respect.* Lanham, MD: University Press of America.

Korczak, J. (2001). The education of educator by the children. *Dialogue and Universalism, 11*(9–10), 51–57.

Korczak, J. (2018). *How to love a child and other selected works* (Trans. B. Platoff, D. Borchardt & S. G. Bye). Chicago: Vallentine Mitchell.

Lewin, A. (1997). Tracing the pedagogic thought of Janusz Korczak. *Dialogue and Universalism, 11*(9–10), 119–124.

Lipiner, L. (2015). *Taking roots: My life as a child of Janusz Korczak, The father of children's rights: Biography of Shlomo Nadel* (Trans. Ora Baumgarten). http:// www.januszkorczak.ca/wp-content/uploads/2015/12/JK_book_En.pdf. Toronto, Canada: Office of the Provincial Advocate for Children and Youth.

Murdoch, I. (1970). *Sovereignity of good.* London: Routledge & Kegan Paul.

Noddings, N. (2014). *The challenge of care in schools: An alterntive approach to education* (2nd ed.). New York: Teachers College Press.

Shner, M. (2012). *Janusz Korczak and Yitzhak Katzenelson: Two educators in the abyss of history.* Tel Aviv: Tel Aviv University.

Silverman, M. (2017). *A pedagogy of humanist moral education: The educational thought of Janusz Korczak.* New York: Springer Nature.

CHAPTER SEVENTEEN

To Inspire Not to Compel: Korczak's Ideas and Practice of Moral Education

Marc R. Silverman

Introduction

KORCZAK'S VISION AND practice of moral education present an unusual opportunity to effectively integrate free development of children with their moral development and, as a result, to base interpersonal and social relationships on justice, truthfulness, caring, cooperation, and compassion.

It is unusual because philosophers and practitioners of education who consider "free development of children" the ultimate goal of education are staunch opponents of those who define such a goal as the moral growth and development of children. In a consistent "free development" theory there is no end of education outside of the individual's own continuous growth. This theory recognizes the child as the most meaningful "subject," making him or her (henceforth, her) the hard core of the educational process and turning society or culture into its soft core. The student uses, shapes, and controls social and cultural norms for growth and self-realization (Lamm, 1976).

In a consistent theory of moral development a clear vision of what constitutes the "good life" and the attempt to accomplish this vision in real life transforms human beings from their existence as biological creatures to human ones. Then, the introduction of moral concepts and ethical modes of behavior to students becomes the "hard core" of the educational process, and the students are regarded as its "soft core." The aim of moral growth guides, shapes, and controls the students (Lamm, 1976).

So how does Korczak achieve an educationally effective integration of the above models, and how does he address the conflicts between them?

To start with, his relationship to these two conceptions of education is dialectical. Utilizing all available sources, including testimonies of Korczak's orphanage graduates and his own writings, it is possible to assume that for him the free development of children is based on two basic principles:

- Offer children love and respect and afford them considerable freedom, albeit guided by their educators, to determine the way they want to pursue their lives.

- Refrain from all forms of domination, coercive manipulation, or indoctrination such as preaching, awarding, and rewarding them, and employing threats or actual acts of physical or psychological punishment against them (Kohn, 1997).

At the same time the development of children is predicated on adherence to the following four guidelines:

- Hold a vision of the "good life" and educate children towards its realization in practice.

- Propagate epistemological humility and opposition to fundamentalism, fanaticism, or murderous intolerance on the one hand, and to emotivism and moral relativism on the other.

- Practice "ameliorative compassion"—the possibility of moral growth and its limitations.

- Do nothing *about* children *without* them. Create and offer dialogical-democratic ways that inspire a combination of caring and justice in interpersonal and social relationships.

How to Translate These Guidelines into Practice

1. **Free development of children.**
Children's rights–Offering children genuine respect and love.
Korczak was an early advocate of children's rights, including the right to keep a secret, and the rights to own personal belongings, to be loved, and to receive

full human respect. The latter entails three further rights: to live in the present (in this day and at this age); to be oneself; and to be in charge of one's own death, e.g., "to take risks, to explore the world, to receive presupposed 'response-ability' for discovering new and challenging situations" (Wolins, 1967, pp. 123–124).

Constitutional education and a "constitutional" educator.

Korczak's establishment of the Children's Court is a very powerful testimony to his commitment to children's rights in real-life practices. Reflecting on the motivations and goals in investing so much in the court, Korczak expressed his ambition to be "a constitutional" educator and to create a constitutional system of education:

> If I am devoting a disproportionate amount of space to the Court, it is because I believe that it may become the nucleus of emancipation, pave the way to a constitution, make unavoidable the promulgation of the Declaration of Children's Rights . . . . The child has been given no right to protest. We must end despotism. (Wolins, 1967, p. 312) . . . I declare that these few cases have been the nub of my training as a new "constitutional" educator who avoids maltreatment of children not because he likes or loves them, but because there is a certain institution which protects them against the educator's lawlessness, willfulness and despotism. (Wolins, 1967, p. 351)

Such an educational system not only champions and grants equal rights to children as human beings who are in the process of physical, intellectual, social, emotional, and ethical growth, but also strives to nurture them. Besides, it gives rise to educators who try not to impose their wishes and whims on the students and refrain from being manipulative. The Children's Court demonstrates the solid philosophical basis of Korczak's educational work, which was respect for a unique nature of every child.

The following passage exemplifies the emotional and ethical dimensions underlying the children's court:

> A teacher turns up his nose at the contents of children's pockets and drawers. A little of everything: pictures, postcards, bits of string, tags, pebbles, pieces of cloth, beads, boxes . . . A story, often highly involved, is attached to each item. A tiny shell is a dream of a trip

to the seacoast . . . . The eye of a doll, broken a long time ago, is the sole reminder of a long lost love . . . . It happens that a brutal teacher, unable to understand and consequently disdainful, angry over torn pockets, and stuck drawers . . . in a fit of bad temper collects all those treasures and consigns them with the rubbish to the stove. A gross abuse of power, a barbarous crime. (Wolins, 1967, p. 30)

The above quote shows how much attention Korczak paid to every aspect of the children's lives. It also illustrates his metaphorical imagination, accompanied by a positivist, scientific attitude toward small details (e.g., "a tiny shell is a dream of a trip to the seacoast"). Korczak's imagination allowed him to unravel the way children relate to objects and their emotional meaning for them. Many of Korczak's colleagues admired his ability to read children; decode their emotions, behavior, and experience; and pay respect to every creature.

2. **Moral education of children.**
Korczak's vision of a "good life."
The very possibility of embarking on any educational project necessitated for Korczak a clear definition of its ultimate goal. Thus, an understanding of a "good life" is an imperative of education and not a luxury. Korczak sought ways of inspiring the children in his care to internalize and strive for this vision in their own lives.

Here is a list of the key principles that constitute Korczak's conception of the "good" or a "good life":

*   Faith in people's ability to improve themselves and, to a certain degree, the world.

*   Respect for every creature—the inanimate, the living, and the human.

*   Growth of self-awareness as the capacity to learn one's own abilities and weaknesses, and to channel the latter positively.

*   Investment of productive, creative, faithful, and thorough work in improving human life.

*   Development of interpersonal and social sensitivity, especially sensitivity to injustice.

- Growth of reflective critical abilities to discern evils in oneself and the society, and of active ethical care to repair what can be repaired.

- Construction and preservation of human relations and social ties based on dialogue, cooperation, justice, and compassion (See Cohen, 1994).

The list of children's commendable personal and social actions that Korczak regularly posted on the bulletin board in the orphanage provides a more practical understanding of Korczak's vision of the "good." Among them are keeping order, accepting responsibility, promoting the common good, caring for one's fellow, acting friendly, providing moral satisfaction, offering material assistance, behaving honestly, etc. (Frost, 1983).

Epistemological humility and the opposition to fundamentalism and moral relativism.

Korczak fully understood and shared the fear that the exponents of the "free development of children" approach held regarding the possibility of falling into the trap of the evils of *direction-fullness*—totalitarianism, fundamentalism, fanaticism, and so on. In the words of Sir Isaiah Berlin (1969):

> One belief, more than any other, is responsible for the slaughter of individuals on the altars of the great historical ideals.... This is the belief that somewhere, in the past or in the future, in divine revelation or in the mind of an individual thinker, in the pronouncements of history or science, or in the simple heart of an individual thinker, there is a final solution. This ancient faith rests on the conviction that all the positive values in which men have believed, must in the end be compatible and perhaps entail one another. (p. 167)

In the view of the "free-development" exponents, establishing an ultimate end of education beyond children's personal continuous growth blocks their freedom to choose their own way to self-realization.

Providing constitutional education and "epistemological humility" (exercising humility and caution regarding the incontestable correlation between one's own conception of the good and the Good itself) are Korczak's remedies to the evils described above. While embracing a vision of the "good life" and educating towards translating it into real-life practices, people at the same time are called upon to always remember that their conception of the good is their approximation of the Good but not the Good itself.

Coming from the opposite direction, Korczak's insistence on the importance of a moral vision in education is an antidote to the strong possibility of the exponents of the "free development of children" approach falling into another trap—of emotivism, moral relativism, and an ethos of "everything goes." The absence of a moral compass leads to the transgression of *direction-lessness,* which is no less pernicious than the transgression of *direction-fullness* and perhaps paradoxically often leads people to embrace the latter's mendacious forms (MacIntyre, 1984).

"Ameliorative compassion"—the possibility of moral growth and its limitations. Korczak also took serious issue with the optimistic view of human nature that serves as another central tenet of the "free development of children" approach. Rousseau (2001), the father of this approach, opens *Emile* with the claim that, "God makes all things good; man meddles with them and they become evil" (p. 5). Korczak regarded Rousseau's premise and a similar stance by Alexander S. Neill (1971), the founder and director of Summerhill, as decidedly erroneous, claiming "Rousseau begins *Emile* with a sentence, which all the contemporary science of heredity contradicts" (Wolins, 1967, p. 201).

Korczak was certain that human evil exists and that it emerges out of two main sources: innate genetic negative impulses, some of which cannot completely be controlled, and negative interpersonal encounters. He warns educators to refrain from adopting a sentimental view of children:

> A teacher starting out with the sweet illusion that he is entering a little world of pure, affectionate and open-hearted souls whose good will and confidence are easy to win will soon be disappointed . . . . There are just as many evil ones among children as among adults . . . . A birch will stay a birch, an oak an oak, and a thistle a thistle. I may be able to rouse what is dormant in the soul but I cannot create anything. (Wolins, 1967, pp. 246–247)

Admitting that evil is inherent in human nature and cannot be entirely removed, Korczak posed the most decisive educational question of how to strengthen and advance children's will towards goodness and to redirect their will away from badness in a more constructive and life-building way.

Aware of the profound difficulties in confronting effectively the very problematic gap between the life-improving possibilities emerging out of constructive work on the human will, and the serious limitations negative genetic and social forces exercise over it, Korczak developed an educational approach and the pedagogy based on it, which I call "compassionate amelioration." It includes:

- Viewing the difficult actions of a child as an expression of the experience of her present self.

- Granting respect to the child's present self, constituting a tolerant and patient attitude toward her negative behavior and traits.

- Providing pedagogical forgiveness and respect, building relations of trust as a necessary condition for having any educational influence on her.

- Offering the child opportunities for action that will challenge her to improve herself and the society in which she lives.

- Assisting the child to acquire and practice the tools and skills necessary for self- and social improvement.

"Response-ability," the ability to respond in compassionate amelioration, in care and critical-ethical concern to the real worlds, aspirations, and struggles of their charges in their current existential presence is the hallmark of good educators. Korczak constructed and implemented an interrelated web of educational practices, methods, and frameworks, later called the "Korczakian system," that fostered a social climate of "compassionate amelioration" in his orphanage community. Among about twenty frameworks and practices (Silverman, 2017, pp. 143–151), one finds the Children's Parliament and Court, the Court Constitution, the apprenticeship system; gradated citizenship status; ethical-improvement wagers; work assignments, units and points. Each of them independently and through their interrelationship encouraged educational processes that assisted members of the orphanage community to relate to each other through the ethos that integrates a relational-caring ethic and a rational-cognitive one. Still, in Korczak's eyes, the Children's Court and the Constitution, and the proceedings themselves, were the most outstanding among these practices (Silverman, 2017).

Dialogical-democratic ways to inspire children to combine caring and justice in their interpersonal and social relationships.

The structure and substance of the Constitution—law book—that Korczak composed, the way he proposed it should be used in the court proceedings, and the proceedings themselves tend to convert his pedagogical ethos into practice. All the orphanage's children and educators were allowed to lodge a complaint in the court against a pupil or educator whom they felt had offended them.

Korczak himself wrote the code, according to which the judges adjudicated the complaints. Instead of substantive laws that define misdeeds, the code contains 109 bylaws that are essentially guidelines for evaluating the extent to which the offender should be held response-able for the misdeed(s) that the plaintiff has brought to the attention of the court. The first 99 bylaws, numbered in singular units (1, 2, 3, ... to 99), comprise a rich array of reasons that provide "forgiveness" to the offender; while the last 10, numbered by hundreds (100, 200, ... to 1000), find the offenders responsible for their actions.

The severity of the offense is expressed in the sharpness of the language used to formulate the reprimand and in the extent to which this reprimand is publicized within the orphanage community. The most severe are bylaws 900 and 1000: the former warns offenders that expulsion is imminent unless they alter their antisocial behavior, and the latter expels them from the orphanage. Still, the subjects to bylaw 900 are afforded the opportunity to choose a more seasoned member of the orphanage community to assist them in their last back-against-the-wall attempt at self-improvement while an expelled person can apply for re-admission to the orphanage after three months (based on anecdotal and empirical evidence of an ongoing self-reformation).

I consider that the outstanding predominance of bylaws that refrain from reprimanding the accused for the offenses they commit, 99 in number and counted in single units—over the 10 incriminating ones counted in units of 100—in the law book is not arbitrary. It is much more educationally sound and constructive to find compelling justifications to forbear children's misdeeds than to jump at the opportunity to punish them. Although extending such forbearance requires great patience and tolerance, as punishment it is a much easier path and a slippery slope.

Close reading of the constitution's preamble provides a better understanding of the dialogical-democratic ways employed by Korczak and his educational staff. I define three major interrelated practices that assist the child in integrating caring and justice into their interpersonal and social relationships:

1. Lending genuine respect for children as persons and adopting an attitude of educational forgiveness towards them in their ever-emerging presence.

The phrase that the best thing is to forgive regardless of what a person did, is repeated twice. This repetition suggests that Korczak considered such forgiveness as a constitutive postulate of the very possibility of engaging in moral educational work with people in general and with children in particular. Respect for the child's given-ness—her present presence—forbearing her weaknesses is the beginning of effective moral education.

Deep respect and caring for children provide ways to forgive their bad deeds through adopting a compassionate understanding of the many circumstances and causes that diminish their capacity to do good things or increase their capacity to do bad ones. This forbearance is not conceived as a special favor but as an ethical imperative commanding respect for the child's given presence. Indicting children for their present respective personhoods not only demonstrates a lack of respect towards them, it also strongly discourages them and eliminates any possibility to reconsider the problematic aspects of their behavior. Angry accusation locks up children's possible entrance into the gates of self-reformation, while pedagogical forgiveness unlocks and opens them widely.

2. Offering children numerous self-reformation and social reformation opportunities.

The pedagogical nature of Korczak's forgivingness does not mean or grant a *do-wrong* free pass to the child. Instead, the acceptance of the bad deed is immediately followed by and predicated upon the hopeful notion that in the future when an opportunity for the child to repeat this bad deed presents itself, she will "mend her way" and refrain from committing it again.

Korczak's system of education abounds with "offerings" of second, third, and more self- and social reformation behavior opportunities. The abundance of such opportunities clearly demonstrates the hope that the children would undertake "response-ability" on their own to mend their unethical ways. This hope was based on individual and interpersonal reformation opportunities constructed for children, such as:

- Ethical-improvement wagers.

- The possibility of reapplying to the orphanage three months after expulsion from it.

- Upgrading one's own citizen status in the orphanage by virtue of having become more socially cooperative.

- Increasing the scope of one's work assignments and responsibilities as well as becoming competent in the specific type of work.

Korczak's response to a child who sought to raise the level of her citizenship in the orphanage community can serve as a summary of the underlying educational ethos:

> If you have enough good will, intelligence, and the appropriate qualities, you will have full rights in our community, but you have to earn it. Without work, there is no fruit—there is no sunlit sports field, no playground, no summer in the country, fairy tales, semolina cakes in milk. There are no days without a yoke if you don't prove that you really, sincerely, wish to enjoy these conditions. The reward is according to the effort. (Cohen, 1994, p. 102)

3. Not just-caring but Just caring.

Interpreting the last two passages of the constitution's preamble will lead us to the third and final practice in Korczak's conception of moral education. Korczak states explicitly that the pursuit of justice and truthfulness is the raison d'être of the Children's Court. This passage and the ones preceding it suggest that in his conception of moral education, interpersonal and broader social relationships should not be based just on relational caring but also on a caring and concern for just relationships. This third practice entails inspiring children not only to care for each other but also to care about supporting relationships with each other that are just or based on justice. Consequently, educational forgivingness is not only predicated on the hope of future mending of wrongdoings; it is also circumscribed by considerations of justice.

The above practices cannot encourage or tolerate the development of an unjust social climate in which the strong, mischievous, and irresponsible children grow stronger while the weak, industrious, and responsible ones become weaker.

Constructing the mending-one's-way practice fields on these grounds helped children to learn and internalize rational ethical principles of give-and-take, effort and outcome, and input and output. The many social frameworks that engaged the children and in which they engaged, and the interest in and commitment to justice, fair-mindedness, rationality, and truthfulness embodied in the former, encouraged them to seek self-knowledge, and to develop and exercise moral reasoning based on rational thinking, critical reflection, and judgment on the one hand, and care, beneficence, and compassion on the other.

Conclusion

Respect and caring for the development of every child as a unique individual and the aspiration that the child's personal relationship to others and the world should be based on compassion and justice serve as the two foci of Korczak's conception of education.

He employed two interrelated non-coercive means:

- Developing a staff of educators composed of Wilczyńska, the "stipendiary" counselors, and Korczak himself whose relationship with the orphanage children was based on and provided a model of compassionate amelioration.

- Constructing a network of educational practices that were grounded in and fostered a social climate and community that provided corresponding amelioration. All the members of this community—staff members and children—were engaged in daily practices of self-education and the education of others on these compassionate ameliorative grounds.

In my view, the entire educational project created and implemented by Korczak is an attempt to develop a model of humanistic moral education that respects the rights of children, avoids resorting to authoritarian and coercive methods of education, and offers dialogical and cooperative methods that encourage and facilitate their moral development. I believe that Korczak should be recognized as one of the outstanding humanist moral educators of the 20th century.

References

Berlin, I. (1969). *Four essays on liberty.* London: Oxford University Press.

Cohen, A. (1994). *The gates of life.* Rutherford, NJ: Fairleigh Dickinson University Press.

Frost, S. (1983). Janusz Korczak: Friend of children. *Moral Education Forum, 8*(1), 4–22.

Joseph, S. (1999). *A voice for the child: The inspirational words of Janusz Korczak.* London: Thorsons.

Kohn, A. (1997, February). How not to teach values: A critical look at character education. *Phi Delta Kappan.* Retrieved from https://www.alfiekohn.org/article/teach-values/

Lamm, Z. (1976). *Conflicting theories of instruction: Conceptual dimensions.* Berkeley, CA: McCutchan.

MacIntyre, A. (1984). *After virtue: A study in moral theory.* 2nd edition. South Bend, IN: University of Notre Dame Press.

Neill, A. S. (1971). *Summerhill.* Middlesex, England: Pelican/Penguin.

Rousseau, J. J. (2001). *Emile.* London: J.M. Dent, Everyman.

Silverman, M. (2017). *A pedagogy of humanist moral education: The educational thought of Janusz Korczak.* New York: Palgrave-Macmillan.

Wolins, M. (Ed.). (1967). *Selected works of Janusz Korczak.* (J. Bachrach, Trans.). Washington, DC: National Science Foundation. Retrieved from www.januszkorczak.ca./legacy/CombinedMaterials.pdf

CHAPTER EIGHTEEN

Janusz Korczak and John Dewey on Re-Instituting Education

Joop W.A. Berding

Introduction

AT FIRST GLANCE, the lives and professions of two of the most significant educators of the 20th century—Janusz Korczak (1878–1942) and John Dewey (1859–1952)—seem to have nothing in common, not even a vague similarity. Yet there is more than "meets the eye" and in this chapter I have chosen to submit both pedagogues' works and their inherent pedagogical "positions" to a parallel investigation.[1]

To begin with, there is a clear like-mindedness in regard to the status of childhood. Korczak and Dewey consider childhood not as a passage towards adulthood, but as a relatively autonomous phase in an individual's life.

Furthermore, both use an experimental approach when it comes to a pedagogical interpretation of children's reality and education. While neither rejects the validity of scientific research, they both strongly emphasize the importance of teachers' observations of their students and remind practitioners that they are dealing with a "real" child in his or her (henceforth, his) interaction with the "real" world.

Thirdly, Korczak and Dewey reject an "objectivist" approach to education when they imply that, in education, a new reality is constructed, rather than simply reinforcing the status quo of any existing reality. For the most part, the child serves as a creator of his own education, while participating in meaningful activities, and the concept of "participation" is significant here.

Finally, both were deeply involved in the practice of education: Korczak in his Warsaw orphanages (1912–1942) and Dewey in the Laboratory School in

Chicago, Illinois (1896–1904). Each was epoch-making in his own way. I believe the essence of their work was to create new forms of an institutional community life where the participation of children and young adults largely determined day-to-day practices and preserved open communication channels with the outside world.

The more pressing question for me, however, is whether it is possible to find ways to resolve our present-day problems of institutionalized life on the basis of what I call the "re-institutionalization" of education as proposed and exemplified by Korczak and Dewey. No doubt, the humanization of society and its institutions remains a timely task. It is, therefore, relevant to examine Korczak's and Dewey's pedagogical ideas and practical arrangements, in order to determine their applicability to current problems in the educational field—lack of intellectual interest, low motivation, dropouts, etc. Clearly, it would be impossible and perhaps irrational to fully implement either Korczak's or Dewey's ideas today (e.g., Boisvert, 1998; Berding, 1999; Tanner, 1997) but they are still promising enough to investigate further.

In this chapter, I plan to describe the socio-cultural context in which both pedagogues developed their theories and practice with more space being given, understandably, to Korczak, and then to reconstruct Korczak and Dewey's "educational anthropology" and their views of children and childhood. I conclude by addressing the question: "What lessons about 'institutionalized participation' could be drawn from the work in the Warsaw orphanage and the Laboratory School?"

Janusz Korczak

His entire life's work is distinctive for its all-embracing "obsession" (Korczak's own term) for the rights of the child. In 1919, he formulated what he called a "Magna Carta Libertatis," a constitution of the rights of the child. Korczak fights against the injustice done to children by their educators and other adults, and against their marginalized societal position. Korczak's pedagogy, which is definitely non-academic, is all about the defense of the rights of children and the protection of weaker human beings from stronger ones.

He practiced his ideals of community life in several orphanages and described them in his books, for example, a legendary Children's Court—in *How to Love a Child* (Korczak, 1967/1919). Being under a strong influence of a famous

Swiss pedagogue Johann Heinrich Pestalozzi (1746–1827), Korczak was even called the "Polish Pestalozzi." During the short period of time (1932–1934) when the orphanage had its own school, Pestalozzi's activity principles and pupils' responsibilities played a major role in Korczak's school.

Pediatrics, which defined the empirical core of his pedagogical work, was an emerging branch of medicine in the last decades of the nineteenth century; Korczak seriously studied it in Paris and Berlin. Afterwards, during his 30 years as an educator-pediatrician in the orphanage, Korczak observed his pupils intensely and collected numerous data on their growth and development. Unfortunately, all of this data was later lost during the war.

The development of Korczak's pedagogy was also tremendously influenced by his work as an apprentice educator in the summer holiday camps near Warsaw in 1904-1908. The experience of these camps taught him the importance of talking *with* children, instead of talking *to* them (Korczak, 1967/1919).

In August 1942, the history of Korczak's Children's Republic entered a final and tragic chapter, and at that moment "a martyr was made" (Chiel, 1975). Korczak's ideas began to spread around the world in the 1950s–1960s, first in Germany and then later on in numerous countries. There is an abundance of secondary literature of biographical, pedagogical, and, unfortunately, also of a hagiographical nature.

John Dewey

During his long life as an American philosopher, educator, and champion of democratic schooling, Dewey published a number of pioneering articles and books: *The School and Society* (1899), *Democracy and Education* (1916), *Experience and Education* (1938), and more. These works are largely based upon Dewey's experience in the Laboratory (elementary) School at the University of Chicago, where he tried to organize education so that it would be closely connected with the everyday lives of his students. Dewey rejected the mainstream educational system and introduced his approach of learning by doing and problem-solving organized in a lively, experience-based school setting. Communication, conversation, construction, and creativity were the catchwords of this "new" education. Not a verbally transmitted "coagulated culture," but a dynamic and vibrant reality was the starting point for the education that Dewey promoted (Berding, 2015; Dewey, 1899; 1902). He believed in a strong connection between school and informal learning and called for a continuity in the experience of the child (Dewey, 1916; MW9).[2]

Dewey was an important spokesman for the influential New Education Fellowship. In the early 1920s he distanced himself from the extreme "child-centered" practices used in some US schools, whose advocates incorrectly aligned themselves to his ideas. To equate Dewey's "progressivism" with child-centeredness is, therefore, and understandably, in dispute (Berding, 1999). Dewey's major concern is the coordination among the child, the subject matter, and the society.

In his lifetime Dewey experienced a whole range of emotional reponses to his ideas—from an enthusiastic welcome to their total rejection. If during the 1920s–1930s he was seen as sort of a "national prophet" in the United States, in the late 1950s, after American education underwent a pendulum swing, any schools' backwardness was then attributed to Dewey's influence. However, today in the United States and Europe we face a renewed interest in pragmatism and its implications for school practice. Recent studies of Dewey are mostly centered on the notion of participation in an attempt to stimulate discussion about new forms of community life in schools, health institutions, and youth work (De Winter, 1997).

Notions of the Child

Korczak and Dewey display a remarkable similarity in their anthropological views of the child. Both criticize the conception that childhood is merely a passage to "real life" equal to adulthood. In *How to Love a Child*, Korczak (1967/1919) pleads against fetishism of the future. He defends the right of the child to live his life now and today:

> Fearful that the child may be snatched from us by death, we snatch from him—life; not wanting him to die, we won't let him live. Reared ourselves in an inert and corrupting expectation, we are in a constant rush toward an enchanting future . . . we refuse to seek the beauty of today. (p. 132)

> For the sake of tomorrow, everything that makes the child happy, sad, surprised, angry and preoccupied, is disregarded. (p. 134)

In his novel *When I Am Little Again* (Korczak, 1992a/1925), where the main adult character is magically transformed back into a child, Korczak formulates this point as follows:

> Children—these are future people. And so it's a matter of their becoming, it's as if they don't exist yet. But indeed, we are: we live, we feel, we suffer. Our childhood years—these really are the years of life. Why? For what reason do they tell us to wait? Do grownups prepare for old age? (p. 155)

According to Korczak (1967/1919), a child does not come into the world as a blank slate:

> I may be able to create a tradition of truthfulness, tidiness, hard work, honesty and frankness but I shall not be able to make any of the children other than what they are. A birch will stay a birch, an oak an oak, and a thistle a thistle. I may be able to rouse what is dormant in the soul but I cannot create anything. (p. 309)

From Korczak's point of view there is no *makeable* human being. Childhood is not intended to prepare children for an idealized adulthood; it has its own autonomous meaning. The child searches, investigates, and experiments to find his own way through life. Educators should respect children's curiosity and ignorance, and, as Korczak (1992b/1929) puts it, "the mysteries and the ups and downs of that difficult task of growing!" (p. 178). Growing up, says Korczak, is a process that no one can do *for* the child. Educators should wave off the idea of living life *for* the child, and should not try to protect him from every possible evil and danger. In other words, educators should allow children to have their own experiences.

Similarly, Dewey states that a conception based upon a *comparison* of childhood and adulthood leads to a negation of the intrinsic value of childhood. In such a conception, the emphasis is put upon what the child is unable to know or to do *yet* (Dewey, 1916; MW9). For Dewey, however, the immaturity of the child forms "a positive force or ability—the power to grow" (p. 41). *Growth* (Dewey's alternative term for Froebelian "development") is the characteristic of all life. Children live this force to the fullest; they do not wait passively for the world to turn upon them. We find life's energy with both children and adults; both are "engaged in growing" (p. 47). Adulthood is, therefore, not a finality that stops the growth process: adults too have new experiences all the time. So the difference is not between growth or no growth but between the "modes of growth appropriate to different conditions" (p. 47). At the basis of the process of growing are, according to Dewey (1899), four genetically inherited "instincts" or "impulses": social, constructive, the impulse to investigate, and the expressive impulse (p. 30).

So I argue that for both—Korczak and Dewey—education represents first and foremost the process of living and living together. The only way by which a child can be prepared for the future is to have him optimally use all available possibilities and experiences (Dewey, 1916; MW9, p. 61). Both pedagogues expressed genuine interest and involvement in the uniqueness of childhood, a time of life with its own speed and dynamics.

Pedagogical Principles

Korczak and Dewey turn against the dominant image of a passive child who waits for the world to become interested in him. Korczak (1967/1919) describes in detail the lives of babies and older children, and the differences between their temperaments, intellect, humor, life-experience, and the way they encounter the world. Being a doctor, Korczak urges educators to actively relate to the child, and in the tradition of his medical profession, conceptualizes "relation" as a form of research (1967/1919, pp. 101–102). Korczak's pedagogical "mission" is to do away with every pedagogical judgment that does not rest upon an authentic educator's observation and reflection. By placing so much stress on the educator-as-researcher, Korczak might sound like a naïve empiricist, but this is far from the truth. He was the first to acknowledge that it is barely possible to derive any prescription for action from allegedly "hard" empirical facts:

> Through medicine, I learned the art of painstakingly putting scattered details and contradictory symptoms together into a coherent image of diagnosis. And rich in keen awareness of the grandeur of natural laws and the genius of man's searching mind, I am confronted with the unknown—a child. (Korczak, 1967/1919, p. 319)

For Dewey, education is not to set the child's development in motion; education starts with the determination of the actual interests of the child. These interests may help the educator to get a clear picture of the direction in which the development is supposed to go. When and where necessary the educator will stimulate, make corrections, guide, and canalize. The observation of the child's activities remains, for that reason, of prime importance. While observing children, an educator may also take leave from the idealized image of the perfect and innocent child, in which the daily "life and strife," falling and picking up the pieces, seem not to exist. Dewey, on the contrary, stresses the potential weaknesses and uncertainties of the educational process.

For Korczak and Dewey, to have faith in a child, provide him with trust, respect his uniqueness, and follow his growth and development are essential pedagogical practices. Both emphasize different points when it comes to the educability of the child. For Dewey, the organic connectedness of the child's experiences and the accumulated experience of the human species is central. By means of participation, doing something together with grown-ups, the child gains access to cultural riches. Korczak goes one step further: his radicalization of children's needs, their reformulation in terms of rights, and the legalization of these rights in the orphanages' judicial system controlled by the subjects themselves, are an explicit critique of the inability of many societies to adapt to children. Korczak's pedagogical struggle is at the same time social and political in nature; it is against the society in which the *homo rapax* continuously seems to win. Put in a more concise way, the difference between the positions of Dewey and Korczak is that with Dewey one can find much *about* the child, while Korczak chooses unequivocally *for* the child.

The School and the Orphanage as Pedagogical Workplaces

Korczak and Dewey have put their organic ideals of communal life into practice in experimental ways, and by doing so, they have given direction to very specific processes of institutionalization. The orphanage and the Laboratory School can be seen as ideal pedagogical workplaces. What is going on there is "institutionalized participation" of children that is defended and legitimized in different, yet clearly connected ways. Korczak's orphanage, for example, was a self-governing children's republic that was based upon a book of law, a constitution.[3] Offenses might be punished, in which case the court considered one or more articles. For example, Article 200 says: "You [the accused] were at fault. Too bad, it cannot be helped. May happen to anyone. Please do not do it again" (Korczak, 1967/1919, p. 410). Article 400 goes as follows: "Serious fault. (...) You behaved very badly" (p. 411). This article represents "the last resort, the last effort to spare the guilty disgrace. It's a last warning" (Korczak, 1967/1919, p. 410).

Korczak's purposes with regard to this constitutional approach were manifold: to maintain order in a community of around 200 orphans, to monitor the observance of obligations of both educators and pupils, and to take care of people, health, and personal belongings. Korczak (1967/1919) acknowledges without hesitation that he came to this way of living and working with children after a long struggle, and not without faults and drawbacks. Nevertheless, Korczak considered his constitutional philosophy of education as an attempt to build—albeit almost without any illusion—a community in which the weaker were not victimized by the stronger or left dependent upon the educator's arbitrariness.

Besides the court, Korczak's orphanage knew different forms of participation: there was a parliament that consisted of children. Pupils and staff wrote letters to each other. When Korczak was busy and found no time to react immediately to a child, the latter wrote a little note with her remark or question, and put it in a mailbox. Later, Korczak would write back or answer directly. Korczak felt that children must learn to postpone their immediate needs and use some distance. New pupils were assigned a mentor, a somewhat older child who knew the way. Much time was devoted to festivities and plays.

Children and staff, including Korczak himself, were jointly responsible for all the necessary work. Korczak (1967/1919) kept saying that *any* educator should be prepared to wash diapers or clean toilets, no matter the smell. No job was too humble, he observed, and he often did the ones just mentioned above.

Together with his children Korczak composed the first-ever children's newspaper, the *Little Review*. The paper had a network of child-correspondents all over Poland, who transmitted their messages by telephone and mail. The editors were rewarded for their work—sometimes Korczak gave them ice cream or took them to the cinema. He was opposed to child labor without worth, but he supported the principle of paying children if they seriously performed their tasks. In other words, Korczak saw participation as a shared responsibility for living together in all its aspects.

Dewey protested against the domination of a policy that imposed on children the necessity to sit still and listen to the teacher. He realized that the passivity of children was emphasized and that the subject matter presented to them had no psychological connection to their daily lives and experiences. Moving in an opposite direction, Dewey saw his school as a community of mutually dependent individuals. Formal education proceeded from and built upon the innate impulses mentioned earlier. Knowledge was produced by and in the interaction between an individual and society (Dewey, 1899; MW1). Any impulses were connected with the processes and the results of centuries of socio-historical development of the human species. In this way, Dewey tried to solve the fundamental problem of education, that is, how to "co-ordinate" psychological and social factors in education (Dewey, 1895; EW5). Dewey implemented the so-called *occupations* in his school: comprehensive, interrelated wholes of subject matter that covered essential human activities such as housing, food, and clothing (Tanner, 1997). These activities connected to the experiences children gained in their preschool life, their families, and communities helped them to develop structure and system in such experiences. The boundaries between formal school subjects played a minor role. The educational content, as a "purified" (re)presentation of the world in the school (Dewey, 1916; MW9, p. 20) was a response to the interests and needs of childen. Participation in activities was at the same time the goal *and* the most important instructional means of the educational process.

Discussion: Re-Instituting Education

Currently, education, care, and youth work undergo incisive processes of institutionalization. Korczak's and Dewey's critique is aimed at precisely these processes of modernization, formalization, and bureaucratization. In my view, their work must be seen primarily as an attempt to re-institutionalize education. Korczak and Dewey are concerned, not with the abolishment of institutions, but with a thorough and comprehensive revision of their components and of the pedagogical practices carried out. Korczak improves the quality of care and education provided to the orphans, and creates a higher—that is, a more humane—level, very different from ongoing practices of the time. He returns responsibility and control to the children and lets them make decisions about issues of justice and injustice on the basis of the book of law. By doing so he counteracts or at least mitigates pedagogical arbitrariness on the part of the educator. The rights of the child are at the same time acknowledged and limited.

Korczak's constitutional philosophy of education creates both freedom and restriction "in one movement": the law protects because it forbids that one lives at the expense of the other. Korczak's pedagogical work is also of a "political" nature in the sense that the orphanage was meant to be a "republic," i.e., a place where the general good or the common interest was considered of prime importance (Berding, 2017).

For Dewey, school education is much too dissociated from everyday existence and the forms of discovery, invention, and spontaneous learning in and by the community. He bitterly criticizes the formalistic and production-oriented character of schooling. Since the times when education became public and large numbers of children were submitted to the process of schooling, the institutionalization has acquired many more traits of factory-model learning.

In Dewey's view, schools are primarily forms of community life that generate meaning. Accordingly, Dewey presents a different education paradigm where the social interaction between humans and the participation of people in community networks becomes central, and schooling is a derived function. Dewey's emphasis on the importance of coordination between the individual and the society is an indication of his choice for the humanization of institutions which are viewed as forms of community life that liberate their participants instead of repressing them.

Conclusion

Thus far I have shown a number of parallels between Korczak and Dewey that are relevant to numerous issues in education today. The crucial question is how to overcome the obvious drawbacks of our institutions that have their roots in the modern age, and take steps toward new arrangements based on the concept of participation. Korczak and Dewey offer us valuable insights derived from communication, social construction, and participation. This is where I see the closest connections between the pedagogues.

In a heuristic way, many theoretical and practical lessons can be drawn from their pedagogical experiments—lessons, suggestions, and ideas that can help increase the quality of our children's education. Introducing the concept of participation can counteract the domination of objectivism and passivity in large parts of our formal educational landscape.

If we are willing to learn from Korczak and Dewey, we might find ways to overcome verbalism and intellectualism in schools, to connect formal learning with its spontaneous forms, provide time and space for children to grow, and stop dragging them along to yet another test. However, the question is whether educational philosophy on its own can effectively deal with the longed-for re-institutionalization. Korczak and Dewey uniquely understand that this is not only a matter of a "just" pedagogy, but that complex social and political problems are at stake that cannot be solved within the pedagogical realm alone.

References

Berding, J.W.A. (1999). *John Dewey's participatory philosophy of education: Education, experience and curriculum.* Retrieved from http://members.ziggo.nl/jwa.berding/ Berding%20Summary%20PhDdiss.pdf

Berding, J. (2015). John Dewey. In T. David, K. Gooch, & S. Powell (Eds.), *International handbook of philosophies and theories of early childhood education and care* (pp. 49–56). Oxford: Routledge.

Berding, J. (2017). Introduction on Janusz Korczak. http://korczakusa.com/wp-content/ uploads/2016/07/Introduction-on-Janusz-Korczak-by-Joop-Berding-May2017.pdf (Retrieved January 10, 2019)

Boisvert, R.D. (1998). *John Dewey: Rethinking our time.* Albany: State University of New York Press.

Chiel, S. (1975). Janusz Korczak: The making of a martyr. *History of Childhood Quarterly,* 13, 363-372.

Dewey, J. (1895). Plan of organization of the university primary school. *Early Works 5,* pp. 223-243.

Dewey, J. (1899). The school and society. *Middle Works 1*

Dewey, J. (1902). *The child and the curriculum.* Chicago: University of Chicago Press.

Dewey, J. (1916). Democracy and education. *Middle Works 9.*

Dewey, J. (1938). Experience and education. *Later Works 13*

De Winter, M. (1997). *Children as fellow citizens: Participation and commitment.* Oxford & New York: Radcliffe Medical Press.

Korczak, J. (1967/1919). How to love a child. In M. Wolins (Ed.), *Selected works of Janusz Korczak* (pp. 81–462). Washington, DC: National Science Foundation.

Korczak, J. (1992a/1925). When I am little again. In E.P. Kulawiec (Ed.), *When I am little again and The child's right to respect* (pp. 1–158). Lanham, MD: University Press of America.

Korczak, J. (1992b/1929). The child's right to respect', in E.P. Kulawiec (Ed.), *When I am little again and The child's right to respect* (pp. 159–186). Lanham, MD: University Press of America.

Tanner, L.N. (1997). *Dewey's laboratory school: Lessons for today*. New York: Teachers
     College Press.

Endnotes

1 I prefer using the term "pedagogues" and "pedagogical" as references to people
     who work as professionals with children in institutions such as schools and in the
     care and welfare sectors.
2 *The Collected Works of John Dewey, 1882-1953*, ed. by Jo Ann Boydston (Carbondale
     and Edwardsville: Southern Illinois University Press, 1967-1991), LW 14:311
3 For more details, see chapters by Silverman and Efron.

CHAPTER NINETEEN

Lessons from Korczak:
The Post Office as a Case Study

Shlomi Doron

ON JULY 18, 1942, at 4:30 p.m. in the party hall of the orphanage, Janusz Korczak (1878–1942) staged *The Post Office* (1912) for the residents of the Warsaw ghetto. Written by a famous Indian philosopher, writer, and poet, Rabindranath Tagore (1861–1941), the play celebrated love, respect, and trust. My goal here is to briefly describe the content of the play and to show how it might relate to educators today.

Tagore and Korczak

Being contemporaries, Tagore and Korczak never physically met, although there is a considerable resemblance between them. Both experienced hardships in life and referred to sufferings of the children in their care. Both devoted themselves to education: Korczak founded and managed an orphanage in Warsaw while Tagore established and headed a school and an orphanage in Bombay. Korczak was forced to relocate his orphanage three times and went through the stages of the ghetto destruction and reduction of its population. Tagore witnessed poverty and the terrible toll it took on children.

Both were popular children's writers and radio hosts of their time and published books on philosophy, educational psychology, and children's development, which were forbidden by the Nazi regime only to be returned to the public and later to become part of the curriculum and studies in India, Israel, England, the Netherlands, Poland, Russia, and the United States. Today, Korczak's legacy is preserved in 16 volumes in Polish and many selected works in English. Tagore's ideas were also translated into English (e.g., 2005; 2006) and made widely known especially after he received the Nobel Prize in Literature (1913).

The Play, Its Choice, and a Description

Korczak felt close to Tagore and was definitely influenced by his attitude towards children, and on the whole, "the ideas of the Indian philosopher touched a chord" (Regev, 1995, p. 220).

Trying to find more reasons for the choice of the play, I approached Yona Botzian, who, as a young woman, worked at the orphanage. Here are her explanations:

> Tagore was the most famous part of the school curriculum . . . . *The Post Office* was fairly natural, it was a continuation of the educational system, the background was there and Tagore's language was understood . . . . Korczak and Tagore had a dual relationship even before the ghetto was built. They were educators, thinkers and resembled each other in their saintliness! The worse the situation was—and we knew that death was around the corner . . .—the more our love and respect for them intensified. (Personal interview, December 1999)

When in 1933, Goebbels, the Nazi Minister of Propaganda, established the German Censorship Department, Tagore's books with their call for freedom, peace, and equality were among the first to be banned. *The Post Office* describes the sufferings of a dying boy and the importance of his encounters with people from other places as a larger framework for treating children. It was interpreted as referring to a "pure" Aryan child who would be saved once the "parasitic" Jew is removed from his presence, but the child still dies at the end of the play. Clearly, the Nazis could not tolerate this kind of message.

Korczak knew that if he chose the play of a well-known writer, whom many teachers studied in college, it would find an easier path to the audience, and its message would be clearly understood. Didacticism of this nature is typical of Korczak; he believed in conveying messages to children and adults who would be able to connect to the characters through a famous personality or a song, narrative, or a theatrical production.

The Post Office tells the story of an adopted boy who has fallen gravely ill. During the course of his illness Amal looks out of the window, sees and dreams of different individuals passing by, and engages them in a conversation. The play is comprised of two acts with six main characters: Amal, the boy; Madhav, his father; Gaffer, his grandfather; Sudha, a flower girl; an evil doctor; and the royal physician, a good doctor. There are also six secondary characters.

In the first act Tagore introduces Amal, who is lying in bed. His adoptive father informs the grandfather of the boy's illness. The latter is alarmed, and they wait for a doctor to pay a visit. The doctor prescribes bedrest for Amal, which means not to approach the window and expose himself to the "harmful" sun. The boy is bored and still goes to the window to talk with a dairyman who shares with him the places he visits and the people he meets.

Then the watchman comes and asks Amal to stay quiet. He tells him about the next world that everyone will eventually enter. The watchman explains that the big building across the street is the post office, and that the king of the land often sends mail to children. Since this moment, Amal lives in anticipation, awaiting a letter from the king that should help him feel better. The watchman describes the postman to Amal, the kind of job he has, and the faithful service he performs while covering long distances on foot, regardless of the weather. The watchman promises to return the following morning.

In the second act there is a series of dialogues where Tagore mixes illusion, imagination, and reality while Amal's condition worsens, with the secondary characters continuing to pass beneath his window. Amal converses with the headman, who explains to him the importance of the letters received at the post office and promises to convey to the king's headman information about the child's illness. Later, Sudha, a flower girl, arrives. She is in a hurry but promises to return the next day. Then Amal meets with a group of boys playing on the street, and they describe their game to him. In his turn Amal inquires about the letters from the king and how they reach their addressees. The children explain and leave Amal with the promise to return.

At the very end of the play Amal asks for permission to approach the window, but his grandfather explains the dangers that this involves. Still in bed, Amal drifts into his dreams and asks his grandfather and father for the reason why the anticipated letter has not arrived. They try to reassure him that it will. The king's headman finally shows up with a letter and a royal physician who overturns the earlier doctor's diagnosis, recommends keeping the window open and letting the sun in, since it can only be beneficial for the sick child. Amal falls asleep and is still sleeping when Sudha arrives. She asks for permission to approach Amal and whispers in his ear that she kept her promise to return, unlike the others. The play ends with Amal falling asleep (dying).

Evidence of the Play

Firsthand evidence about the play is meager, being confined to five short passages in *The Ghetto Years*, Korczak's diary, which he kept from 1939 to 1942, and a number of testimonies written after the Holocaust by people who had seen the play. On July 18, 1942, Korczak wrote in his diary (1980/1942):

> Yesterday—the play. *The Post Office* by Tagore. Audience appreciation, handshakes, smiles, attempts to engage in warm conversation... What would happen if yesterday's players continued with their roles today? Izhik would imagine he was a fakir. Little Haim would really appear to be a doctor. Adak, the mayor, representing the king. Perhaps this would serve me as a topic of conversation on Wednesday in the boarding school—"illusions" and their role in human life. (p. 191)

On August 1, 1942, Korczak adds the following entry to his diary: "Miss Esterka [director of the play and educator; murdered in Treblinka] is not anxious to live either gaily or easily.... She is dreaming of a beautiful life. She gave us The Post Office as a farewell for the time being. If she does not come back here now, we shall meet later somewhere else" (p. 209).

Thus, untamed India, dreams, imagination, flowers, colors, and the hope that every child would be able to visit distant places are all important to Korczak. He believes in the sanctity of certain values such as the right to dignity and the obligation to treat each child and adult with respect, noting very angrily that these rights and obligations don't exist in the ghetto; perhaps they existed only in distant India.

Analysis of *The Post Office* as Presented by Korczak

Korczak realized that only through public events would he be able to transfer educational messages to his charges and the community as a whole. Accordingly, he availed himself of this tool before many common holidays, in particular Passover and Chanukah. In the ghetto everyone knew that during these periods it was worthwhile to visit the orphanage and observe the preparations for the plays and concerts that were held there throughout the year.

A series of dreams that pass beneath the window of the sick boy, Amal, who has been forbidden to approach it, was very much in tune with Korczak's own message to his charges: teaching them how to die with dignity and without fear. It was also meant to be a message to the entire ghetto community, which was shocked realizing that the child's death in the play in fact symbolized their own fate. *The Post Office* is a *macabre* event in which sick and exhausted children play characters and introduce dreams about freedom, a magical island, flowers, and mail that they have not seen—and will never see. More so, the audience is in a no less pitiful state than the actors.

Korczak foresaw the advent of death wisely and understood that the children's end was at hand. He also realized that a similar fate awaited him (Silverman, 2017), the ghetto, and perhaps the Jewish people as a whole. In anticipating death in this way he chose to handle the uncertainty involved by deploying a ceremonial mechanism in the form of a play.

The play is a reflection of a collective understanding of love, respect, and trust. The characters in the play represent an existing structure: Madhav, who adopted a sick boy, is akin to Korczak; Amal symbolizes the sick ghetto children; the doctor, who forbids the opening of a window or the entry of sunrays, embodies the Nazis who brought in hunger and death instead of sun and freedom; the dairyman could perhaps stand for the whiteness and purity missing in Korczak's world; the boys, wandering around, personify the orphans who outlived their parents because of the Nazis; the king's physician represents salvation and healing. Finally, the window itself signifies the passage from freedom to incarceration, which was the reality of the ghetto. In other words, Korczak chose a play where the world of one sick child and his rights constitute the epicenter, and where the characters lived a parallel existence to the ghetto's daily reality.

Lessons for Educators

First, Korczak describes the modern world by means of a penetrating satire as a world gone crazy, one that is distorted and devoid of values, and that is choking on its own ropes because of social and moral tyranny. In such a world children must be taught how to love, respect, and trust even if sometimes it seems hard. This could be better achieved through illusions, ceremonies, and theatre that combine reality and imagination, life and death, good and bad, and permissible and forbidden. These binary options, according to Levi-Strauss (1974), encapsulate the life experience, and serenity and happiness remaining in the children's world as shown in *The Post Office*.

Secondly, there is the place of God and his disappearance from the world of humans because of their evil and immoral deeds, a world that reflects the chilling reality of the Warsaw ghetto. The play features the departure of God because of acts in the adult world. When children find themselves in a crazy world that seeks to destroy them, death becomes their only salvation, and Korczak tries to prepare them for their last journey.

Thirdly, there is the system of educational and democratic messages. In the play we see the struggle for human rights in general, and children's rights in particular. Apart from the motif of madness and death, plainly visible are the educational lessons of true democracy that Korczak wishes to deliver. Parliamentary reforms, a new constitution, the right to be respected, and the obligation to provide respect are representative of the educational motifs that Korczak wished to bequeath to generations of children and adults alike, as seen throughout his life and in his many plays (Efron, 2005).

Finally, theatre serves as a response mechanism in the face of existing and potential conflicts. Ceremonies and symbols, public events and plays are part of the set of expressions that people choose to actuate in the process of cultural development.

Korczak was a writer and an educator in his every fiber. Emphasizing the importance of Korczak's contribution to education, Kulawiec (1989) stated that the following concepts that Korczak had developed in his educational pedagogy in the first half of the previous century were in many ways similar to Tagore: human egalitarianism, the principle that children too are human beings, an openness to people who are different, an empathetic attitude to those who are suffering; the right to respect that every child and adult has (the obligation to respect all those who are born in God's image and have maintained that image), and the responsibility towards work and an aspiration to peace (Shalauddin, Hoque, & Bhuiyan, 2017).

These concepts are still the focal point of our lives as educators. The present age is witness to complex post-modernistic approaches in the social sciences that are being applied in educational systems throughout the world. Even though Korczak's legacy belongs to the past, it is certainly compatible with the anthropology of education today. Korczak elaborates on subjects such as trust, forgiveness, good, and evil.

And is not trust—and faith in man—the same good that can be maintained, developed as a counterweight to evil, that at times can only be removed with great difficulty? How much more understanding and patient is life than no small number of educators (Brendtro & Hinders, 1990, p. 237).

By constructing a public event around a theatre play Korczak sought to convey clear messages to the people around him in general, educators and the audience in particular as he demanded the right for children to be honored and live, to be loved and respected.

References

Brendtro, L., & Hinders, D. (1990). A saga of Janusz Korczak, the king of children. *Harvard Educational Review, 60*(2), 237–246.

Efron, S. (2005). Janusz Korczak: Legacy of practitioner-researcher. *Journal of Teacher Education, 56*(2), 145–159.

Kulawiec, E. (1989). Teachers and teaching: Yanoosh Who-o-o?: On the discovery of greatness. *Harvard Educational Review, 59*(3), 362–366.

Korczak, J. (1980 [1942]). *The ghetto years 1939–1942*. Western Galilee, Israel: Ghetto Fighters' House.

Korczak, J. (2003 [1942]). *Ghetto diary*. New York: Yale University Press.

Levi-Strauss, Cl. (1974). *Structural anthropology*. New York: Basic Books.

Regev, M. (1995). Janusz Korczak and the play *The Post Office* by Rabindranath Tagore at the orphanage in the Warsaw ghetto. *Maagale Kria*, 23–24, 215–220. (In Hebrew).

Shalauddin, M., Hoque, M. S., & Bhuiyan, T. (2017). Cognitive study of image schema and dying-mind in Tagore's near-death experience poems. *Rupkatha Journal of Interdisciplinary Studies in Humanities, IX*(2), 303–320.

Silverman, M. (2017). *A pedagogy of humanistic moral education: The educational thought of Janusz Korczak*. New York: Palgrave Macmillan.

Tagore, R. (1996 [1912]). *The post office*. New York: St. Martin's Press.

Tagore, R. (2005). *Selected poems*. Toronto: Viking Penguin.

Tagore, R. (2006). *The Tagore omnibus: Volume 1*. New York: Penguin Group.

CHAPTER TWENTY

From Despair to Agency: The Call from Janusz Korczak

Kristin R. Poppo

Bulletproof Teen
Run, if you can
Hide, if you can't
If neither, fight
The fighting isn't to save you
It's to save the next class, the next hall
It's to give them more seconds
To get there, to stop it
I am a child, a teenager
But, I am also a bulletproof vest
A diversion
A fighting chance for the others
Hope in the form of a distraction
I am blood and flesh
But I need to be Kevlar and fabric
Minimal casualties
Minimal children dead
Minimal little girls and boys
Minimal college applicants
Minimal honors students
And minimal teachers and coaches
But, not none.
The constitution doesn't allow for none.
That document is living
But will I be?
—Katie Houde, *Facebook post, 2018*

I have struggled to define the anguish I see in today's youth. And yet, Katie Houde, a teenager from Boston, says all that I find challenging to explain in a short poem. Mass shootings are not the only threat that our children face. Terrorist threats in a post-9/11 world, erratic weather stemming from climate change, economic volatility that is global in scope, and superbugs that resist current medications are all realities for our youth. From these events, narratives exist in the minds of young adults that lead toward apocalypse. Hearing such angst as an educator and a parent, I am deeply concerned about the psyche of youth. Anxiety and depression are on the rise amongst young adults, and yet, we often put the blame on our youth by pointing out that their challenges are a result of their increased obsession with cell phones and video games. While I see these technology trends as disturbing, I see them as symptoms rather than causes. The underlying cause is that we live in a time when fear of a human-induced apocalypse is real, and for many children and young adults there is a profound hopelessness relative to the future.

Although I cannot change the meta-story, as a college provost I seek to create a learning community in which young adults feel honored and respected. My hope is that such a community will provide a means for children to engage ethically in an increasingly challenging global environment. As I look for models for such a community, it is the children's homes of Janusz Korczak that stand out. Although Korczak was eventually murdered, his legacy is global. One of his former orphans who survived the Holocaust wrote,

> We used to say that Korczak was born to bring the world to redemption. What was so special about him was that he knew how to find a way to a child's soul. He penetrated the soul. The time spent at the orphanage formed my life. All the time, Korczak pushed us to believe in other people and that essentially man is good.... When the war broke out and I was starving and ready to do anything, I didn't, because something of Korczak's teachings stayed with me. (Korczak, 1999, p. xix)

Similar testimonies from many of Korczak's children affirm that he created environments that fundamentally transformed the psyche of his children from hopelessness and strife to hope and compassion. My hope is that we can lessen the emotional toll of today's world on our youth by reflecting on Korczak's writings and enacting more compassionate communities for children and young adults.

The Context

Each year, the American College Health Association completes the National College Health Assessment surveying over 30,000 students from 2008 to the present. The trends are alarming. The increase of anxiety, depression, and suicidal ideation amongst college-age students is very concerning. There are many theories as to why such trends are occurring. Hunt and Eisenberg (2010) propose that the increase in help-seeking behavior results in a perception that there are greater mental health issues amongst today's youth. In fact, there are both greater help-seeking behaviors and increased feelings of mental anguish as evidenced by direct student survey below (see Table 20.1).

TABLE 20.1

	2008	2013	2018	Percent Increase
Felt things were hopeless	47%	44.7%	53.4%	+6.4
Felt very lonely	59.7%	56.5%	62.8%	+3.1
Felt very sad	63.7%	59.5%	68.7%	+5.0
Felt overwhelming anxiety	49.1%	51.0%	63.4%	+14.3
Felt so depressed it was difficult to function	30.6%	30.9%	41.9%	+11.3
Seriously considered suicide	6.4%	7.5%	12.1%	+5.7

(American College Health Association, 2008; 2013; 2018)

Other psychologists point to technology and social media, changes in parenting and families, and systematic changes in education as the net cause of increased mental angst (Henriques, 2014). As I reflect on these perspectives, I agree they compound the mental health issues of today's youth, but these phenomena are, in part, a reaction to some of the root causes based on societal conditions of the 21st century.

The events of 9/11 heralded a new narrative both nationally and globally. The one remaining superpower was vulnerable, and thus, not only was the psyche of the United States of America changed, but there was a ripple effect around the globe also. Terrorist attacks touched many global centers, and a new level of fear came into the consciousness of those of us who, in the past, had been sheltered. As the decade progressed, global economic markets collapsed and the prediction of environmental collapse became more compelling. Within the United States, gun violence and mass shootings erupted on an unprecedented scale. The smartphones that reassured us that we could always communicate with our children became the means through which our children learned 24/7 of the latest catastrophe. Technology, which brought us comfort in knowing our children are safe, reminded us just how fragile our safety is.

This national and global vulnerability is having a profound impact on our youth. Although many of my peers tell me that they too lived in fear during the nuclear drills during the Cold War, the nature of the current threats brings the collective anxiety and hopelessness to a new level. Recently, when speaking to a group of young adults, I was alarmed that most of them believed there would be a significant event resulting in catastrophic global casualties during their lifetime. *Brave New World* and *1984* are no longer warnings to the masses; they are mainstream expectations. Young adults' convictions that these outcomes are likely are based on their knowledge of the multitude of threats, including nuclear weapons, bioterrorism, super-viruses, environmental devastation, etc. As educators, how can we help these youth remain positive in the unfolding global drama rather than powerless objects in a terrifying world?

Understanding the Child/Human

Korczak wrote extensively and worked with children in the early part of the 20th century in a way that was different from many developing child-centric pedagogies. When one of his former orphans stated above that Korczak (1999) "penetrated the soul," it speaks to me of his ability to deeply understand how children feel, think, and develop (p. xix). As I have moved from working with elementary students to college students, I recognize that young adults and adults are still struggling with some of the same "work" as they try to grow into their full humanity.

I have proposed that there are four states of being that are experienced by children that need to be fully understood by educators in order to create a learning environment in which children can flourish (Poppo, 2006). These states of being include enduring vulnerability, discovering uniqueness, joining community, and making meaning. As I have moved fully into the higher education context, I recognize that understanding students and these states is critical to creating an environment where students can move from hopelessness to agency.

Enduring vulnerability. One of my favorite stories of Korczak as an educator was when he invited a group of his students to the X-ray laboratory and then brought a young child from the orphanage into the room. The child was frightened by being in front of a group of strangers in a dark room with loud equipment. Korczak had the child stand behind the X-ray machine, and his students, training to be teachers, watched the child's heart beat at an alarming rate. Korczak (1999) said to the group: "Don't ever forget this sight. How wildly a child's heart beats when he is frightened and this does even more so when reacting to an adult's anger with him, not to mention when he fears to be punished" (p. 153). This experience was meant to elicit empathy and compassion. As educators, this is where our work begins, by trying to understand how our students think and feel.

In his works, including *When I Am Little Again* (1992), Korczak provides keen insight into the mind of the child, writing about a child's small size, their relative weakness, and vulnerability. As educators, we often focus on our frustration in dealing with difficult children rather than understanding how frightened children are when a person, who is older, more powerful, and perhaps even many times their size, communicates their frustration with loud words, threats, and even violence. Although this experience is particularly frightening for children, I am convinced that, as adults, we also share such feelings of vulnerability. For this reason, it is critical for educators to remember this when interacting with students. Enduring vulnerability is difficult work and often exhausting, and responsiveness to a vulnerable state is particularly important today. It is only when students feel safe in the educational institution that they can begin understanding themselves, which at its best allows them to respond compassionately to the vulnerable in their community and the world.

Discovering uniqueness. One of the most distressing outcomes of the "No Child Left Behind" era is that in teaching to the test, we have limited opportunities for our students to engage in a wide variety of experiences that help them to discover their unique gifts and talents. At the same time, in an age of economic uncertainty, college students often focus solely on accessing a job without engaging in intellectual and experiential exploration to truly decipher their passions and their inner selves.

Korczak began his relationship with each child with a period of discovery. He wrote, "There is in every human being a spark, which may kindle the flame of happiness and truth. It is our task to assist the growth of that which begins to sprout strong shoots even before man draws his first breath" (Korczak, 1967, p. 150). Korczak studied the child because he truly believed in the value that each child brought to the world. Korczak also recognized the need to create an environment where a child's individuality could flourish, no matter how challenging this could and would be for the educator. As he describes other educational institutions of his day, it is apparent that little has changed. He wrote,

> Contemporary educational ideas strive to make the child more convenient to handle and consequently, attempt, step by step, to put to sleep, to stifle and destroy everything which constitutes the child's will and freedom—the things which temper his spirit, which make up the driving force behind his demands and intentions. He is well behaved, obedient, good, convenient, but no consideration is given to the fact that his inner life may be indolent and stagnant. (Korczak, 1999, p. 126)

The challenge of indolence and stagnation is that, at its best, it creates a world of automation devoid of intellectual exploration and beauty. At its worst, it allows evil to eclipse the good as a charismatic leader can spread fear and hatred to automatons who are trained to obey, including carrying out atrocities that may be legal, but are clearly not ethical. Korczak had faith in human potential. He saw the job of the educator to engage in co-discovery with the child.

The lack of a true sense of self and a deep understanding of the unique contributions one can make to the world can result in despondency and withdrawal. If people perceive themselves and are perceived by others as mere numbers, tools, or objects, human community is at risk. Discovering one's uniqueness can only result in a search to see uniqueness in others. It inspires agency and compassion, and perhaps even hope. Youth without hope is the greatest tragedy I can envision.

Joining community. In my earlier paper (Poppo, 2006), I put forth that the educational mission to teach students to compete and win in a global economy was shortsighted and problematic. Instead, I wrote that the "greatest educational challenge today may not be to succeed and win in a global economy, but to live in a global community" (p. 33). Ten-plus years later, I am more convinced than ever that we need to teach our students to engage productively in cooperative teamwork rather than engage in individualistic, competitive, and nationalistic pursuits. Korczak was ahead of his time in creating a pedagogy that engaged all children in building a healthy community where violence was not permitted between children nor used as a means to enforce discipline. Children were expected to contribute positively to the greater community by overcoming their own selfishness and obstinacy.

Korczak trusted that most children would amend their poor behavior if they were given the opportunity to see how their behavior adversely impacted others and were provided the opportunity to grow in community. He wrote, "Politicians and legislators make rules and decisions about children, which often fail to work. But who asks the child for his opinion or consent? Who is likely to take note of any advice or approval from such a naïve being?" (Korczak, 1999, p. 142). Politicians, legislators, and educators continue to make the same mistake while Korczak shows us a different way by providing a context where children have agency, where they hold each other accountable, and where they largely take care of themselves and each other under the guidance of adults. He shows a human capacity for living together in a caring and healthy community.

Unfortunately, today, community is a foreign concept for many young people, and yet, learning to live in communities is absolutely critical to their personal and our collective existence. Korczak taught his children to flourish together by engaging them in collectively running their home and solving both collective and individual challenges.

Making meaning. The final process in which all of us are engaged is making meaning. For many this includes faith in the broadest context, as Tillich (1957) used it in *Dynamics of Faith*. Faith is an "ultimate concern," which defines a worldview—an understanding of the world and how it functions—and guides behavior

(p. 1). For young adults today, it may include a worldview devoid of hope and characterized by despair. Korczak (1999) was certainly no stranger to disenfranchised youth, stating,

> Alongside the children whose lives are fairy tales, who are trusting, friendly, and happy, there is a majority to whom, from their earliest days, the world teaches the gloomy facts of life in harsh words: poverty, abuse, neglect and indifference corrupt them. They become angry, distrustful, withdrawn and resentful—But not bad. (p. 143)

Korczak worked with the children who were full of anguish and despair. He saw his work to be transforming how they see and engage in the world. In his orphanage, children were protected, valued as individuals, and challenged to live in a compassionate community. This experience was transformative.

Korczak's transformation of children provides me hope for the transformation of today's youth from a worldview of hopelessness and despair to one of agency and compassion. Addressing his orphanage graduates, Korczak (1999) wrote,

> I cannot give you God, for you must find Him in quiet contemplation. In your soul. I cannot give you a Homeland, for you must find it in your own heart. I cannot give you love of Man, for there is no love without forgiveness, and forgiving is something everyone must learn to do on his own. I can give you but one thing only—A longing for a better life, a life of truth and justice; even though it may not exist now, it may come tomorrow. Perhaps this longing will lead you to God, Homeland and Love. (p. 144)

While Korczak maintains the opportunity for faith, the meaning he emphasizes most is the longing for a better life, a life of truth and justice. I am struck with how he sends forth his children with a longing that can be universal and not bound by human-created divisions fueled by religion, nation, race, etc. I also recognize that it encourages agency. It speaks primarily to how we are called to act in the world. It provides meaning that guides action.

At a time when there are few answers and much angst, we are faced with a generation looking for meaning. Korczak helps youth gain this meaning through service, relationship, and community. As we learn the boundaries of human knowledge, perhaps we can value the wisdom that compassion in pursuit of justice is enough. We can teach children, and each other, that consistently acting for the greater good is enough. The greatest meaning resides in the will to work toward a more ethical, caring, and just world.

Developing Agency

Hopelessness and anguish emerge from the understanding of the size and level of the problems one faces and our limited ability to impact outcomes. The poem of Katie Houde is tragic as she shows that in a moment of crisis the most she can do is delay the perpetrator in her school from killing others by acting as a diversion—perhaps this act would save another student. Her life is so easily expendable in a nation where the right to own guns supersedes her right to grow up. In a world where one's life has less value than the right to own a gun, despair is understandable. When children get lost in this despair, they do not claim their agency.

My hope is that our young generation can regain a sense of agency. This is not an easy task, but is exactly the task that Korczak took so seriously. He not only helped children understand their capacity for action, he created an environment that would serve as a model for their own vision of a better world, the environment where children engaged in every aspect of its function and governance. Korczak recognized their vulnerability, their unique nature, and their need to learn how to live in community, and develop their own meaning and passions. He created a community where this could occur, and as a result, created a blueprint for education of the complete person. At the end of this education, a person emerged who was capable of confronting the challenges of the world in a way that did not result in the sacrifice of others.

Korczak provides educators with a place to start. It is a place where we can begin by understanding and nurturing our students and recognize that we are role models and agents for their greater good. It is through the giving of ourselves that we can empower youth to discover their own agency in the hope of becoming a force for the good. In Katie Houde's poem, she has agency. Part of her agency is that she will act to protect other children in a school shooting if it comes to that. Her greater agency is that she has made it known to the adults around her that she will not be silent. She will speak truth to power that the

Constitution without a contemporary interpretation places her life below the right of a disturbed person to own and use a gun. With this agency, she has emerged as a beacon of hope for her generation.

My hope is that this generation of children can and will find a way to emerge as actors in a dysfunctional world. There are examples. Children are suing the government over its failure to act on climate change. The Parkland students are a definitive force for gun control. Children are seeking empowering meaning in a difficult world. As teachers, we can work to create classrooms where students discover the power they have to live in functional communities and reach beyond those communities to impact the greater good. Acting for the good is meaningful. Meaning pushes back despair. The retreat of despair makes room for light. Our youth deserve to be in the light so they can work to build a better tomorrow.

References

American College Health Association. (2008, 2013, 2018). *National College Health Assessment*. Baltimore, MD: ACHA.

Henriques, G. (2014, February 21). What is causing the college student mental health crisis? *Psychology Today*. Retrieved from https://www.psychologytoday.com/us/blog/theory-knowledge/201402/the-college-student-mental-health-crisis

Hunt, J. and Eisenberg, D. (2010, January). Mental health problems and help-seeking behavior among college students. *Journal of Adolescent Health, 46*(1), 3-10.

Korczak, J. (1967). *Selected works of Janusz Korczak*. Washington, DC: National Science Foundation.

Korczak, J. (1992). *When I am little again*. Lanham, MD: University Press of America.

Korczak, J. (1999). *A voice for the child: The inspirational words of Janusz Korczak*. London: Thorsons.

Poppo, K. (2006). A pedagogy of compassion: Janusz Korczak and the care of the child. *Encounter: Educating for Meaning and Social Justice, 19*(4), 32–39.

Tillich, P. (1957). *Dynamics of faith*. New York: Harper & Row.

CHAPTER TWENTY-ONE

Found Poetry:
An Interview with Julie Scott

Interviewers:
Tatyana Tsyrlina-Spady, Peter C. Renn, and Amy Spangler

1. How did you learn about Korczak, and why did you decide to use his ideas?
I first heard of Korczak in 1998 on a trip to Poland with the Holocaust and Jewish Resistance teachers program. I came across his name at the Emanuel Ringelblum Jewish Historical Institute in Warsaw, Poland, and then again on a monument at Treblinka, along with other monuments to him in Warsaw. However, the most meaningful encounter was at the Ghetto Fighters' House in Israel at the Janusz Korczak of the Children exhibit (see Resources). Korczak really intrigued me. I found that my ideas about how children should be treated were very similar to his, so I started reading, first *Homage to Korczak* (1989), then Lifton's (1988) *The King of Children*. At this point I decided to start teaching about him.

My interest in Holocaust education began during the summer of 1994 when I visited the Washington, D.C. Holocaust Museum (see Resources) . . . . Of course, I had heard of Auschwitz and Dachau, and don't get me wrong—I had a minor in history and taught social studies for quite some time, but had never had any in-depth study into Holocaust history. After I returned to my school, I asked my principal if I could introduce an elective on the Holocaust. I started learning from there, which included strict and rigid professional development to prepare for teaching this complex history. That first year I had a local Holocaust survivor, Eva Lassman, visit my classroom and tell us her story. She was the first Holocaust survivor I had ever heard speak in person, and this made the history really come alive for both my students and me . . . . This is how I learned about the program that took me to Poland and Israel in 1998 . . . . Additional training and experiences followed.

2. Was there any specific moment that inspired you to start practicing your Found Poetry project?

Yes, it was a 2010 survey of college students on *empathy* that demonstrated its steady decline, by 40 percent, compared to students in the 1970s and 1980s. This really bothered me because I consider empathy an important quality for anyone to have, especially for young people. I always focused on it in my unit, but I felt that after teaching my students about Korczak and his work with orphans, following it up with something about honoring him could really tap more into a better understanding of empathy. That year, Mariola Strahlberg, president of the US Korczak Association (see Resources), contacted me while searching out teachers who were teaching about Korczak. I ran the idea by her, and she liked it. I had already taught Found Poetry, so it wasn't new to me to teach students how to use primary and secondary sources for this activity. That's how it started.

3. Could you describe how Found Poetry works? Is it part of the curriculum, and if so, then for what age group and for how long?

I use this project with eighth graders, but it can be adapted to any secondary grade level.

Found Poetry uses excerpts from primary or secondary sources to create a poem. Students find words and phrases they want to use and, in this case, mostly words from, or about, Korczak. I have assembled excerpts from a variety of sources, including picture books about him and the orphans, Korczak's *How to Love a Child*, and more. I teach repetition for emphasis. My students know ahead of time that we have a theme of celebrating the life and works of Janusz Korczak.

The steps I follow with the students include: showing examples of past poems (see Appendix 1) and working through the packet while utilizing the document camera to model and teach them how to pull out strong words and phrases. Students have a direction sheet, which I go through very carefully using checklists (see Appendix 1). We begin with brainstorming and highlighting things we talk about—what direction we can go and, again, using repetition in the poetry. I also ask them to either draw or trace their illustrations. I allow tracing because I understand not everyone can draw very well, and I don't want them to get hung up on the illustration before even getting the poem done. We work on these poems for a couple of weeks. I approve all of the rough drafts ahead of time and monitor the students' work all the way through the project.

4. *Do you write poems as well?*

I do write poetry. Some of it is hanging in my classroom where students have illustrated it for me. When teaching Found Poetry I usually take a book from my shelf, put it under my document camera, and model by pulling lines from the text and composing a poem. . . . I wrote a poem about Korczak when I was in Poland in 2005. In fact, on both of my trips I kept a journal to ensure I remembered my experiences. I decided to share my journal entry made on Thursday, July 14, 2005, and also my first poem about Korczak here:

> Treblinka has meaning to me because it was in Poland, in 1998, that I met my personal hero, Janusz Korczak. He perished at Treblinka in August of 1942, and he had many chances to save himself. I always wonder what I would have done had I been in his shoes. Could I have gone to my death like that, or would I have saved my own skin? I guess I can only hope I would have done the brave and noble thing. As I thought about Janusz Korczak today I put my thoughts down into a poem. It probably isn't very good, but it expresses my true feelings. . . .

Korczak, You Are My Hero

Korczak,
you are my hero.
I only met you seven years ago,
yet, you are my hero.
In a selfish world,
with so few selfless souls,
your memory is a beacon, calling to me, challenging me,
and you are my hero.

If only I possessed your courage and strength.
If only I exemplified your devotion and love,
if only . . .

But, you will remain my hero, always.
You led by example, even to your death.

I met you again at Treblinka,
and I hope some of you
left Treblinka with me.

I met you seven years ago,
and I returned to Treblinka to mourn you again,
but also to celebrate the memory or your goodness.
You are my hero.
Korczak.

5. Do other teachers at your school participate? Do you have administrative support?

I have had two colleagues whom I mentored in teaching the Holocaust and teaching this project. One teacher has moved on to the high school, and the other still works to include it in her curriculum. I've always had strong administrative support with this project and my Holocaust unit. The administration allows me to attend conferences during the school year and some of this support comes from the positive publicity it brings the school district.

6. What is the attitude of your students and their parents?

I have never received any pushback from students, parents, staff members, or administrators in regards to this project or my Holocaust unit. I have a very positive reputation as a language arts teacher of over 30 years in my district. The curriculum I teach is respected and honored. Many of the students come into my classroom having an older brother or sister who experienced it or they've already heard about the Holocaust unit. They are excited to study it.

I have had students who were extremely sensitive, so I've had to be very careful if I thought something might upset them. I have had parents share at parent-teacher conferences and the feedback was very positive. I had one parent who was very resistant to even listening about what the student had to say, but by the time the unit was completed, she was glad they shared what they had learned.

When my students complete this Korczak poetry project, towards the end of the school year, they are very connected to the man and the history. They are totally engaged in the project, they feel safe expressing themselves and their feelings, and the outcome is very moving, heartfelt poems. As a Found Poetry project students know that every one of them is capable of writing something meaningful.

I forge strong, lasting relationships with my students. Some have returned to my school and completed their student teaching with me. With any of these encounters, the first question is almost always, "Are you still teaching about the Holocaust?" Then they'll say it was the only thing they remember from middle school, which is always a little disconcerting; but they remember. Recently, a former student who works in New York City at the Center for Social Justice (see Resources) Facebook messaged me to thank me for inspiring her to do that work.

Due to my training from the Holocaust Museum in Washington, D.C., my approach to teaching and talking about Korczak and the orphans is not to scare or traumatize students. I don't believe in showing students graphic photos of the Holocaust. The students are already very interested; they'll Google things, but I warn them to be careful and that if we need to talk about it later, then they need to let me know. I begin by teaching about life before the Holocaust to show the pre-war people as humans and not just victims in piles of bodies. I ask for students to send me pictures of themselves with family at parties, barbecues, hanging out with their friends, playing at the beach or soccer (and other sports), and I match them up with the pre-Holocaust pictures of Jewish families so that the students can see that while it is 70-plus years later, we're really not so different. It helps my students to connect with the hopes and dreams of the people from before, to realize they were human beings exactly as we are today. Again, I'm careful, and the Holocaust Museum has guidelines not to use simulations because we can't re-create walking in someone else's shoes.

7. What steps should any teacher take to integrate this activity in her/ his classroom? Have you developed any guidelines for teachers and for students—participants?

The guidelines have all the links (see Appendix 1). You can't teach about Janusz Korczak in isolation; it has to be in context. I assume if teachers are interested in doing this, then they already have some type of Holocaust instruction with their students. For me, it is important to mentor teachers in my building teaching this for the first time.

I have created my own curriculum using primary sources, diary entries, and personal photographs from past trips. My philosophy is to share everything that

I have composed. I use PowerPoint and a document camera. I teach the Holocaust thematically and chronologically starting with life before the Holocaust
and the Nazi rise to power, and ending with lessons on heroes of the Holocaust,
those few bright and shining stars in Europe who were willing to hide or rescue
Jews (less than 1 percent of the population), Jewish resistance (uprisings and
partisans), the "White Rose" (German college students who defied the Nazis),
and I finish with my last lesson on Janusz Korczak. I am hopeful my students
will remember some of the names of these heroes, as opposed to the perpetrators of this horrific genocide. I don't allocate a lot of time to Hitler. I mostly
show things students can relate to (e.g., the Hitler Youth program and the Nazis' use of propaganda). I show a video called *Heil Hitler: Confessions of a Hitler
Youth* (Holch, 1991), but I don't want them to get mired down and obsessed with
Nazism. I teach them about different groups: collaborators, perpetrators, by-
standers, and victims. This curriculum is prepared with notes and documents,
in a visual format, and shared with other teachers. I even teach aspects of the
unit if another teacher doesn't feel comfortable teaching it.

I suggest teachers use a Parking Lot activity so students can place questions on
Post-it Notes. If teachers can't answer them, I do it for them. My students have the
option of writing down their questions if they don't feel comfortable asking them
in class, but most prefer to talk, and we have excellent in-depth conversations. Prior
to the unit, parents are notified with an email, but I don't send a permission letter
because I feel I don't need permission to teach my curriculum. Sometimes parents
will come in, usually when a Holocaust survivor visits from Seattle.

8. How is the poetry presented?

Students can read the poems in class, but it is purely voluntary. Last year,
students knew I was preparing for a conference presentation and I had plenty
of volunteers who came in and read their poems for me to record. Otherwise,
poems are shared in the school hallway; all of them go up.

9. Did you notice any changes in your students after they were involved in your Found Poetry project?

This is a hard question to answer because it is observation based and the
unit is towards the end of the school year when they leave and go to high school.
Sometimes they'll share with me when they come back to visit or I'll run into

them at basketball or volleyball games, and other school district events. As far as immediately, during the project and after, what I see the most is their pride in their work. With any project in my classroom, I set high expectations, and students know the final product has to be what I call "gallery worthy." Because I've taught these units for so long, some of the things I have noticed after the civil rights unit or the Holocaust unit is that students will report things to me. Perhaps someone was bullying another student on the bus or something happened in the hallway and students talk about stepping in, because it was the right thing to do.

Initially, I start teaching about Korczak on the first day of school. By the time we are finished with the Holocaust unit, they've heard his name many, many times. The last assignment is to describe the two or three topics that resonated most with them, things they will never forget. I would say nine times out of ten, Korczak is someone they will write about. As far as my Holocaust unit, when our district had two middle schools, the high school history and English teachers could always tell students who came from my classroom. They stood out from other students due to their knowledge and care about this topic. In fact, two of my former students have won the writing and art contest sponsored by Temple Beth Shalom.

10. How has leading this project changed your life?

I have been using Korczak's practices. He is my personal hero in history. It obviously opens doors for me professionally. I've become closer to the Korczak Association of the USA, where my students' poems and illustrations are presented on their website. I present at conferences on teaching Korczak, and share this work with my colleagues. I constantly reevaluate what I do in my classroom. Originally, I started this project because I needed something new, a meaningful end to our Holocaust unit. The story of Janusz Korczak and his orphans breaks the hearts of students. When reading picture books on Korczak to my students (*A Hero and the Holocaust: The Story of Janusz Korczak and His Children* (Adler, 2002), *The Champion of Children: The Story of Janusz Korczak* (Bogacki, 2009)), I tear up and have to stop at times because I'm getting choked up. I wanted to change the emphasis for the poetry project from his death, as students had a tendency to focus on this, and went with the theme of celebrating his life and accomplishments. It really changed the tone and content of the poems.

Eighth grade is the perfect age to do this project. I treat my students like young adults, and they are really drawn to issues of social justice, right and wrong, and fairness at this age. In high school, they begin to believe they know everything; even more than their teachers sometimes, so it's a beautiful, perfect age group because they really latch onto it. As far as working on it, this is the type of project you want an administrator to come into your classroom to observe because students are totally focused on discussing the phrases they have highlighted and used in their poems, talking about their poems, reading each other's poems, and often making suggestions.

Finally, I take great pride in the work my students produce for this project. It is an extremely rewarding project because of the meaningful poems they write. In fact, some of them are students who are not really interested in poetry, but they write it because of their interest in Korczak and his story.

11. What are the overarching social-emotional goals that you have for your students as a result of participating in the Found Poetry unit?

To summarize, these goals are the following:

- It is for my students to feel empathy. By focusing on children, teens (and family) during my Holocaust unit, and teaching about Korczak and his orphans, the history is much more relatable for my eighth-grade students. Social awareness is another social-emotional goal. I am hopeful that my students will leave my classroom appreciating differences and that through the lessons I teach on the civil rights movement, the Holocaust, and Janusz Korczak, that they "stand in others'" shoes as much as possible.

- The ability to be a responsible decision maker is also a goal. I try to achieve it through fostering respect for others, awareness, and concern for how one's actions may affect others; students will develop a deeper sense of social responsibility. Students will begin to balance their own well-being, while keeping the well-being of others in mind (school, community, and beyond).

- I also hope that the students will manage to establish meaningful relationships with trusted adults. My school is a high-poverty-rate school, and some students do not have any kind of trusting relationship with an adult. By the time they complete this poetry project (April–May), my classrooms are more like a family.

I don't just teach about Korczak, I use his ideas to demonstrate how children should be treated in my classroom. I live Korczak! I want my students to meet someone in history who really understood and truly loved children, and who would not leave his children, even when facing death. Janusz Korczak is an extremely compelling person to young people, and a historical figure whom they don't just learn factual information about, but truly connect with, honor, and respect. This is vividly shown in the work they produce in writing and illustrating their Found Poetry to honor his life, work, and sacrifice.

References

Adler, D. A. (2002). *A hero and the Holocaust: The story of Janusz Korczak and his children*. New York: Holiday House.

Bogacki, T. (2009). *The champion of children: The story of Janusz Korczak*. New York: Francis Foster Books.

Holch, A. (1991). *Heil Hitler: Confessions of a Hitler youth*. [Video file]. United States: Home Box Office, Inc. Retrieved from https://www.youtube.com/watch?v=JJ6umV7CVY8

Homage to Korczak. Excerpts from his writings, poems in his honor, children's drawings (1989). Yad Layeled: The Korczak Society of Israel.

Korczak, J. (2018). *How to love a child: and other selected works, Volume 1*. Elstree, England: Vallentine Mitchell.

Lifton, B. J. (1988). *The king of children: A biography of Janusz Korczak*. New York: Farrar, Straus & Giroux.

Resources

The Center for Social Justice: https://www.centreforsocialjustice.org.uk/

Holocaust Center for Humanity: https://www.holocaustcenterseattle.org/

Janusz Korczak Association of the USA: http://korczakusa.com/

Janusz Korczak of the Children exhibit: https://www.gfh.org.il/eng/Exhibitions/188/Janusz_Korczak_of_the_Children

The Jewish Foundation for the Righteous: https://jfr.org/The United States Holocaust Memorial Museum: https://www.ushmm.org/

Bringing Irena Sendler and Janusz Korczak into the Classroom: Contemporary Topics for Curricular Integration

Tilar J. Mazzeo

WHO WAS IRENA Sendler (Mazzeo, 2016)? And what is she doing here, in a book on the legacy of Janusz Korczak? The simple answer to those questions is that Irena Sendler—or Irena Sendlerowa (1910–2008), as she is known in her native Poland—was a social worker; trained at the Polish Free University in the 1930s by the visionary pedagogy professor and activist, Dr. Helena Radlinska; and who during the Second World War and the German occupation of Warsaw worked with a network of close friends and associates to save more than 2,500 Jewish children from disease and, ultimately, death and deportation to the Nazi concentration camps in Poland. In order to persuade parents to let her smuggle their young children out of the ghetto and give them new non-Jewish identities, she promised to record on a secret list the children's real names, so that after the war their parents could find them in their foster homes and in the orphanages. She and the partners in her network could not know that more than 90 percent of the children's parents would perish, most of them at the death camp at Treblinka. The list of Irena and her compatriots, in one form or another, however, did outlast the war and helped the surviving child-refugees recover their family stories, Jewish identity, and, in some fortunate cases, their relatives. To educators, her story is perhaps best known as the subject of the school-based play "Life in a Jar" (1999) created by the young middle-school students who interviewed Irena Sendler in the 1990s and brought her story to media attention in the United States.

To Holocaust historians, the part of Irena Sendler's story that is most poignantly memorable is the fact that she was among those who stood in the ghetto on that sweltering August morning in 1942 when Dr. Korczak and his orphanage co-teachers calmly walked at gunpoint with nearly 200 children to the cattle cars and, finally, to their deaths together at Treblinka. As one witness, Nachum Remba, described the last moments of the march, "I shall never forget this scene as long as I live. This was no march to the train cars, but rather a mute protest against this murderous regime . . . a procession the like of which no human eye has ever witnessed" (Lifton, 1988, p. 345). In Irena Sendler's memory of the scene, "When that day in August of 1942, I saw that tragic parade in the street, those innocent children walking obediently in the procession of death and listening to the doctor's optimistic words, I do not know why for me and for all the other eyewitnesses our heart did not break" (Janusz Korczak Association of Canada, 2018). Among those 200 children, 30 were children Irena Sendler and her network had already saved once by bringing them to Dr. Korczak, and she had been a regular visitor to the orphanage and, especially, to the children's amateur theatrical performances.

Irena Sendler's personal and professional connections with Janusz Korczak, however, pre-dated the war and the creation of the Warsaw ghetto. Irena Sendler and many of the other women in her clandestine wartime network were former students of Janusz Korczak and considered the "Old Doctor" a mentor and friend. Their work was deeply informed by his writings and teachings and by his commitments to pedagogy, social justice, the empowerment of children, and the use of theater and role-playing in the educational setting. The purpose of this short chapter is to suggest ways in which the stories of Irena Sendler and her network of both young people and adults offer possibilities for framing and incorporating the legacy of Janusz Korczak in curricula and classrooms especially at the middle-school level.

This chapter is focused around three thematic issues that connect current curricular standards and contemporary topics to the work of Sendler and Korczak and with the National History Day[1] annual contest, which was one of the routes through which Sendler's work came to public recognition in North America.

Refugee Issues in Civic Education and History

Early in her career, Sendler's interest was in assisting impoverished families and refugee populations. The establishment of the Warsaw ghetto in October of 1940 created a large community of both internally and externally displaced refugees in the city. While conditions inside the ghetto were perilous for families relocated to the quarter from inside Warsaw, the most vulnerable populations were those who arrived to the ghetto from other parts of Poland and were weakened from journeys made under difficult conditions. So Sendler's first efforts to smuggle children out of the ghetto focused on saving the orphaned children of external refugees. The younger children were placed in foster care outside the ghetto, and the pre-teen and teenaged children frequently joined Sendler's network as couriers and worked guiding small children out through the sewer systems.

Refugees and issues of populations displaced either through conflict, climate change, or economic collapse are central to the civic debates across North America and Europe. The National Education Association and the United Nations High Commission on Refugees,[2] to which Canada and the United States are party states, both provide excellent resources on incorporating teachings about refugee-status topics in curricula.

What educators may be less familiar with is the role that Korczak's work and legacy, and especially his 1928 pedagogical treatise "The Child's Right to Respect" (Korczak, 2009), played in inspiring and shaping the United Nations' Convention on the Rights of the Child (Walther, 2003), which was widely ratified in 1989 and based on the 1959 "Declaration of the Rights of the Child."[3]

Korczak's thinking on these topics was shaped, as well, by the children's newspaper, *The Little Review*, that was integral to the children's learning at his orphanage and published by the children from 1926 to 1939. Core to the newspaper were the beliefs that children should write for children and could do so on substantial and weighty issues.

And, finally, Korczak's ghetto diaries (1979), running from May to August of 1942, offer a personal consideration on the refugee crisis of the ghetto, particularly as it pertained to children and the school, and may be selectively appropriate for classroom units, especially when combined with contemporary photographs of the ghetto.

Educators may wish to consider ways to:

- Incorporate the 10 principles of the "Declaration of the Rights of the Child" into classroom conversations and learning materials on refugee-focused units.

- Combine contemporary refugee-focused units with units on the history of the Holocaust and genocide.

- Engage students in the legacy of *The Little Review* as a learning tool in these units.

- Encourage students to use personal documents such as letters, journals, and photographs in pedagogical storytelling and learning.

The Children's Parliament and the Children's Court

Among Korczak's most firmly held educational beliefs as a mentor, activist, and school director was the conviction that institutions should be both child-focused and, to the extent possible, child-led. This was a principle that he passed on to a generation of social workers, including Irena Sendler and her collaborators, and Sendler was not surprised to discover, during one particularly dangerous rescue operation in the Warsaw ghetto involving Korczak's orphanage, that the doctor sent children to help other children out of danger. This belief was put into practice through the Children's Parliament, along with its corollary, the Children's Court.

The creation of a constitutional republic required the early involvement of children as youth-citizens in the institutions of democracy. Korczak believed that it was not reasonable to expect that children would live under the authority of adult-citizens until the age of 18 and then, overnight, enter into full political participation as prepared citizens.

Korczak's legacy is very much alive with respect to this model, and we should anticipate more discussion of the Children's Parliament. The most integrated contemporary example of the application of Korczak's principles is the work of the Children's Parliament in Scotland, which offers resources to educators and communities[4] and is connected to recent legislation lowering the voting age in Scotland to 16; the model has recently been adopted as well in schools in Australia as a pilot program.[5]

It is worth noting that, in teaching about issues of suffrage, a number of cities in the United States have lowered the voting age to 16, the federal voting age of 18 notwithstanding, and that a number of countries in the world are actively debating legislation to lower the voting age or have suffrage for minors, including Brazil, Malta, Scotland, and Austria. There have been calls in some cases for voting rights for children as young as six in Britain, although no country to date has adopted a voting age lower than 16 (acast, 2018; Weaver, 2018).

I would urge educators to think of how to:

• Foster international connections with schools in the United Kingdom and Australia piloting Children's Parliaments in educational programming.

• Incorporate discussions of the youth suffrage movement with learning units on women's suffrage and civil rights history.

• Include the use of the Children's Parliament and Children's Court in lessons on civics and democratic process and in classroom management, along with engagement strategies.

• Integrate and foster children's agency across the curriculum.

Role Playing and Theater

One important aspect of children's learning to become citizen-activists in Dr. Korczak's pedagogy was the value of role-playing and performance. Children performed and embodied characters as a means of developing agency and new roles in their lived experience, and it was a practice that went hand-in-hand with the Children's Parliament and the Children's Court.

As was earlier mentioned in this book, Korczak authored several children's books, including *King Matt the First* (2004), the story of a young boy who becomes king and wants to reform his republic and end war. Other titles included the sequel, *Little King Matty and the Desert Island* (1990), and *Kaytek the Wizard* (2012).

Some schools choose to work with the "Life in a Jar" play (n.d.), written with the involvement of the Kansas middle-school students whose National

History Day work helped to popularize Irena Sendler and her story in North America some decades ago. The costs for hosting the play, however, are substantial. For schools with more limited budgets or for independent classrooms, educators may wish to consider Korczak's books as texts for student engagement and, perhaps, dramatization.

These themes of children's empowerment, child rulers, and magical, adult powers granted to young people in Korczak's books have clear resonance for students, but they provide as well an excellent platform for integrating, as above, the study of civics and the history of the Holocaust and refugee displacement into the classroom through literature with specific contexts. These texts are readily adapted for dramatic performance in classrooms.

I would encourage educators to

- Include Korczak's children's books as reading on their school curricula.

- Encourage students, where they participate in National History Day projects, to consider dramatic and documentary options and to consider Korczak's legacy and children's rights as a topic.

Korczak's legacy offers rich opportunities for empowering young people and engaging them in democratic institutions and in the world.

References

Acast. (2018, December 5). Talking politics: Democracy for young people [Audio file]. Retrieved January 16, 2019, from https://play.acast.com/s/talkingpolitics/democracyforyoungpeople?autoplay
Children's Parliament. (2019). *Children's Parliament: Giving kids a voice*. Retrieved January 16, 2019, from www.childrensparliament.org.uk
Janusz Korczak Association of Canada. (2018, May 13). *A ceremony to honour Irena Sendler*. Retrieved January 16, 2019, from www.januszkorczak.ca/a-ceremony-to-honour-irena-sendler.
Korczak, J. (1979). *The Warsaw ghetto memoirs of Janusz Korczak* (E.P. Kulawiec, Trans.). Washington, DC: University Press of America.
Korczak, J. (1990). *Little King Matty and the desert island.* (A. Czasak, Trans.). London: Joanna Pinewood.
Korczak, J. (2004). *King Matt the first.* (R. Lourie, Trans.). New York: Algonquin Books.

Korczak, J. (2009, November). *Janusz Korczak: The child's right to respect*. Strasbourg: Council of Europe Publishing.

Korczak, J. (2012). *Kaytek the wizard*. (A. Lloyd-Jones, Trans.). Brooklyn, NY: Penlight Publications.

Life in a Jar: The Irena Sendler Project. (n.d.). Retrieved January 16, 2019, from https://irenasendler.org/about-the-project

Lifton, B.J. (1988). *The king of children: A biography of Janusz Korczak*. New York: Schocken Books.

Liverpool City Council. (n.d.). *2168 Children's Parliament*. Liverpool, BC. Retrieved January 16, 2019, from www.liverpool.nsw.gov.au/community/2168-childrens-parliament

Mazzeo, T. J. (2016). *Irena's children: The extraordinary story of the woman who saved 2,500 children from the Warsaw ghetto*. New York: Gallery Books.

Nast, P. (2002-2019). War and migration. Washington, DC: National Education Association. Retrieved January 16, 2019, from www.nea.org/tools/lessons/63678.htm

United Nations High Commission on Refugees (UNHCR). (2001-2019). Teaching about refugees. Retrieved January 16, 2019, from www.unhcr.org/teaching-about-refugees.html

Walther, S. T. (2003). United Nations. Declaration of the Rights of the Child. Retrieved January 16, 2019, from www.unicef.org/malaysia/1959-Declaration-of-the-Rights-of-the-Child.pdf

Weaver, M. (December 6, 2018). Lower voting age to six to tackle bias against young, says academic. *The Guardian*. Retrieved January 16, 2019, from www.theguardian.com/politics/2018/dec/06/give-six-year-olds-the-vote-says-cambridge-university-academic

Endnotes

1 For more details see www.nhd.org
2 See more: the National Education Association: http://www.nea.org/tools/lessons/63678.htm; United Nations High Commission on Refugees: https://www.unhcr.org/teaching-about-refugees.html
3 See www.januszkorczak.ca/legacy/4_The%20Child's%20Right%20to%20Respect.pdf; https://www.unicef.org/malaysia/1959-Declaration-of-the-Rights-of-the-Child.pdf
4 For more details see https://www.childrensparliament.org.uk
5 For more details see https://www.liverpool.nsw.gov.au/community/2168-childrens-parliament

PART IV: ASSIGNMENTS

1. What are main similarities between Korczak's and Dewey's approaches to pedagogy?

2. Following Korczak's ideas, how could a teacher instill the sense of responsibility for oneself and others in his/her students?

3. What is the difference between a teacher's *sentimental love* and an educator's *pedagogical love*? Prove with Korczak's quotes.

4. How to translate Korczak's theory of moral education into practice in modern American schools? Give examples.

5. Comment on the following Korczak's (2018) statement about teachers and tutors: "We are not miracle-workers—and we do not wish to be charlatans. We renounce hypocritical longing for the perfect child" (*How to love a child and other selected works* [Chicago: Vallentine Mitchell, p. 329]).

6. How does Korczak's legacy help modern youth to regain agency and to be heard and respected? How could teachers utilize it in their work in the classroom?

PART V
Transform and Play:
Creating Different Educational
Realities Inspired by Korczak

CHAPTER TWENTY-THREE

Guiding Children for Virtue

Tonia Bock, Darcia Narvaez,
Ralph Singh, and Mary S. Tarsha

HUMAN BEINGS LEARN from their immersion in community. In fact, they are bi-ologically shaped by their social experiences. Ideally, their experiences from birth are those of love and care, creating a prosocial and cooperative nature. When early supportive care is missing, humans will exhibit various forms of dysregulation. Un-fortunately, many children are not receiving the supportive care they need early in life and arrive at school anxious, stressed, and unprepared to learn. This impairs not only their intellectual development but also their socio-emotional and moral development. In this chapter we discuss some of the causes of children's ill prepa-ration, describe ways to structure classrooms to foster virtuous human beings, and explore how educators can address students' needs, integrating the pedagogical philosophy of Janusz Korczak.

The Industrialized Child

Now we know what the elements are that comprise tender care for young children and how important they are for neurobiological development (Narvaez, 2014). Rapid development occurs in the first six years of life, and the quality of these early experiences needs to be especially supportive. And we recognize now more than ever that the developing brains of young children need certain experi-ences to grow properly.

The human species evolved a caregiving system to provide for the needs of young children—the *evolved nest* that includes soothing perinatal experience, responsiveness to needs by multiple familiar adult caregivers to mitigate distress, frequent positive touch and co-sleeping, breastfeeding on request for several years, self-directed free play with multi-aged mates, positive social climate, and support for mother and child (Hewlett & Lamb, 2005; Narvaez, 2018).

The absence of the evolved nest is having harmful effects on human potential (Narvaez, 2014). Young children are regularly left in childcare centers, undermining key developments such as secure attachment, which is rooted in neurobiological development (Carter et al., 2005). Moreover, stressed parents often use techniques for early care that are detrimental to young children's body and brain development: artificial feeding and mechanical and electronic gadgets to keep their baby preoccupied and quiet instead of being "in arms" socializing with the family. Such practices set children up on a less-than-optimal trajectory and teach them insecurity, low self-esteem, lack of trust, and self-centeredness from not getting their needs met and carrying around a wounded self (Narvaez, 2014). Korczak (1967a) spent many hours observing and studying children who suffered from wounded selves as a result of unmet needs. He keenly diagnosed this pain as potentially pervasive, sometimes being carried over into subsequent generations:

> There are some rare children whose age is not just their own ten years. They carry the load of many generations and . . . under the action of a slight stimulus . . . the latent potential of pain, grievance, anger, and rebellion [is released]. Then it is not a child but the centuries weeping. (p. 8)

His acute awareness of the inner workings of children and their sufferings was developed through years of working as a *wychowawca* (in Polish), a special type of teacher or educator who dedicates his/her entire life towards understanding, seeing, caring for, and providing for children. His vocation as *wychowawca* was not limited to pedagogy or instruction. Rather, he lived out his professional role by taking responsibility for the physical, social, and moral development of the child (Korczak, 1967b; Lewowicki, 1994).

What can educators and caregivers outside of the home do to repair children's maladaptive neurobiological systems? They can provide a *sustaining* environment that both reconstitutes critical brain functions and meets basic needs (Narvaez, 2010) and maintains neurobiological supports such as procedures for and skill building in self-calming, social pleasure, and communal imagination. Students can learn ways to calm themselves and enhance self-regulation. They can also learn to *rewire the social brain* areas with socially pleasurable activities through self-directed free play with others of different ages, social art, and music making. Educators and caregivers can help grow an *imagination that is communal*—that keeps the welfare of others in mind, and includes a sense of attachment to a positive group, feeling connected to the rest of humanity and to the natural world.

Educators can create sustaining environments, help foster development of the social brain, and expand children's communal imaginations because of the privilege entrusted to them as teachers. Korczak (1967c) fully recognized this privilege because he was self-aware: "every word of mine enters a hundred minds, every step is watched by a hundred pairs of vigilant eyes" (p. 61). He knew the power of his vocation and practiced self-reflection in order to continually better his pedagogical skills. Korczak also emphasized the importance of persevering in these endeavors, describing that even when the entire classroom seemed to dismiss his instruction, later on one or two children would demonstrate proof that the teaching was effective.

The Need for Moral Character Development: The RAVES Model

Though it may be necessary and wise to provide to children what was missed in early life, this is just getting back to the starting gate. If our aim is for moral character development, we must do more. Today not only are children missing the early experiences that foster health, well-being, and sociality, they are typically not immersed in a society and daily activities that emphasize moral character development. They do not receive the close guidance and supervision needed for moral cultivation as a few generations ago when the neighbors took a role in guiding and watching out for children in the local community.

Educational institutions, because they are a constant presence in the lives of children, must fill this role. They can take a more deliberative approach to moral character education (Narvaez, 2006; 2007). Korczak continually repeated that knowledge alone is not enough nor is love alone an effective means to foster child flourishing (Korczak, 1967a). What is needed, then, is the translation of a well-developed theory into an effective model that can facilitate the much-needed skills required for moral character development.

To this end, we propose the RAVES model, a research-based approach, which offers educators the guidelines to foster moral character while teaching academics. The aim is to help children grow into intelligent and morally agile adults with high moral quotients (MQ) as well as high IQs. The RAVES model begins with high expectations for ethical behavior alongside achievement. It is also designed to provide high community support for reaching these goals. The acronym RAVES stands for Relationships, Apprenticeship, Virtuous models, Ethical skill development, and Self-authorship (see Table 23.1).

Relationships in the RAVES Model. Secure attachment relationships are fundamental to a good life (Carter et al., 2005). Such relationships are characterized by social trust and interdependence built through emotional presence, as well as verbal, nonverbal, emotional, and cognitive consistency.

There are two aspects to establishing caring relationships in the RAVES model. First is initiating a caring relationship between student and educator. Caring means that an educator shows respect by tuning into the needs of the child and honoring the child's culture and preferences. Children need the experience of *being-with* another person who is emotionally present and engaged in the moment. Korczak was a moral exemplar when it came to respectful relationships. His pedagogical philosophy proposes a relationship of equality (Boschki, 2005) when the teacher is not above the student nor is the pupil below the educator.

Oftentimes, parents wish their children would develop into better versions of themselves (Korczak, 1967d). Korczak viewed this as a potential violation of children's intrinsic right to develop into their own unique person. He did not view children as developing into adults nor did he see childhood as a preparation for an adult life. Rather, he deeply respected both the child as a person and the period of childhood, demonstrating that both called for protection from the adult community (Reiter, Asgad, & Sachs, 1990; Sheridan & Samuelsson, 2001). Korczak reminds us that at times adults are focused on their own struggles, and consequently, fail to see children as people. He relates this back to other points in history when society failed to see and acknowledge the rights of women, peasants, and other oppressed groups of people (Korczak, 1967b).

When children experience deep respect for their personhood, it helps open up their uniqueness. The carer-for, the adult, sets aside the self to feel-with the other, to develop mutual reciprocal communication that shows active listening and fosters trustworthiness (Noddings, 2002), understanding that this may take longer with some students (Watson & Ecken, 2018). Students need experiences of *being cherished* where caring is customized to their needs and preferences, where forgiveness is ready and available, and where the child's unique spirit and "best self" are evoked. Students also need *responsive, playful* relationships where child-like spontaneity and positive humor are fostered.

The second aspect of establishing caring relationships is a *sustaining community* of caring relationships. What should an educator pay attention to in building a sustaining community? The Child Development Project (Battistich, 2008) helped discover many of these components:

1. **Foster student motivation.** Educators can create a motivating climate for students by allowing developmentally appropriate autonomy (providing self-direction and building self-efficacy and self-regulation) as well as by encouraging positive student interaction.

2. **Foster community fellowship.** A climate of fellowship can be nurtured by promoting solidarity, diversity, and oneness (emphasizing unity, the common good, and connectedness), establishing trust (e.g., building a class narrative or "our story"), and creating nurturing leadership.

3. **Cultivating human potential.** Educators can bring out the best in their students by nurturing their creativity, using developmental discipline (building skills for self-control and social connection), and creating a supportive physical structure (promoting an aesthetic environment).

4. **Building a democratic organization.** Educators can structure democracy by providing open governance, establishing open communication channels, and promoting community building.

Apprenticeship in the RAVES Model. Educators using the RAVES model establish an apprenticeship context of modeling and guidance. The Minnesota Community Voices and Character Education project (Narvaez, Bock, Endicott, & Lies, 2004) advocated a four-level *novice-to-expert* instructional approach to teach ethical skills (described in the Ethical Expertise section). Though expertise in a particular area takes many years to develop, classroom instruction can be designed to move students along the path toward expertise. Educators using this approach often employ more than one level at a time to include a range of student developmental readiness.

Level 1 involves immersion in examples and opportunities for plunging students into multiple, engaging activities. Students learn to recognize broad patterns in the domain, acquiring *identification knowledge*. They develop gradual awareness and recognition of elements in the domain.

Level 2 focuses on facts and skills. The teacher guides students' attention to the elemental concepts in the domain in order to build *elaboration knowledge*— increasing associations of how the skill operates and how it relates to other knowledge. Skills are gradually acquired through motivated, focused attention and practice of subskills.

In Level 3, students practice procedures. The teacher coaches students in applying skills and ideas throughout the domain to build an understanding of how best to solve problems. Capacities are developed, and students ultimately attain *planning knowledge*.

Level 4 integrates knowledge and procedures. Students gradually integrate and apply skills across many contexts, and learn how to take the steps in solving complex domain problems, thereby demonstrating *execution knowledge*.

Virtuous Models in the RAVES Model. For any aim, we all need examples, stories, and guidance that supportive communities provide. The kind of life that is considered virtuous is conveyed though the culture in which a child is immersed. Stories can be a powerful influence for shaping our beliefs, guiding our actions, and providing role models for behavior. Children learn who they can and should become from the stories we tell them (MacIntyre, 1981). How we treat children are stories they internalize. What stories guide virtuous behavior? Adults can pass on the stories of the community. In doing so, it is important that adults understand that their own characters are "under construction" by the activities they pursue and by how they use their imagination.

Stories to Light Our Way (Singh, 2010) from the Wisdom Thinkers Network (see Resources) is a set of positive multicultural stories to guide children's moral character development that align with social and emotional learning goals (SEL; Elias & Berkowitz, 2016) as well as with academic benchmarks. Like Korczak's stories, stories from Wisdom Thinkers present virtuous examples of ethical skills. "The Real Bargain," drawn from the life of Guru Nanak in the Sikh tradition, features Young Nanak, who is faced with the choice of making a good bargain in the market to prove his skills as a trader to his father. Young Nanak chooses to use the money to feed and clothe a group of poor people, thinking it a better "bargain" to share with those in need. This sets up a clear conflict with what his father and society consider a bargain and the ideals or ethical approach. However, as a testimony to Nanak's "victory" in taking action for the poor, to this day each Gurdwara (Sikh Temple) features a free community meal where all are welcome to share the food regardless of their backgrounds. In this way, "The Real Bargain" spawns discussions on inclusive communities, poverty, and our social responsibility or social justice. Educators have integrated the story in several ways into the classroom, including reader's theatres, math games, and service-learning projects focused on sharing food or supplies.

According to RAVES, children should be immersed in a community whereby they *hear* about the importance of the particular skill or virtue, *practice* active experiences of the virtue with others, and *find pleasure* from the virtuous behavior. Educators can help connect virtue to students' lives in several ways:

1. Link the classroom work to local community needs.

2. Promote global awareness while connecting students' work to issues around the world.

3. Develop global citizenship skills: sociopolitical awareness of the world and ecological consciousness.

4. Cultivate flourishing: developing an engaged and purposeful life and helping students' communities flourish in the process.

Ethical expertise in the RAVES Model. Ethical skills can be taught across the curriculum and extra-curriculum (Anderson, Narvaez, Bock, Endicott, & Lies, 2004; Narvaez et al., 2004). They are developed through a novice-to-expert pedagogy in the apprenticeship context described above until the individual is able to self-author (described next). To teach ethical skills, educators should model, emphasize, and discuss them with their students. Due to a variety of ethical skills, the RAVES model organized over two dozen important skills into four broad categories: ethical sensitivity, ethical judgment, ethical focus, and ethical action, listed in Table 23.2 (Narvaez et al., 2004). Some skills could fit multiple categories.

Ethical sensitivity (Narvaez & Endicott, 2009) involves picking up on the cues related to ethical decision making and behavior, and interpreting the situation according to who is involved, what actions could be taken, and what possible outcomes might ensue. Ethical sensitivity skills facilitate four main functions: acquiring, organizing, and interpreting information about the ethical situation, and expressing oneself appropriately. The "information" can represent perceived events, perceived relationships, currently experienced emotions, background knowledge of events and relationships, and also existing attitudes accessed from memory (e.g., LeDoux, 1996). Expressive skills such as empathy and compassion are developed as students observe and imitate role models and reflect on their experience and performance.

Ethical judgment (Narvaez & Bock, 2009) entails reasoning about the possible actions in the situation and judging which action is most ethical. Ethical judgment is a critical piece in the decision-making process. To make a sound decision or effectively solve a problem, a person must have some basic cognitive skills that enable them to thoroughly complete the decision-making process. These basic cognitive skills include understanding what the ethical problem is, knowing what ethical codes can be applied to the situation, using reasoning to determine the best decision, and planning how to implement it.

Ethical focus or motivation (Narvaez & Lies, 2009) is prioritizing the ethical action over other goals and needs, either in the particular situation or as a habit. If an individual is not driven by his or her own ethical identity, he or she may take actions that harm others. Similarly, if one does not have an ethical goal in mind when taking action, one may behave in ways that harm the self or others. Ethical focus is nurtured when a person learns to respect others, act responsibly, and develop a positive identity.

Ethical action (Narvaez, 2009) involves understanding how to behave ethically and how to follow through despite obstacles. Ethical action skills include both (1) interpersonal skills such as conflict resolution and negotiation, leadership, assertiveness, and basic communication, and (2) personal skills such as taking initiative, courage, perseverance, and working hard. A person without all or most of these skills may have a difficult time behaving ethically, no matter how much he or she might feel motivated to do so. These skills make it possible to follow through and complete the identified ethical activity.

Self-authorship in the RAVES Model. Educators can guide student self-authorship and self-regulation for life tasks. Autonomy is particularly important for moral functioning (Narvaez, 2011). Moral self-authorship capacities include skills like moral self-monitoring (e.g., Am I taking all sides into account in making my decision?) and moral self-regulation (e.g., Can I take this moral action on my own without additional support?).

Using our suggested terminology, children's self-authorship was a central tenet of Korczak's pedagogical method. He respected each child's free will and encouraged children to reflect upon their actions and behaviors in order to gain greater awareness of themselves and others around them (Korczak, 1967d). One strategic way in which Korczak fostered self-authorship was through the creation of a children's government with its own legal code. Through this democratic system, children were able to self-author their own lives and shape the community around them, practicing the skills of self-monitoring and self-reflection.

Those with good self-monitoring are able, for example, to change strategies when a particular course of action is not working. Virtuous individuals must be autonomous enough to monitor their behavior and choices. Once developed, virtues must be maintained through the selection of appropriate friends, activities, and environments (Aristotle, 1988).

Self-regulation is key to skill development. It has to do with preparing students for post-instruction by helping them to build capacities for independent action and to get support they need.

Conclusion

The RAVES model was designed to provide a framework for establishing an intentional approach to fostering moral character in schools. The overall aim is to build well-functioning community members who have the skills to participate in a democratic society. RAVES starts with warm, supportive relationships. Then educators follow an apprenticeship model, mentoring students through virtuous examples, ethical skill development, and helping them learn to self-author. RAVES was built with children from the US in mind so it is oriented to meeting many of their basic needs that these days are not fulfilled elsewhere in their lives. Other nations may be better at providing the elements of the model outside the classroom.

RAVES is not a manual or curriculum. Instead, educators must decide how to modify their regular instruction to integrate the model into their daily practice. In the Minnesota project, RAVES was presented to local teams of educators and community members who then decided what aspects to adopt and adapt for their local needs. Each implementation was unique and took time to prepare and enlist collaborating teachers. Those who implemented deeply (across homeroom/advisory period, in school-wide projects) showed the greatest effects when measured against a comparison group (Narvaez et al., 2004).

As with the RAVES model, Korczak's pedagogy was based upon understanding the child, entering into their world, and above all, respecting and loving each child as an equal person (Lewowicki, 1994). Korczak is a moral exemplar who lived the tenets of the RAVES model in his own time and in his own cultural way. The numerous similarities between his pedagogy and the RAVES model indicate a "grammar of ethics" and point to a universal call to respect the dignity of all children (Korczak, 1978, p. 6). Through committed efforts to implement practices that foster respect for the child, teachers will create classrooms with students who are ready to learn, and children will grow in socioemotional and moral intelligence, toward wisdom like that of Janusz Korczak.

References

Anderson, C., Narvaez, D., Bock, T., Endicott, L., & Lies, J. (2004). *Minnesota community voices and character education: Final report and evaluation*. Roseville: Minnesota Department of Children, Families and Learning.

Aristotle. (1988). *Nicomachean ethics* (W.D. Ross, Trans.). London: Oxford.

Battistich, V. A. (2008). The Child Development Project: Creating caring school communities. In L. Nucci & D. Narvaez (Eds.), *Handbook of moral and character education* (1st ed.). Mahwah, NJ: Erlbaum.

Block, J. (2007). *Pushed: The painful truth about childbirth and modern maternity care*. New York: Lifelong Books/Da Capo/Perseus.

Boschki, R. (2005). Re-reading Martin Buber and Janusz Korczak: Fresh impulses toward a relational approach to religious education. *Religious Education, 100*(2), 114–126.

Carter, C.S., Ahnert, L., Grossmann, K.E., Hrdy, S.B., Lamb, M.E., Porges, S.W., & Sachser, N. (2005). *Attachment and bonding: A new synthesis*. Cambridge, MA: MIT Press.

Elias, M. J., & Berkowitz, M. W. (2016). Schools of social-emotional competence and character: Actions for school leaders, teachers, and school support professionals. Naples, FL: National Professional Resources.

Hewlett, B. S., & Lamb, M. E. (2005). *Hunter-gatherer childhoods: Evolutionary, developmental and cultural perspectives*. New Brunswick, NJ: Aldine.

Korczak, J. (1967a). *Selected works of Janusz Korczak*. Published for the National Science Foundation by the Scientific Publications Foreign Cooperation Center of the Central Institute for Scientific, Technical and Economic Information, Warsaw [Available from the US Dept. of Commerce Clearinghouse for Federal Scientific and Technical Information, Springfield, VA.]. http://www.janusz-korczak.ca/legacy/1_Introduction.pdf

Korczak, J. (1967b). How to love a child. *Selected works of Janusz Korczak*, 404–405. Retrieved on November 27, 2018, from http://www.januszkorczak.ca/legacy/3_ How%20to%20Love%20a%20Child.pdf

Korczak, J. (1967c). Educational factors. *Selected works of Janusz Korczak*, 1–80. Retrieved on November 27, 2018, from http://www.januszkorczak.ca/legacy/ 2_Educational%20Factors.pdf

Korczak, J. (1967d). Child's right to respect. *Selected works of Janusz Korczak*, 355–377. Retrieved on November 27, 2018, from http://www.januszkorczak.ca/legacy/

Korczak, J. (1978). *Ghetto diary* (J. Bachrach & B. Krzywicka, Trans). New York: Holocaust Library.

LeDoux, J. E. (1996). *The emotional brain: The mysterious underpinnings of emotional life*. New York: Simon & Schuster.

Lewowicki, T. (1994). Janusz Korczak. *Prospects*, 24(1–2), 37–48.

MacIntyre, A. (1981). *After virtue: A study in moral theory*. Notre Dame, IN: University of Notre Dame Press.

Narvaez, D. (2006). Integrative ethical education. In M. Killen & J. Smetana (Eds.), *Handbook of moral development* (pp. 703–733). Mahwah, NJ: Erlbaum.

Narvaez, D. (2007). How cognitive and neurobiological sciences inform values education for creatures like us. In D. Aspin & J. Chapman (Eds.), *Values education and lifelong learning: Philosophy, policy, practices* (pp. 127–159). New York: Springer Press International.

Narvaez, D. (2008). Triune ethics: The neurobiological roots of our multiple moralities. *New Ideas in Psychology, 26*, 95–119.

Narvaez, D. (2009). *Ethical action: Nurturing character in the classroom* (EthEx Series Book 4). Notre Dame, IN: Alliance for Catholic Education Press.

Narvaez, D. (2010). Building a sustaining classroom climate for purposeful ethical citizenship. In T. Lovat and R. Toomey (Eds.), *International research handbook of values education and student well-being* (pp. 659–674). New York: Springer Publishing Co.

Narvaez, D. (2011). Neurobiology, moral education and moral self-authorship. In D. de Ruyter & S. Miedema (Eds.), *Moral education and development: A lifetime commitment* (pp. 31–44). Rotterdam: Sense Publishers.

Narvaez, D. (2014). *Neurobiology and the development of human morality: Evolution, culture and wisdom*. New York: W.W. Norton.

Narvaez, D. (2018). *Basic needs, well-being and morality: Fulfilling human potential*. New York: Palgrave-MacMillan.

Narvaez, D., & Bock, T. (2009). *Ethical judgment: Nurturing character in the classroom* (EthEx Series Book 2). Notre Dame, IN: Alliance for Catholic Education Press.

Narvaez, D., Bock, T., Endicott, L., & Lies, J. (2004). Minnesota's Community Voices and Character Education Project. *Journal of Research in Character Education, 2*, 89–112.

Narvaez, D., & Endicott, L. G. (2009). *Ethical sensitivity: Nurturing character in the classroom* (EthEx Series Book 1). Notre Dame, IN: Alliance for Catholic Education Press.

Narvaez, D., & Lies, J. (2009). *Ethical motivation: Nurturing character in the classroom* (EthEx Series Book 3). Notre Dame, IN: Alliance for Catholic Education Press.

Noddings, N. (2002). *Educating moral people: A caring alternative to character education.* New York: Teachers College Press.

Reiter, S., Asgad, B., & Sachs, S. (1990). The implementation of philosophy in education: Janusz Korczak's educational principles as applied in special education. *The British Journal of Mental Subnormality, 36*(70), 4–16.

Sheridan, S., & Samuelsson, I. P. (2001). Children's conceptions of participation and influence in pre-school: A perspective on pedagogical quality. *Contemporary Issues in Early Childhood, 2*(2), 169–194.

Singh, R. (2010). *Stories to light our way.* Elbridge, NY: Wisdom Thinkers Network.

Watson, M., & Ecken, L. (2018). *Learning to trust,* 2nd ed. San Francisco: Jossey-Bass.

Resources

Wisdom Thinkers Network: http://www.wisdomthinkers.org

TABLE 23.1.
THE RAVES MODEL FOR MORAL CHARACTER DEVELOPMENT[1]

Each concept in model	Defining each concept
Relationships	Attachment, positive social climate, basic needs met, village of support
Apprenticeship context	Modeling, guidance
Virtuous models	Narratives, role models, expectations of virtuous behavior
Ethical skill development	Sensitivity, judgment, focus, action
Self-authorship	Independence, autonomy

[1] The research was initiated when all authors were at the University of Minnesota under the grant USDE OERI Grant # R215V980001. Materials to help educators set goals, identify activities related to RAVES activities, are available at https://cee.nd.edu/curriculum/

TABLE 23.2.

FOUR BROAD ETHICAL SKILLS WITH MORE SPECIFIC SKILLS FOR EACH

ETHICAL SENSITIVITY	ETHICAL REASONING
Understand emotional expression	Understand ethical problems
Take the perspectives of others	Using codes & identifying judgment criteria
Connecting to others	Reasoning critically
Responding to diversity	Reasoning ethically
Controlling social bias	Understand consequences
Interpret situations	Reflect on process and outcome
Communicate well	Coping and resiliency
ETHICAL FOCUS	**ETHICAL ACTION**
Respecting others	Resolving conflicts and problems
Cultivate conscience	Assert respectfully
Help others	Taking initiative as a leader
Being a community member	Planning to implement decisions
Finding meaning in life	Cultivate courage
Valuing traditions & institutions	Persevering
Developing ethical identity & integrity	Working hard

CHAPTER TWENTY-FOUR

Bets and Postcards:
Fostering Children's Self-Efficacy

Wojciech Lasota

A New Approach

IN 1899, KORCZAK (1983) wrote: "Children are human beings already, not *in the future* but right now.... We can speak to their minds and they will respond, let's speak to their hearts, they will feel us" (p. 31).[1] Years later, on the eve of WWII, Korczak (1939) echoed this sentiment, reinforced by his 40 years of experience: "The keynote: a child is as equally a valuable human being as we are" (p. 5).

Korczak and his associates took this concept seriously as an imperative in their day-to-day work, which was dedicated to organizing the institution where everyone was equally appreciated and where the use of violence—a dominant method of disciplining children at the time—was banned. The question then became: How can one effectively address challenges connected with conflict, ownership, participation, safety, cleanliness, and bad habits without violence? In response, Korczak introduced a unique set of methods based on the recognition of human rights of children and adults. Two of these methods, Bets and Postcards, gradually grew out of his practice. Korczak did not preemptively create rules or codes but observed and met challenges as they arose.

Bets became a way of addressing the needs of those children who were aware of their bad habits and wanted to eliminate them but struggled to do so. The Postcards method was helpful in working with the children who wanted to feel appreciated and recognized by their peers and teachers, and to have their personal successes publicly acknowledged.

I focus on these specific methods (actively used in the Orphans' Home and Our Home) because they reflect the core of Korczak's approach and allow establishing balance between the enactment of self- skills (self-confidence, self-control, or self-awareness), and co- skills (co-operation, co-responsibility, or co-existence).

Bets

Once a week, children living in Korczakian orphanages were invited to one-on-one meetings with adult mentors with the goal of helping them eliminate such bad habits as fighting, lying, cursing, and lack of care regarding their personal hygiene and chores. The key method used was Bets. And as simple as it sounds, its implications were more complex and sophisticated. Here is an example.

A boy would like to stop swearing but struggles to do so. He meets with a helping adult, and their conversation goes as follows:

Adult: What do you want to bet on?

Boy: I'd like to stop cursing.

Adult: How many times a week do you curse?

Boy: About 40.

Adult: How many times do you want to curse next week?

Boy: I don't want to curse at all!

Adult: Will you be able to go from 40 to zero?

Boy: I don't know.

Adult: So maybe go down to 30 for a start? You can curse 30 times next week.

Boy: OK.

Adult: The bet is on. Meet me here in a week and tell me about your progress. If you succeed, you will get two candies. If you don't, you will give me two candies.

The above illustrates a basic structure of the bet. The child, who asks for and voluntarily attends the meeting, is prompted to identify his struggle and propose his own goal. The adult's job is to simply listen to the child and enable him to enact a feasible, measurable, and tangible goal while proposing an outcome for which the costs and benefits are equal. Here is how Zalman Wassercug (1927), one of Korczak's educators, explained Bets:

The first visit, a boy bets that, this week, he will not engage in offending people more than ten times. He struggles the whole week to suppress his habit and finally wins: "He did not affront more than nine times." As a reward for this achievement, he gets three candies. He also bets that he will reduce the number to eight times. The challenge is even fiercer than before, and it so happens that he is defeated. Like so, the weeks of failures and successes pass until he reaches a zero, which means that he has entirely avoided offending others. Still, he bets for a few more weeks and then there is the real victory—he does not have to bet anymore, it is now a habit. (pp. 27–28)

The crucial part of this method is an unconditional trust in children's ability to identify and improve their own behavior. The adult's role is not to control or correct the child but to build favorable conditions in which a child will have the courage to discuss his or her (henceforth, his) struggles and honesty to present the results of their bet, successful or not. The adult is also responsible for demonstrating to the child that his authentic effort is priceless, and even if he fails first, there is always another chance to try and to finally succeed. Wassercug (1927) further described this method:

"Bets" are surrounded by an atmosphere of complete truthfulness. It is not about silly candies, but something greater—struggling with yourself.... Bets reflect vitality and the will of the child's fight wrestling with one's self. The main goal here is self-improvement, which is a principal foundation of the human soul. (p. 29)

Postcards

The essential goal of using Postcards was to appreciate, thank, and commemorate, both publicly and individually.

The Common Good

There were many ways and forms for contributing to the children's community, one of which was the use of so-called duties or chores. Practically all the work at the orphanage was scrupulously divided into small tasks. Children were supposed to choose their duties for the entire month, at the end of which they could choose the same or go for a different task. After the first year, Korczak, as quoted by Medvedeva-Nathoo (2012), wrote,

> This year has finished as a triumph for us. One housemother, one teacher, caretaker and cook—for a hundred children. We have freed ourselves from staff of nondescript quality and the tyranny of hospice workers. The master, worker and director of the Home has become—the child. (pp. 197–198)

The success of this system was largely made possible by the Postcards method. Due to the number of children and the division of necessary duties among them, many residents were unsatisfied with the nature of their tasks. From Korczak's perspective, it was crucial to convince them that their efforts were all equally important for the community, even if they did not enjoy their particular job. Korczak also hoped to show them that each communal duty provided a unique opportunity for self-development. If a child enjoyed his duty, it was presented as an exercise in identifying, "How to do that duty the best?" If children did not like their duties, the exercise was introduced as a challenge, "How to cope with a difficult situation?"

For Korczak, both kinds of efforts were valuable, and he tried to point out their value through the system of Postcards. Here is how it worked. The monthly duration of each child's duties was divided into portions, 30 minutes per day, and 30 portions per month on average. Those who collected 500 different types of duties received a special postcard. After accumulating six postcards in two years, there came a chance to gain a special title—'The Worker,' which was a great honor for the children and was in principle possible because they could have more than one duty, which incentivized labor. There were also additional opportunities to gain postcards, such as for "voluntary help," which children would choose if they felt it was the right thing to do.

Most importantly, postcards were issued by the Parliament of the Orphans' Home and always remained precious for the children. Many of Korczak's charges were Holocaust survivors, who lost almost everything during WWII, but chose to save photos and postcards from the Orphans' Home as their most valuable items.

> The picture postcards were awarded on set days and were accompanied by an established ritual. The children would await the moment

with growing excitement. Receiving a postcard, handwritten by Korczak, who was their great leader, was a particular point of pride for them. Some children received several such postcards at one time. One could easily imagine how much of a special occasion it must have been for them. (Medvedeva-Nathoo, 2012, p. 193)[2]

Self-Improvement

Postcards were also signs of individual achievements for children who had struggled in a particular area of self-improvement (e.g., waking up early in the morning). Overall, the objective of the two methods—Bets and Postcards—might look similar but there is a crucial difference between them. While Bets remained a private activity that emphasized intrinsic motivation, the Postcards, on the contrary, were oriented towards the public value of one's self-improvement. A postcard served as physical proof that the Parliament recognized and appreciated someone's self-improvement and considered it beneficial for the orphanage in general. Postcards were also given to people from outside the orphanage for such accomplishments. Korczak (1967) recalled, "The shoemaker who never used to be on time, promised, and then brought the boots and shoes on the expected day and hour for a whole year. He was awarded a punctuality card by the Parliament" (p. 351).

Today's Adaptations

Janusz Korczak and Maria Falska (director of Our Home) were aware that many educators wanted to replicate their methods, and they always recommended not to copy but to adapt them to the particular context. Korczak and Falska worried that a mere copy would override the key objective: to center and build on children's agency in their self-improvement and self-governance. Furthermore, these methods were crucially interconnected, bound, and dependent within the ecosystem of their orphanages. If taken out of context, a specific method would not function and could actually do more harm than good.

Taking into account Korczak and Falska's warnings and the context-dependent nature of these activities, I argue that Bets would be more easily and effectively implemented than Postcards. While Postcards as a method demands complex institutional activities and organizational structures, Bets only requires the cooperation of a child and facilitation of an adult. This is why I discuss the use of Bets in a more detailed way.

Recommendations: Bets

1) Find an appropriate space for your meetings, quiet and away from others—one in which conditions engender trust, center the child's sense of agency, and value their privacy. Make sure you have enough time for an easygoing conversation that does not devolve into an interrogation. If you think it is necessary, let the parents know that you will implement a new method and explain it to them.

2) Train yourself in effective Bets conversations. Find someone with whom to practice. Run through the following scenario and try switching roles (see Table 24.1 on opposite page).

While reflecting on Table 24.1, I suggest you address the following issues:

1. Do you think Bets could be useful in your work? How so?

2. Do you have any suggestions for how to improve it? What conditions should be met?

3. I recommend using the following table for monitoring your agreement, but it is optional (see Table 24.2). Please think about your own technique for creating motivation. Whatever you decide (whether it's Korczak's sweets or not), it should meet the following criteria:

   • The reward should be real and tangible.

   • It should be attractive to children, but at the same time, it should be very cheap (or free of charge), and easy to prepare or to acquire. Children who lose the bet should be able to have easy access to these things.

TABLE 24.1.
GUIDELINES FOR PLACING BETS

Version for Children	Version for Adults
Preparation:	Preparation:
Imagine you are a child and you need to speak with your teacher.	Imagine you are a teacher/educator. You will speak with a child.

- The reason for your conversation is that the child has an issue/problem/goal that he would like to deal with. It is the child's role to state his challenge, and the educator's role is to help specify and clarify that challenge/goal.
- The challenge should be tangible, authentic, quantifiable, and feasible, and should directly respond to the child's issue/problem/goal. The challenge could enable a child to develop a positive habit or change a negative one. For example, it could include a way to start learning Spanish (e.g., learn one word a day) or it could be about eradicating a bad habit—limiting the amount of time one spends on a smartphone or the amount of sweets one eats.

Version for Children	Version for Adults
- Invent an issue/problem/goal. - Use the following statements as guides to begin your conversation. After that, please improvise, remaining in your role as a child.	Use the following questions to help guide the conversation, writing down the child's answers and the nature or a mechanism of their bet.

Type of a Conversation	Type of a Conversation
ADULT: What do you want to bet on? CHILD: I'd like to... (Describe what you'd like to change: e.g., to start/stop doing something).	YOU: What do you want to bet on? 'CHILD': [states his bet]. YOU: How many times a week do you do something (or want to do something)? 'CHILD': (states the number—be sure to write it down) YOU: How many times would you like to (do something) next week? CHILD: (provides the answer) YOU: Will you be able to do this ____ many/so few times OR decrease/increase that number)? CHILD: ... ____ <u>IF A CHILD SAYS, 'NO':</u> YOU: Maybe you should make it easier and do that (not too many/too few times)? 'CHILD':... YOU: You agreed to [do something X times OR decrease/increase that number to X]. The bet is on. Meet me here in a week and tell me about your progress. If you succeed, you will mark 'Yes!' in our table (see below). If not, mark 'Not yet' here in our notebook. Is that OK? CHILD: ...

TABLE 24.2.
TRACKING BETS

Name	Date of bets	Date of next meeting	Subject of the bets	Did you succeed?
				Yes!
				Not yet!

4. The method must be self-imposed by the child rather than determined by an adult.

5. The teacher's central task is engendering trust and writing everything down. You should avoid defining the child's goals or commenting on their efforts, past, present, or future. You may be working with a child who has failed to win a bet thus far and feels that bets should be less ambitious or has ideas for how to improve this approach, but you should refrain from interfering.

Recommendations: Postcards

1. Identify or develop some sort of an institution which could become an awarding body. For example, you could create a students' council for your class. To avoid any biases, postcards should never be awarded by a teacher or any other individual. The awarding of postcards should be as fair-minded and democratic as possible.

2. As a class, select and document areas of appreciated activity, which might, for example, include the following:

   • Community contributions: cleaning the classroom, watering plants, passing out materials, etc.

   • Heroism: speaking up against and defending other children from acts of bullying, actively including children who have been excluded from group activities, demonstrating a protest against unfair behavior or favoritism, treating everyone equally, etc.

- Personal growth: honoring students who have achieved personal goals that benefit the group, whether it's not being late to class for two months straight, improving a grade from a D to a C, reading two books per week for three months, or something similar.

3. Identify and document the rules for awarding postcards. Do this by arranging an open debate about the process addressing the following questions: What tasks do we count? How do we count them? When should people be awarded? If the area is unquantifiable (e.g., "heroism"), then what and when should we recognize as a success? It is crucial to create rules that are simple, trustworthy, and concrete.

Here are some sample guidelines:
- We recognize and count the following: *Community contributions* will be measured in terms of time (e.g., 10 minutes of cleaning), *Heroism* in terms of specific deeds or actions, and *Personal growth* will be self-identified.
- One unit of time is equal to 10 (15, 20, 25 . . .) minutes. If you collect 250 units, you will be awarded a postcard.
- Members of the community can report other students that behaved in an extraordinary way by helping to defend someone, saying something brave, etc. Depending on your agreement, you can award postcards for a single deed or a collection of deeds for the month.
- Students can write down on the board whether they have achieved a specific personal goal. Postcards can be awarded for a single achievement or a specific number of achievements per month.

4. Work with the class to design and create postcards. Postcards could be many things: photos, toys, sculptures, ready-made objects, etc. I recommend they meet certain criteria: be cheap and easy to prepare, be tangible objects and not consumables like candies but more like a keepsake. Finally, they should acknowledge the student's achievement as both personal and social.

Bets and Postcards: How to Succeed

There are some essential requirements that should be followed to make the implementation of these methods successful. The first is to establish and maintain a friendly climate within an educational institution. Bets and Postcards can help to foster such a climate, but without it already in place, these methods will be impossible to enact effectively.

A friendly climate means trust; students need to know that their teacher will always help them in their self-improvement, that a high level of independence will be provided to every child in their personal growth and search for different ways, and that the teacher will stay away from imposing any strategies on them. Children always seem to know when a teacher is invested in their self-efficacy. In the case of Postcards, there is an additional requirement that the teacher and students are flexible and open to adaptation, which is necessary for successful cooperation and the ability to effectively address both institutional and individual mistakes.

The second condition is acquiring patience. Children need lots of time and practice to understand and become familiar with these methods. Predictably, students will struggle to win bets and postcards in the short term, so it is important to find ways of helping them overcome these challenges and develop a long-term perspective.

The third condition is more difficult and reflective of Korczak's approach. Do not view children's resistance to these methods as their failure to enact them, but rather as the teacher's need to improve them with regard to students' demands and necessities. For example, when Korczak first introduced the concept that students would be able to resolve grievances before a court of peers, the children derided it, refused to participate, and even sabotaged it. Rather than forcing his system on the students, Korczak attempted to understand what exactly they disliked about the process, revised it, and then re-implemented it. Among other changes, he added one crucial point: children could take to court both other children and adults. This *small* change in the protocol produced a greater one: children not only accepted the Court of Peers as a viable process for resolving conflicts, but it became a cornerstone of Korczakian institutions for decades.

Conclusion

Bets and Postcards were part of the complicated and sophisticated methods and ways that gave a structure to everyday life in Korczakian institutions. The whole system of the content and usage of these methods was designed around Korczak's assertion that a child is an equally valuable human being and therefore entitled to the same rights as adults.

If we believe in children's agency and potential, they should have an opportunity to identify and adjust undesirable behaviors or habits themselves. The Bets method provided this kind of an opportunity. If we also believe that children's efforts towards caring about the common good and also towards their self-improvement should be recognized and awarded, then we should create special occasions for children to do good things and to be appreciated and recognized. Thus, Postcards[3] served as a protocol to do just that.

I am convinced that these Korczakian methods could and should be implemented today. While it is rather impossible to copy and paste them, it is still quite possible and worthwhile to learn more about them, and then modify and adapt them to any social conditions.

References

Korczak, J. (1939). *Pedagogika żartobliwa* [Playful pedagogy]. Warsaw: Wydawnictwo J. Mortkowicza. Retrieved from http://www.dbc.wroc.pl/Content/13804/RP1342_Pedagogika_zartobliwa.pdf

Korczak, J. (1967). *How to Love a Child: The Children's Home*. In *Selected Works of Janusz Korczak*. Jerzy Bachrach (Transl.). Washington, D.C.: The National Science Foundation. (Original work published 1920). Retrieved from: http://www.januszkorczak.ca/legacy/CombinedMaterials.pdf

Korczak, J. (1983). Rozwój idei miłości bliźniego w XIX wieku [Development of the idea of loving your neighbor in the nineteenth century]. In Maria Falkowska (Eds.) *Myśl pedagogiczna Janusza Korczaka. Nowe źródła* [Pedagogical thought of Janusz Korczak. The new sources]. Warsaw: Nasza Księgarnia. (Original work published 1899.)

Korczak, J. (2018). *How to Love a Child: The Orphan's Home*. In *How to Love a Child: And Other Selected Works* Vol. 1. (S. Bye et al., Trans.). London: Vallentine Mitchell. (Original work published 1920.)

Medvedeva-Nathoo, O. (2012). *Oby im życie łatwiejsze było* [May their lot be lighter]. Ryszard Reisner (Transl.) Poznań: Uniwersytet im. Adama Mickiewicza. Retrieved from http://www.januszkorczak.ca/wp-content/uploads/2016/12/Janusz-Korczak_2012.pdf

Wassercug, Z. (1927). Zakłady [Bets]. *Dos Kind*, 7, 27–29 (A. Geller, Trans. from Yiddish). The text is available in Polish in KORCZAKIANUM (Museum of Warsaw).

Endnotes

1 The author expresses his appreciation to Dr. Denise Grollmus for her help in composing and editing this chapter.

2 For more details about the postcards and their examples, see Medvedeva-Nathoo (2012), pp. 100–132, 191–206.

3 A note from the editors: American teachers might consider using digital badges, which are familiar to children today and could produce the same effect as a physical postcard.

CHAPTER TWENTY-FIVE

It Is Hard to Be in Charge: What Can We Learn from *King Matt the First*?

Tamara Sztyma

BEING ONE OF the most famous books by Janusz Korczak (1923), *King Matt the First* is a great example of how to talk with children about serious and difficult topics. In this chapter I first touch upon the historical context and ideas expressed in *King Matt the First*, and then briefly introduce an unusual exhibition inspired by this book at the POLIN Museum of the History of Polish Jews in Warsaw.

Historical Background

Korczak was writing *King Matt* during a very challenging time. WWI ended on November 11, 1918, and radically transformed Europe. The three empires—Germany, Russia, and Austro-Hungary—fell apart, providing independence to many new nations, including Poland; the latter regained it after 126 years of partitions.[1]

However, winning back independence was just the beginning of a long process of rebuilding the state, which was impoverished; ravaged by war; politically, economically, and socially fractured; and consisted of many national and ethnic minorities. Similar to other new states in Europe, Poland introduced a parliamentary democratic system. In January 1919, the first legislative Parliament (The Sejm) was elected and convened. The Constitution of 1921 granted equal civil rights to all citizens of Poland, regardless of their origin or religion, although this mutual understanding was not easy to achieve. Numerous conflicts arose from competing national interests; cultural, religious, and economic differences; and also from mutual distrust.

There were two irreconcilable visions of the state—one that would celebrate a nation state where only Polish Catholics could enjoy full civil rights, and the opposite with the view of Poland as an open democratic state, inclusive, and respectful of its every citizen. In December 1922, the first Polish president was shot and killed only a week after the election by a follower of Endecja, a nationalist political group opposed to the participation of minorities in ruling the country.

King Matt the First Was Born

Korczak published this book at the beginning of 1923 in the midst of the above events as an attempt to explain to the children what was happening in the hopes that it would help them to become good citizens. This issue occupied him particularly in the first years of the Second Polish Republic when the new state and a new democratic society were born. According to some optimistic thinkers at the time, Poland was supposed to provide for everyone, including poor Jewish orphans in Korczak's care.

In 1918–1919, the orphanage children's newspaper, *Tygodnik Domu Sierot*, published a series of Korczak's journalistic texts directly addressed to children, entitled *What is Going On in the World (Co się dzieje na świecie)*, where he made an attempt to explain the causes and the course of the First World War, the essence of independence, and the process of building a parliamentary democratic system in the newly established state. Korczak was doing this in a simple way— by referring to experiences familiar to children, such as everyday arguments on different issues among peers and their attempts to solve them. He believed it was the most efficient way for adults to talk with children about complicated matters. Moving further in this direction, Korczak decided to write a novel for children, *King Matt the First*, in which he created an image of a young king with whom the children could easily identify. Through the adventures of this little protagonist, Korczak planned to explain the nature of power and the responsibility that governing a nation entails (see Image 25.1).

The book tells us a story of a 10-year-old boy who inherits the throne following his father's death, and very soon afterwards, a war breaks out with the neighboring states. Despite his victory in the war, Matt realizes how devastating the experience was. He is then faced with the need to restore the ravaged and war-torn country. The boy is striving to understand what power is all about. He wants

to be a good ruler, but once in a while
he finds it very difficult. Matt seeks
advice from his counselors and other
kings, argues with his ministers, sometimes acting like a tyrant and forcing
others to follow his orders. Gradually,
he learns what reforms and democracy
are about and decides to organize his
state according to democratic rules
with open parliamentary debates and
the participation of the population in
governing the country. More precisely,
he establishes two parliaments—one
for children and one for adults—as
he wants children to make their own
decisions about their most pressing
issues. It turns out that reaching de-

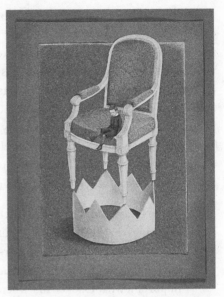

IMAGE 25.1

cisions is not all that easy; each person strives for something else, opening the
door to fights. Some of Matt's reforms appear too farfetched and unrealistic (for
example, he orders that children and adults swap roles: children should go to work
and adults to school). In the country where children take control over adults,
general chaos ensues, and the possibility of a new war arises on the horizon. Matt
learns that governing a state is a great responsibility, and that good intentions do
not always protect you from making mistakes.

This amazing book takes the form of a classical philosophical tale with a
protagonist who, through his adventures and experiences, reflects upon the
nature of different truths and ideas, and constructs his worldview.

Korczak's Pedagogy as the Foundation of the Book

Korczak was one of the first to perceive children as independent and fully
capable human beings. He sought new methods based on partnership, dialogue,
and cooperation rather than pressure or demands. He understood the role of an
educator as someone who would provide support, explain the world, and build
emotionally positive and respectful relations.

In one of his articles Korczak (2008) states, "The child's experience is deeper, stronger and more vivid . . . . We can only understand—he can feel and see" (pp. 18–19). He also claims, "Children find it hard to say what they feel and what they think about, because one has to speak in words. And it's even more difficult to write. And children are poets and philosophers" (2003, p. 100).

With his strong belief in a deep emotional connection between an adult and a child, Korczak emphasizes the necessity for adults to always remember that they were once little and they were dreamers. He calls for cherishing the "inner child" in adults. This thought is most beautifully presented in the preface to the first edition of *King Matt the First* accompanied by his own photo as a 10-year-old boy:

> When I was a little boy you see in the photograph, I wanted to do all the things that are in this book. But I forgot to, and now I'm too old. I no longer have the time or the strength to go to war or travel to the land of the cannibals. I have included this photograph because it's important what I looked like when I truly wanted to be a king, and not when I was writing about King Matt. I think it's better to show pictures of what kings, travelers, and writers looked like before they grew up, or grew old, because otherwise it might seem that they knew everything from the start and were never young themselves. And then children will think they can't be statesmen, travelers, and writers, which wouldn't be true. (Korczak, 1986, p. 1)

This philosophical reflection on equivalence and interdependence of children's and adults' worlds led Korczak to some serious practical decisions. He became one of the strong proponents of children's rights and joined the International Save the Children Union that developed the Declaration of the Rights of the Child, endorsed by the League of Nations General (Geneva Declaration on the Rights of the Child, 1924). Korczak wanted children to participate in social life and make decisions about the issues that concerned them, which brought him to the idea of a "citizenship of children" or a "republic of children." Korczak insisted that children should be treated as equal members of society and that from their early days they should participate in social life. He transformed his orphanages into self-governing communities with their own children's courts and newsletters, and active children's involvement in preparing meals, keeping the house in order, and taking care of younger orphans.

The symbolism of King Matt's image. It is not an exaggeration to say that King Matt was Korczak's secret ally, his childish *alter ego*. Matt's attitude to the children of his country is just a fairytale representation of Korczak's own pedagogy. Matt was a child but he could rule his country, and he was empowered the way Korczak wished every child were. Korczak granted him the right to decide, to gain his own experience, and to learn from his own mistakes. And so Matt realizes that "children are part of the people . . . and also a nation" (Korczak, 1986, p. 167) and that they should participate in governing the state. As a king, he allows them to do so, and he provides them with the parliament. Matt admits, children know best what is good for them, and due to this they should be allowed to make decisions about matters that concern them.

Moreover, Korczak endows Matt with a number of his own features and also with dreams about how to make everyone happy and the world a better place to live. Korczak's whole literary, journalistic, and teaching endeavor was aimed at preventing anyone's exclusion. He called for everyone to start taking responsibilities for the world, and in contrast to the revolutionary way of reforming it, he believed in a gradual evolution. In this regard it is worthwhile to quote the conversation Matt held with the "sad king" upon a visit to his country:

"And what is a king for?" asked Matt naively. "Not just to wear a crown—but to bring happiness to the people of his country." [. . .] "But how could you bring happiness?" [. . .] "What I did was to make various reforms. Oho, that's interesting, thought Matt" (Korczak, 1986, p. 120).

Matt is dwelling on this topic while walking with his friend, a court doctor, whom we can perceive as another figure of Korczak in the book:

"Are all the children healthy like me?"

"No, Matt, there are very many children who are weak and sick." [. . .]

"But can't something be done, so everyone could have nice little houses with gardens and nourishing food?"

"That's very difficult. People have been thinking about that a long time, but so far nobody has come up with a good idea." [. . .]

"Do you think I could?"

"You could, of course you could. A king can do a lot. . . ." (Korczak, 1986, p. 127)

The narrative of *King Matt* as a parable of Korczak's vision of humanity. *King Matt the First* does not have a usual happy ending for children's books. Despite his good intentions, Matt does not succeed. The story of a little king, who wanted to make people in his country happy and bring children and adults equal rights, remains a beautiful utopia. This also reflects Korczak's vision of people and his meaning of life.

He emphasized the idea that everyone should continue to question reality instead of holding to one's initial conclusions and facts. He was against any form of dogmatism, following Socrates' wisdom: "I know that I know nothing." Much more important for him than eventual success were the work and efforts needed to attain one's goal. And so, although Matt's bold ideas end in failure, the king's good intentions, hard work, and efforts to change the world make him a hero.

Korczak did not believe in happy endings, as he realistically saw the difficulties of raising good human beings and improving the world. Instead he shared the skepticism and sadness of a philosopher who knows that it is so easy to fall down. However, he was convinced that people should keep on acting and trying. "One cannot leave the world as it is," he announced.

In King Matt's Poland: A New POLIN Exhibition

In November 2018, the ideas and lessons of civic education contained in *King Matt the First* became an inspiration for an exhibition organized at the POLIN Museum in Warsaw to commemorate the 100th anniversary of Poland's independence. Following in the footsteps of Korczak, who talked to children about democracy and the toils of governing when Poland was being re-created, the museum invited its visitors into a similar conversation. The exhibition also provided a great opportunity to remind Poland and the world of Janusz Korczak—apart from his heroic death, people are less aware of his pedagogical and social teachings (see Image 25.2).

In the exhibition, the historical challenges involved in reconstructing the Second Republic of Poland and the activities of Janusz Korczak were interwoven with the fairytale land of the literary narrative of *King Matt the First* and the universal reflection on basic notions from the social and political sciences. The exhibition's title, *In King Matt's Poland*, has in a way deconstructed the metaphorical message of Korczak's novel by indicating that the author created

IMAGE 25.2

his fictional world based on an interwar reality. The central questions that the exhibition posed—What are responsibilities, freedom, power, state, democracy, and self-governing communities?—seem universal, timeless, and as vital today as they were 100 years ago.

In one part of the exhibition, visitors could literally *enter* the pages of the book and move around to get acquainted with the narrative and with the main problems that beset the little king. This section of the exposition was beautifully illustrated by Iwona Chmielewska, an acclaimed artist and author of many books in which images complete the written word, forming a symbolic message together.

In the case of King Matt, Chmielewska was inspired by the photo of Korczak as a 10-year-old boy. Through changing colors—his black-and-white boy's uniform was transformed into royal scarlet—the artist practically realized the Old Doctor's dream and bestowed upon him the title of king. She put a golden crown on his head: a symbol of royal authority and, in a universal sense, of authority in general. In the book illustrations, the crown usually symbolizes problems faced by the young king. All sorts of relations between the boy-king and the golden prop that changes details are the true essence of the novel. Now and then, the crown is too heavy, but occasionally, it is too light; sometimes it signifies fun and in other times concern. It changes shape, too: sometimes, it serves as a bandage, and in other situations, it works as a regular baseball cap. The emotional message is completed by the little boy's gestures: climbing up on a huge throne, angrily striding across a conference table, floating in a crown-parachute above the country or unable to see when the crown slips over his eyes, then jostled by children running around him (see Image 25.3). Children, viewing the exposition, were able to touch the scarlet boy, to play with his crown and, thus, step into his shoes and feel the weight of the responsibility he was forced to bear. Is it possible to make everybody happy? What are the reforms about? How much do they cost?

In the following part of the exhibition, the questions that occupied
Korczak and his little king transposed
themselves into the language of contemporary civic education. Visitors
were invited to a large, open space
full of fun and games, where everyone—both adults and children—was
encouraged to participate in a conversation and reflect upon universal
and fundamental issues pertaining to
the organization of both a state and
a smaller local community (see Image 25.4). The games were organized
around the following six issues: What
is a community, society, state, and a

IMAGE 25.3

nation? How do people manage to agree and make decisions in regard to their community? What state structures are involved there? How does a democratic republic function? How does a self-governing community operate? What does it mean to govern, make decisions, and manage a budget? And finally, what are the rights of people, citizens, and children?[2]

IMAGE 25.4

Conclusions

Following Korczak's pedagogical vision, the exhibition was meant for "big and small adults," and it was not supposed to provide ready-made answers but aimed more at offering experience. It encouraged reflection on the past and on our current situation. It allowed visitors to spend quality time with children, in direct accordance with Korczak's words: "When I am playing with or simply talking to a child, the two equally mature moments of my and his or her lives intertwine" (Korczak, 1993, p. 453). The great interest the exhibition evoked immediately after its opening and the many positive responses received from visitors testify to the importance and validity of Korczak's legacy in general and his books for children in particular. No doubt, they can inspire many new educational and social projects.

References

Geneva Declaration of the Rights of the Child. (1924). Retrieved from UN Documents Database, http://www.un-documents.net/gdrc1924.htm

Korczak, J. (1923). *Król Macius Pierwszy* [King Matt the first]. Warsaw-Kraków: Towarzystwo Wydawnicze.

Korczak, J. (1986). *King Matt the First* (R. Lourie, Trans.). New York: Farrar, Straus and Giroux.

Korczak, J. (1993). *Prawo dziecka do szacunku* [Child's right to respect], *Dzieła* [Works], Vol. 7. Warsaw: Oficyna Wydawnicza Latona.

Korczak, J. (2003). *Prawidła życia* [Rules of life], *Dzieła* [Works], Vol. XI/1, p. 100. Warsaw: Wydawnictwo Instytutu Badań Literackich PAN.

Korczak, J. (2008). Nasz Przegląd 1926 [Our review], (*Dzieła* [Works], Vol. 14/1, 18-19. Warsaw: Wydawnictwo Instytutu Badań Literackich PAN.

Sztyma, T., & Czerwińska, A. (Eds.). (2018). *In King Matt's Poland. The 100th anniversary of regaining independence.* (Z. Sochańska, Transl.).Warsaw: POLIN Museum of the History of Polish Jews.

Endnotes

1 The rules of the partitioning powers were harsh; political and civil freedoms were restricted, the use of Polish in schools and offices was limited, and in some cases even banned. Poland suffered a lot.

2 In the description of the main ideas of the exhibition I also used and summarized the curatorial text published in the exhibition catalogue (T. Sztyma, *An Exhibition for Small and Big Adults: What Questions Do We Want to Ask, on This Specific Occasion?* Warsaw: POLIN Museum of the History of Polish Jews, pp. 23–28).

Photo Credits

25.1 – An illustration inspired by the book King Matt the First, at the 2018 exhibition In King Matt's Poland. The 100th Anniversary of Regaining Independence at the POLIN Museum of the History of POLISH Jews in Warsaw, Poland. Artist Iwona Chmielewska, used with permission.

25.2 – A photo from the 2018 exhibition In King Matt's Poland. The 100th Anniversary of Regaining Independence at the POLIN Museum of the History of POLISH Jews in Warsaw, Poland. Photographer Magdalena Starowieyska, used with permission.

25.3 – An illustration inspired by the book King Matt the First, at the 2018 exhibition In King Matt's Poland. The 100th Anniversary of Regaining Independence at the POLIN Museum of the History of POLISH Jews in Warsaw, Poland. Artist Iwona Chmielewska, used with permission.

25.4 – A photo from the opening of the 2018 exhibition In King Matt's Poland. The 100th Anniversary of Regaining Independence at the POLIN Museum of the History of POLISH Jews in Warsaw, Poland. Photographer Maciek Jaźwiecki, used with permission.

CHAPTER TWENTY-SIX

Nash Dom Camps:
A Unique Space of Childhood

Irina Demakova

Introduction

MY JOURNEY TO Korczak started in 1990 in Israel when, together with 30 fellow academics and teachers from Moscow, I participated in the Korczak seminar run by famous Warsaw researcher and former student of Korczak, Alexander Levin.[1] Impressed and moved by Korczak's heritage, I have never stopped studying it nor doubting its timely nature. What is more—my personal ties with Korczak's pedagogy keep growing stronger, and to this day I am passionate about the necessity of applying it. Since then, on the institutional level there have been serious developments as well: the Russian Korczak Society was born on June 6, 1991, and almost immediately it initiated the opening of Korczak Centers in Moscow, Saint Petersburg, Kazan, and Perm, with the Korczak youth chapters launched at state universities in Khabarovsk, Kursk, Saratov, Ulyanovsk, and other Russian cities.

The Korczak Society has matured over the past three decades and it now has two major foci. The first is studying Korczak's legacy to learn how to better apply his unique humanistic values, goals, and principles to work with children, youth, and teachers, and also how to disseminate this knowledge to all interested parties. The second is its practical implementation in schools, colleges, and teachers' continuing education courses. I have experience with all of the above, but here I will limit myself to articulating the results of my research before concentrating on the practice-oriented work of organizing and supervising numerous summer and winter camps for children and youth (ages 6 through 17).

The Space of Childhood

Drawing on a combination of Korczak's ideas and David Feldstein's (1997) psychological concept of *the space-time of childhood*, I have proposed my own term and concept: *the space of childhood*. In addition to coining the term itself, I have identified its meaning and specified effective ways of humanizing this *space*. The *space of childhood* is a sociocultural phenomenon that has a considerable effect on the child's development, serving as a hub of activities, which, while being closely related to the adult space, still affords a high degree of autonomy. This is an explored environment (natural, cultural, social, and informational) adapted to the purpose of achieving educational goals. However, the terms "environment" and "space" are not synonymous in this regard. It comes across clearer in Russian, where *environment* implies something that exists regardless of human efforts, and *space* is the result of such efforts and, to be more specific, of the *educational exploration* of the environment.

Most importantly, our research has proven that the *space* of social education does not develop of its own accord—rather, it grows within the educational reality as the result of intentional efforts. Only under such circumstances does it improve and humanize a child's life. More critically, children must perceive this space as their own *territory,* assuming responsibility for preserving and protecting it from harm. I am convinced that every teacher should provide all "inhabitants" of this *educational territory* with a certain level of interaction and emotional and intellectual challenge to stimulate children's inquisitive stance toward the world and to encourage their creative search for answers to important life questions.

Clearly, every participant in the social education process must assess his or her competence when a child, confronted with a new situation, activity, interaction, or communication, wonders how well he or she (henceforth, she) is prepared for it. If it proves an affirming space this means that the space of social education has played a stabilizing role in the child's development.

Drawn mostly from the works by Janusz Korczak and some modern scholars, I have formulated a few basic principles that facilitate humanizing the space of childhood: recognition of the inherent value of childhood, respect for general children's rights, and especially, the right to freedom in the social education process.[2]

Recognition of the inherent value of childhood. This principle reflects Korczak's belief in the absolute value of childhood. The Polish educator repeatedly emphasized the significance of a happy childhood in personality formation and opined that without this the whole life of a person might be impaired. He wanted his students to experience the joys of childhood for at least several years. Korczak (2018) wrote:

> Years of work have made it even more clear that children deserve respect, trust, and kindness; that they enjoy a sunny atmosphere of gentle feelings, cheerful laughter, lively first efforts and surprises; of pure, bright, loving joy; where work is dynamic, fruitful, and beautiful. (p. 317)

Recognition of the rights of the child. Korczak (2018) offered a unique interpretation of these rights. He believed that every child is entitled to the respect of her ignorance and cognitive labor, her failures and tears, the mysteries and deviations of the hard labor of growth, the current hour and the present day, the mystery of correction, and efforts and credulity. Similarly, in terms of actions, each child has the right to be what she is, participate in discussions and judgments which concern her directly, experience considerate attitude towards her problems, express her ideas, organize her life independently, use her virtues and conceal her faults, protest, make mistakes, move, possess property, play, etc. What is more, these rights were actively implemented by Korczak.

Recognition of children's freedom in the social education process. Korczak believed that freedom means choice and agreement rather than anarchy or permissiveness. "So is everything permissible?" Korczak (2018) asked himself. His answer:

> Never: of a bored slave we'll make a bored tyrant. With our prohibitions, after all, we harden the will, albeit toward restraint and renunciation; we cultivate inventiveness on restricted terrain, skill in slipping out of others' control, we arouse the critical faculty. And this is precious as a one-sided preparation for life. In allowing that "everything goes," in indulging whims, let's be all the more cautious not to stifle desires. One way, we weaken the will, another, we poison it. (pp. 33–34)

Discussion: Children's Camp *Nash Dom* (Our Home)

Nash Dom camp has three key elements:

1. First, it is a unique, humanistic institution grounded in Korczak's recognition of both the intrinsic value of childhood and of the child's right to freedom in an educational environment. It also presupposes the establishment of dialogue between an adult and child as key to their relationship, and forgiveness as the primary condition of any successful pedagogical activity.

2. It is an international camp. Over the years, we have provided training to over 300 volunteer camp counselors and team leaders from many countries, including the Netherlands, Germany, Italy, Switzerland, USA, etc.

3. It is an integrated camp that, to date, has welcomed approximately 4,000 children, ranging from the wealthy to the socially underprivileged. We accept children with physical and mental challenges as well as those in good health, orphans as well as at-risk children.

The year 2018 marked the 26th anniversary of Nash Dom. This is in itself quite remarkable, and it allows us to draw several relevant conclusions.

First, the camp's underlying philosophical and psychological foundations have remained unchanged, and at their core lies Korczak's idea of the inestimable worth of each child and her rights.

We continue to follow our camp traditions, developing and expanding Korczak's Memorial Day and implementing Korczak's educational practices and methods. The most cherished tradition features arranging camp activities within what are called "families" (not teams or groups) to evoke a sense of life at home. *A family* is a play-therapy formulation that helps heal and make up for what some children desperately miss—having two loving parents. In our camp every child has two team leaders, usually a young man and a woman, referred to as "parents."

In this way, Korczak's "course of action," his legacy, remains intact, and its value preserved. Our camp's flag features a golden clover leaf against a green background, replicating the flag at Korczak's original orphanage. Furthermore, during the camp season we celebrate Korczak's birthday and observe Memorial

Day in his honor. We consistently implement many of Korczak's own practices, such as a message board, a newspaper, fight lists, and others.

Nash Dom camp is governed by children, just as it was in Korczak's orphanages. This tradition dates back to 1993, when the Children's Parliament was formed by election and the Camp's Constitution was adopted. Meetings of the Parliament are held daily, with decisions made and implemented by children with the help of team leaders and the Camp director. Such authentic self-government helps regulate the relationships from both within and outside of Nash Dom.

Every camp day is special, and each has its own name. For example, we usually have Love Day, Family Day, the Day of Many Holidays, the Upside-Down Day, the Nash Dom Birthday, the Day of Birds, and the Workshop Day, to name just a few. The Self-Governance Day is one of the most desired and long-awaited days, when children from *older families* become heads and group leaders.

All inhabitants of Nash Dom, children and adults alike, devoutly observe the following major camp activities: the all-camp gathering called the "Sbor"; the all-camp concert by candlelight (the "Svetchka"); a family concert, also by candlelight; the "Freshmen Meet and Greet"; the "Families Presentation"; and, finally, the Gratitude Concert which marks the end of the camp season with expressions of appreciation to everyone involved in the camp.

At the end of the 2016 summer camp, we asked counselors to reflect on what they had learned about themselves, their charges, and their work by responding to the phrase, "This summer I have learned that..." Here are their responses:

- I need to study how to stop, how to pay attention to children, and that a child's agreeable personality does not mean that this child needs less care and love than the others. I have also learned that not every child is ready to accept help. (Anna K.)

- Children made me open up from an unexpected place, a place I did not even know I had. Each child helps to plant a little seed of love, warmth, and smile within me.... I am changed. (Mariya K.)

- Children are not always to blame for what they do, and they may help us and suggest the right way out. Counselors are human beings, and although we are strong people, we also have our weaknesses. (Denis M.) (Demakova & Denisova, 2016).

Conclusions

Over a quarter of a century has passed. Looking back, one wonders, what's next? What will be preserved and what is destined to be left behind?

No doubt, in this ever-changing world some adjustments are to be expected, especially considering that today's child spends a lot of time on electronic devices. We encounter children who don't know how to make friends, how to play, or how to daydream. The ever-pervasive Internet readily provides answers to virtually any question, imposing often-unhealthy role models on our youth and yielding ineffective behavior patterns. Rather than having the freedom to invent their own ways and devise their own strategies, children have no choice but to mimic what they see.

Still, Korczak's holistic vision of the child, with all her physiological, psychological, and social elements, guides us. The philosophy of Nash Dom is rooted in trust, love, and respect. Our work requires acknowledgment and appreciation of every personality and everyone's uniqueness. We don't aim at "fixing" parents' mistakes within our short time together. Rather, we aim to accept every child as they are.

We assign great value to establishing positive relationships between group leaders and children. This process begins immediately. From the first meeting at the train station before leaving Moscow up until our last minute with the children, we focus on cultivating relationships that celebrate childhood, a unique space where transformational experiences abound. The key component in establishing these relationships is a trust born in dialogue, where all decisions are made through discussion. Hugs and smiles are the most important forms of communication. By hugging a child we pass along the emotional warmth that is vital for meaningful relationships. We teach children to be responsible and aware of what they do; we trust their creative efforts; we inspire them with music and history; we lead them by example; we teach them to reflect before speaking or acting; we teach them compassion and independence. These experiences transform and inform their lives—and ours.

References

Demakova, I.D., & Denisova, V.V. (2016). Anticipating the 25th anniversary of *Nash Dom*: Korczak's Camp in Russia. *Russian-American Education Forum: An online journal, 8(2)*. Retrieved from www.rus-ameeduforum.com

Feldstein, D.I. (1997). *Sotsialnoe Razvitie v Prostranstve-Vremeni Detstva* [Social development in the space-time of childhood]. Moscow: Flinta.

Gazman, O.S. (1996). *Pedagogika svobody: Put' v gumanisticheskuju tsivilizatsiju XXI veka* [The pedagogy of freedom: On a way to the humanistic civilization of the XXI century]. *New Values of Education, 6*, 10–37.

Korczak J. (2018). *How to love a child and other selected works*, Volume 1. London and Chicago: Vallentine Mitchell.

Endnotes

1 A note of appreciation: I am grateful to my Korczak associates Dr. Alina Shipova and Ms. Varvara Denisova, and to my American translator and consultant Ms. Erin Grimm.

2 This principle implies that the child is recognized not only as a natural (biological) and social (cultural) being but also as an existential (or free) human being (Gazman, 1996).

CHAPTER TWENTY-SEVEN

The Janusz Korczak Contest of Youth Literature

Shirane L.A. Halpérin

Introduction

YEAR AFTER YEAR, new technologies are taking over more traditional—and sometimes healthier—means of education in schools at every level. However, their consequences are not always positive (e.g., the decrease of literacy skills), which becomes especially serious when it happens in the elementary grades, when many important life habits are being developed. For example, reading is highly important for a child's cognitive development and has a strong impact on his/her life achievements (BOP Consulting, 2015). Moreover, reading tends to increase the development of empathy and tolerance (Gleed, 2014). Already 20 years ago, the US Department of Education (1998) found that the more students read, the better their grades are. Nevertheless, the National Assessment of Educational Progress ran a test regarding reading skills amongst American children and the result was worrisome: 38% of them were below the basic level (US Department of Education, 1999), which remains a serious issue in the United States today (OECD, 2013), and in many other Western countries.

American children spend an average of 180 days a year, or an average of 6.8 hours a day, at school (Craw, 2018; US Department of Education, 2008). This is a considerable amount of time, and hence, school is and must be the place where these tendencies and habits could and should change. Consequently, what if the solution was to go back to the basics, or in other words, to reconsider the use of traditional resources such as books, which, on the one hand, will ameliorate children's chances for their future and, on the other hand, will help promoting some forgotten and yet fundamental values?

The Concept

The Janusz Korczak Contest of Youth Literature is an annual literature contest in which participating children have the opportunity to choose their favorite book within a given collection. Inspired by the work and values of Janusz Korczak, the contest is based on his humanistic legacy. It was first initiated in 2008 for two elementary grades in France by three considerate adults: Béatrice Rosenberg, the founder of an elementary school and the Honorary President of *L'enfant et la Shoah - Yad-Layeled France*; Annie Falzini, a bookseller of youth literature; and Eglal Errera, a writer of children's books. In 2014–2015, it was extended to more grades.[1] Belgium, Luxembourg, and Switzerland soon joined the project (although the present chapter only uses the example of Switzerland where the contest has been supported by the Department of Public Education of Geneva's cantonal government and has been steadily growing since 2014). The participants are mostly students from Grades 3 to 8 in both private and public schools (a primary level in the Swiss system), or, in other words, ages 6 to 12 years.

The Process

At the beginning of every school year any teacher can register for the contest in Geneva and Lausanne. The contest committee in Paris chooses a new topic each year, except for "The Children in War," which returns every three to five years due to its major historical and psychosocial importance, and its unfortunate present-day relevance. Regardless of the topic, each is inspired by the thoughts and actions of Janusz Korczak, and the context of the book is always set within the wide world of children, with topics such as "Disabilities," "The Gift," "Home," "Change of Life," and "Exile."

The same committee then selects three to four books related to the chosen topic.[2] During the fall, the students receive their selected books in accordance with the children's age. The contest embraces three categories of books for age groups 6–7, 8–9, and 10–11. After the books are received, it is up to teachers to decide how they want to proceed. Generally, throughout the school year, students read the books, discuss the chosen topic, and also talk about Janusz Korczak and children's rights in general. Whenever possible, students meet with the writers and/or illustrators of the chosen books.

The reading and discussion process lasts until May, when all children are asked to select their favorite book. This is done by filling in a voting bulletin, which presents an excellent way of having children learn how to a handle a collective process using democratic tools. It stimulates students' active participation and develops their free expression and open-mindedness.

At the end of the school year, the Swiss Korczak Association organizes an event inviting all participating classes (see Image 27.1). First, a master of ceremonies presents a musical quiz about the different books; children have to listen to songs or music tracks and link each of them to one of the books. Then there comes the announcement of each category's winner that always brings a lot of enthusiasm and excitement. Prior to the closing ceremony, an invited speaker gives a talk on a related topic and answers questions, engaging participants in a lively discussion.

For example, when in 2015 the topic was "The Children in War," a survivor of Rwanda's genocide talked about her fight to survive, escape, and adjust to a new life. During the 2016 contest, "The Gift," a teacher-presenter recounted how

IMAGE 27.1

in her childhood she used to lack self-confidence and how her school principal helped her, reassuring all pupils that each one of them was special, unique, and brilliant, which became a true gift in her life. In 2018, a pediatrician spoke on the topic of "Disabilities" and described her own lower-limbs palsy due to poliomyelitis in infancy that did not prevent her from achieving her life goals.

Each year, during this final presentation, it feels like there is never enough time to answer all of the children's questions. But if the participants manage to approach the speaker outside the conference hall . . . beware! The person will not be able to leave the area for the next hour . . . at least (see Image 27.2)!

IMAGE 27.2

The Results

In only four years of existence in Switzerland, there was an increase in the classes' participation of more than 600 percent: during the 2014–2015 school year, 250 children took part in the contest while more than 1,600 children are attending it in the 2018–2019 school year. Currently in France, Switzerland, and Belgium together, the contest embraces more than 15,000 children. This happens mostly due to a word-of-mouth process and demonstrates the interest and appreciation of both students and teachers. The project is thus continuously expanding and will certainly attract more children from larger parts of Switzerland. So far, only two cities from the French part of Switzerland have been taking part in the contest, although the situation might change to a new reality—adding the entire French and German parts, and possibly the Italian as well.

Additionally, the success of the contest can also be measured by the reactions of the participants. Nora, 10 years old, "loved participating in the Korczak Contest," and Camille, 12 years old, explained that "the ceremony was a great moment, very touching for all the kids" and she "really recommend[s] this exercise of reading such books at school, it taught [her] a lot!" This enthusiasm is also reflected by the adults involved: Mireille, a teacher whose class took part in the contest twice, spoke about "magnificent and magical moments in the class" and explained that after the contest, the books even "went around in the families." Finally, Sigrid Baffert, one of the awarded writers, shared her emotion:

> I am deeply touched and proud that [my book] won the Janusz Korczak Award. If I had to win only one prize, this would be the one I would have chosen. Because of what it represents, because of what it carries. When I think about this great man Korczak— the modernity of his ideas continuously impresses me—I hear life force, courage. I hear freedom of thought. I hear impertinence, transmission, humor, and creativity. (La Lettre, 2018)

The Reasons for Success

Everyone involved in the contest benefits from this unique and extremely rich experience: writers, illustrators, organizers, guests, teachers, and particularly students. For the latter the benefits are both obvious and undeniable: children learn a lot while participating in the contest. Furthermore, as acknowledged by teachers and children, this knowledge stays with them for a long time, unlike many facts studied at school and quickly forgotten! Not only do they learn a lot, but also, they learn about important and essential values and topics that will serve and help them on a daily basis. While the contest does not aim at shaping and changing students' personalities, it contributes to the formation of their minds, simultaneously increasing their ability to exercise critical thinking and develop self-reflection and empathy, as well as tolerance and open-mindedness.

Gradually, it helps the participants to sharpen their understanding of the surroundings by focusing on real and current social topics instead of keeping children in an excessively protective shell that prevents them from being exposed to the reality of life. Reading about such topics in children's books and trying to understand them through fiction is an excellent way to address sensitive issues in a non-scary way.

The contest also introduces the children to Janusz Korczak and his Declaration on the Rights of the Child. This allows a deeper look into his life and its historical context. Thus, the participants are able to learn about a great man and a model, as well as approach a crucial part of the history of the 20th century, the Holocaust, that definitely deserves to remain in the memory of future generations.

In addition, children become more knowledgeable about Korczak's works, which in many ways teach them tolerance and mutual respect, values that have become more and more rare in our present day and time. Therefore, it is essential for children to understand and apply them from the youngest age and on the broadest scope possible.

Of course, teachers are not forgotten in this contest! Although the contest constitutes a small part of the annual academic program, it is still considered an unusual and funny activity by many children, increasing their participation in other day-to-day school activities, reinforcing their attention span, and thus offering greater gratification to their teachers. It also allows students to create a special bond with their teachers especially through deeper discussions and the sharing of personal problems and experiences. I believe this bond is the most precious tool that enables children to reach their full potential at school and to mature into successful young adults.

In other words, there are many reasons that may explain the success of this project. To begin with, the contest helps enhance education in the field of children's rights that has generally been rare or even nonexistent in elementary school curriculum. Moreover, it generates students' interest in Korczak's life and teachings, while emphasizing important and necessary values such as tolerance, equality, and respect. The contest promotes the children's right to free expression through their active participation, which is highly important in today's world. It also aims at promoting reading skills and an interest in literature while fighting against some of the negative consequences of our digital world: screen addiction and lack of literacy skills. In addition, it provides access to literature to children who otherwise might not receive such a chance at home. Lastly, the contest introduces the children to the history of World War II and to the Shoah,[3] and it helps raise their awareness about important, sensitive, and contemporary social topics, such as war, disabilities, diseases, exile, etc. The contest also helps to develop children's ability and motivation to become actors for transforming society and for making the world a better place.

Conclusion

The Janusz Korczak Contest of Youth Literature has had a huge success in a short period of time in France, Switzerland, Luxemborg, and Belgium. Such a contest is relatively easy to launch and implement at an elementary school level, starting on a small scale and progressively growing. Our experience proves that it is an efficient, useful, and powerful tool that can be used by teachers to share an important part of history and teach fundamental rights and values to their students.

References

BOP Consulting, The Reading Agency. (2015, June). *Literature review: The impact of reading for pleasure and empowerment.* Retrieved from https://readingagency.org.uk/news/ The%20Impact%20of%20Reading%20for%20Pleasure%2and%20Empowerment. pdf

Craw, J. (2018, February). *Statistic of the month: How much time do students spend in school?* Retrieved from http://ncee.org/2018/02/statistic-of-the-month-how-much-time-do-students-spend-in-school/

Gleed, A. (2014). *Booktrust Reading Habits Survey 2013. A national survey of reading habits and attitudes to books amongst adults in England.* Retrieved from https://www.djsresearch.co.uk/Free/published/1576-booktrust-reading-habits-report-final.pdf

La Lettre, Association suisse des Amis du Dr Janusz Korczak, Vol. XXXVIII, N°88 (2018, October). *On Nous Écrit.* Retrieved from http://www.korczak.ch/doc/let/let_20181101_fr_0.pdf

OECD (2013). *OECD Skills Outlook 2013: First results from the Survey of Adult Skills.* Retrieved from https://www.insidehighered.com/sites/default/server_files/files/Skills%20volume%201%20(eng)--full%20v8--eBook%20(01%2010%202013).pdf

Official Website of "Association suisse des Amis du Dr Janusz Korczak." Prix Janusz Korczak de Littérature Jeunesse, Règlement du Prix. Retrieved from http://www.korczak.ch/?m=25

Official Website of "Le Prix Janusz Korczak de Littérature Jeunesse." Retrieved from http://www.prix-janusz-korczak-de-litterature-jeunesse.fr/

US Department of Education, Office of Educational Research and Improvement, National Center for Education Statistics. (1998). *The condition of education 1998, NCES 98-013.* Washington, D.C., U.S. Government Printing Office. Retrieved from https://nces.ed.gov/pubs98/98013.pdf

US Department of Education, National Center for Education Statistics. (2008). *Average number of hours in the school day and average number of days in the school year for public schools, by State: 2007–08.* Retrieved from https://nces.ed.gov/surveys/sass/tables/sass0708_035_s1s.asp

US Department of Education, Office of Educational Research and Improvement, National Center for Education Statistics. (1999, March). *The NAEP 1998 Reading Report Card for the Nation and the States, NCES 1999-500.* Washington, D.C. Retrieved from https://nces.ed.gov/nationsreportcard/pdf/main1998/1999500.pdf

Endnotes

[1]   For more details see the official website of the contest: www.prix-janusz-korczak-de-litterature-jeunesse.fr, 2018.

[2]   For updates see the official website of the Association Suisse des Amis du Dr Janusz Korczak: www.korczak.ch, 2018.

Photo Credits

27.1 – A photo from The Janusz Korczak Youth Literature Contest, organized by the Swiss Korczak Association. A photo by Daniel Halperin, used with permission.

27.2 – A photo from The Janusz Korczak Youth Literature Contest, organized by the Swiss Korczak Association. A photo by Daniel Halperin, used with permission.

Part V: Assignments

1. How do Korczak's strategies and methods relate to today's shift towards building social emotional competencies in children? Which of Korczak's ideas in particular could be used in this regard and why?

2. What are the main challenges of using Bets in schools today? State pros and cons of this method.

3. Define ways of utilizing Postcards in teachers' reward systems in modern classrooms.

4. Suggest how to utilize the Found Poetry (Julie Scott) method/project/approach in your own classroom.

5. How does Korczak's holistic vision of a child change summer camp practices? Could these ideas be used in extracurricular activities in schools?

6. What are the principal conditions of successfully utilizing children's literature contests in today's schools and making them tools of civic education?

7. How would you define the term "Korczak inspired pedagogy"?

Respecting and Developing Children: A Valuable Collaboration with Janusz Korczak

Lukas Ritson and Caitlin Murphy

LET'S GO OUT into the country, Korczak used to tell his charges, understanding that these simple words could fill a child's heart with excitement and wonder. Those were the words he said to them getting on their last journey. Indeed, the power of nature conjures up an image of freedom where a child can be wild, unsupervised, and fearless—climb a tree and shout into the forest. Or hide behind a log and make him/herself so small that he/she (henceforth, he) goes into another world altogether, a world where one can simply *be a child*. Nature has this immense effect on children. Just the idea of being in the natural environment can transport a child who is on his way to a concentration camp into a world of imagination and hope.

Korczak (2007) reflected, "When I approach a child, I have two feelings: affection for what he is today and respect for what he can become" (p. 17). This respect for children is deeply embedded in Korczak's teachings. Placing the child at the center of learning emphasizes benevolence, allowing the child to learn without judgment. Korczak embraced children's independent spirit and encouraged them to learn and exist as their own true selves.

The democratic system within his orphanages eliminated hierarchies and championed every child. It also promoted equality, bringing adults to the children's level, and facilitating values, courage, and citizenship while teaching the children the discipline they could learn through action, a type of self-education. The orphanage was a democracy, and its numerous institutions, like the Children's Court, put this into practice, offering children the opportunity to learn self-assessment, understanding, and forgiveness.

Children "have a right to be taken seriously.... They should be allowed to grow into whoever they were meant to be—the unknown person inside each of them is our hope for the future" (Korczak, 2007, p. 19). As educators, we have a universal obligation to support the development of our future leaders. To maximize this learning outcome, we need to maximize learning resources. One of our greatest resources and teachers is just outside the walls where you find yourself right now—the natural environment. But before we go outside and walk down that path, we should first reflect on Korczak's (2007) observations:

> Know yourself before you attempt to get to know your children. Become aware of what you yourself are capable of before you attempt to outline the rights and responsibilities of children. First and foremost you must realize that you, too, are a child, whom you must first get to know, bring up, and educate. (p. 2)

Being in the presence of children shows us who we really are. The innocence of a child and their curiosity for life can make us question our own behavior and life principles. Korczak highlighted the importance of conscious teaching: educating oneself in order to empathize with children. Recognizing that we are all children walking each other home can help nurture the notion of equality between young and old, creating the space to explore vulnerability and to develop understanding based on a foundation of trust.

In any relationship we need to feel trust and know that our needs are valued. We are living in an age where technology enables us to spark a relationship by connecting instantly, but we have never felt so disconnected as a species. As a result, we crave connection more than ever before, and our children are suffering. We face a growing tide of self-indulgent, inconsiderate, dependent, negligent young adults who are disconnected from themselves and our planet. What can we do right now to create change?

Let's begin with *fear*. Our own relationship with fear informs our existence and has a domino effect on the emotional development of children. Most fears stem from a place of love: wanting the very best for our children, keeping them safe and secure, and seeing them succeed. It is a primal instinct to protect our young, but in a modern society this fear has dramatically transformed how we educate children: in schools they strive to be "the best" by achieving high results, but when the outcome is not what a child expected, an overwhelming sense of failure can develop.

Feelings of discomfort and concern about the future belong to adults. When we place our fears on children they become distorted; the child has not encountered the life experiences and range of emotions associated with our problems. It is disrespectful to our relationship with a child to let our fears dictate their lives. To truly focus on the development of children and attend to their needs, our own fears need to be acknowledged and set aside. This awareness encourages our own and children's growth and enables their independence.

Developing a child's voice is what will keep them safe and make them successful, as this is how they learn to navigate their world in the absence of adults. But they are not able to develop the skills and personal traits to survive on their own if we are constantly dictating to them what to do.

In an era when children didn't have physical safety, Korczak's focus on emotional development was essential to their well-being. By introducing the performance of plays to the orphanage, Korczak welcomed a range of exciting characters and magical worlds the children could step into—far removed from their own reality. On the surface, theatre was a safe haven of escapism for the children, but the subtext had much greater meaning. Underneath the action and storyline, the children were gaining knowledge of emotions, exploring their creativity, and identifying their sense of self in a turbulent, confusing world.

In our efforts to ensure children's safety, mindfulness is how we can collectively create change. Only through this practice can we start building resilient, compassionate, fulfilled young people.

Another reminder comes from Abraham Maslow (1908–1970), who considered that we begin life by needing a level of physiological satisfaction in order to move onto the next stages: safety and security, love and belonging, self-esteem, and finally self-actualization (Journal Psyche, 1994–2018). Today, children are not reaching the basic required amount of physical satisfaction, resulting in an emotional imbalance. Unable to proceed to the next stages of growth, they then seek emotional fulfillment in all the wrong places.

In our modern culture when children are deprived of this kind of fulfillment, they will seek answers outside themselves: the adrenaline rush of video games, the physical satiety of food, and the attention from others on social media. These behaviors build unhealthy habits and promote negative values including materialism and consumerism. The outcome is an unfulfilled, lonely child with low self-esteem. With screen time increasing in many children's lives, it is no surprise that children today are spending half the amount of time outdoors than they were just one generation ago.

Korczak believed that nature must play an integral part in nurturing children. Children inherently know how to embrace the natural world. With our cities growing and suburbs sprawling, it is becoming increasingly necessary for us to support children in building a meaningful relationship with nature, nurturing respect for the environment and all living things. Acts of love and kindness, like those involved in children's caring for the environment and each other, are critical in creating conscious, caring, resilient, and self-sufficient learners. As Michael Gurian mentioned, "Our brains are set up for an agrarian, nature-oriented existence that came into focus five thousand years ago" (cited in Massy, 2017, p. 425).

Respecting the child comes in many forms: from an awareness of our own fears, to supporting their healthy relationship with nature. By reflecting critically on ourselves and contributing to knowing ourselves better, we pledge our availability to children. Utilizing Korczak's books and legacy as a resource for reflection is one of the most powerful tools for personal development in contemporary education.

The next step in creating change is collaboration: finding those partnerships with people who are doing things differently and comparing our own practice to theirs. Opening ourselves up in this way could evoke some fear: vulnerability, fear that we may not receive the validation we seek, realizing that we are not perfect.

By applying Korczak's philosophies for children to our own lives, as educators, we give ourselves permission to say, "I am who I am. That is my power." This is a message from us to our children. That is the beauty in empowering children; they will gain the confidence to speak out about what they need in relationships. It takes boldness, persistence, and a willingness to be the child's equal that will bring the walls down and allow a relationship based on respect to flourish.

Korczak didn't set out to change the world. His teachings came from a place of love and compassion, showing the capacity of one person to make a difference. He believed that adults could learn the most by allowing children to teach them. Children need guidance and education, but they also need to be celebrated. In order to make an impact, we, as educators, naturally look to those whose ideas have changed the world. These thought leaders make us question our abilities, provoke an emotional response in us, and motivate us to create real change. But it is important to remember that these heroes of ours all started within a single community, with *one child*. That is something we can draw inspiration from. If we let go of the idea of making grand gestures and begin to understand what is at the heart of our fulfillment as educators, we will find our own sense of worthiness and this will have a monumental impact on the children in our care. And that is what they will hold onto for the rest of their lives.

References

Journal Psyche. (1994–2018). *Tag archives: Theories of Abraham Maslow. The quest for self-actualization.* Retrieved on April 21, 2019, from http://journalpsyche.org/tag/theories-of-abraham-maslow/

Korczak, J. (2007). *Loving every child: Wisdom for parents.* Chapel Hill, NC: Algonquin Books of Chapel Hill.

Massy, C. (2017). *Call of the reed warbler: A new agriculture, a new earth.* London: Chelsea Green Publishing.

Appendix

Found Poetry Project: Janusz Korczak

Julie Scott

Guidelines

AFTER STUDYING THE Holocaust, the life and death of Janusz Korczak, and watching two YouTube videos on Janusz Korczak, students will use excerpts from selected sources to create a found poem on the life of Janusz Korczak.

- Teach the process of found poetry (model examples).

- Read through excerpts together as a class, while students highlight text they plan to use in their found poem.

- Watch videos and have students write down information, facts, words etc. for use in their poems.

- Create and illustrate poems.

  - Poem has to be at least 10 lines in length.

  - Present Korczak's life in a chronological manner.

  - Use of repetition, as a poetic device, is encouraged as a point of emphasis.

  - Illustration (large) that ties into the content of their poem, or the life of Janusz Korczak, fills the background.

  - Illustrations can also be smaller, with more than one, to create a collage of pictures tied into the life of Janusz Korczak.

  - Encourage illustrations drawn by pencil, charcoal, colored pencil, or crayon.

Videos on YouTube

Irena Sendler Remembers Janusz Korczak
http://www.youtube.com/watch?v=5nrDWJVOscA

Janusz Korczak: Hero to Children in the Warsaw Ghetto
(This Week in Jewish History)
https://www.youtube.com/watch?v=4_jHNKbIXu4&feature=emb_logo

Sources used for excerpts with this project

Adler, D. (2002). *A hero and the Holocaust: The story of Janusz Korczak and his children.* Picture Book. New York: Holiday House, Picture Book.

Bogacki, T. (2009). *The champion of children: The story of Janusz Korczak.* Picture Book. New York: Francis Foster Books.

Lifton, B.J. (1988). *The king of children: The life and death of Janusz Korczak.* New York: St. Martin's Griffin.

Additional excerpts from *How to Love a Child* by Janusz Korczak (from Janusz Korczak Association PDF online).

Students' Poems about Korczak

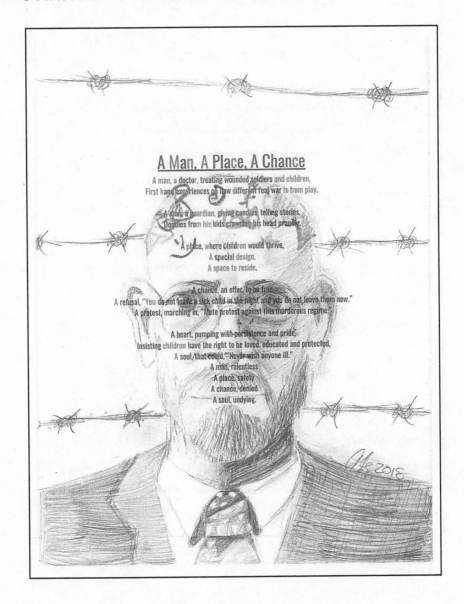

A Man, A Place, A Chance

A man, a doctor, treating wounded soldiers and children,
First hand experiences on how different real war is from play.

A man, a guardian, giving candies, telling stories,
Doodles from his kids crawls up his head proudly.

A place, where children would thrive,
A special design,
A space to reside.

A chance, an offer, to be free,
A refusal, "You do not leave a sick child in the night and you do not leave them now."
A protest, marching in, "Mute protest against this murderous regime."

A heart, pumping with persistence and pride,
Insisting children have the right to be loved, educated and protected,
A soul, that could, "Never wish anyone ill."
A man, relentless
A place, safety
A chance, denied
A soul, undying.

His Spirit Survives

Janusz Korczak was a man of truth.

The most important rule was that of forgiveness.

He wanted to do more than make children well.

Korczak gave his children love and attention.

He always made time for his children.

Janusz Korczak devoted his life to helping children—

Gave out candies, told stories to earn their trust.

"I always felt best among children"

Korczak let his children govern themselves—

To learn right from wrong.

August 6, 1942 trouble arose for Korczak and his children.

Calmly leading his children, refusing to leave them—

people screaming in horror all around.

Korczak led his children with love to Treblinka extermination camp.

His spirit survives in all he achieved for his children.

A young boy, humble and bold,
yearned to heal all, new and old,
Now a man with a glorious smile and selfless twinkle in his
eyes,
    He dreamed of a kingdom of peace and
endless golden skies,
The children adored him, their pasts now faded scars,
Hearts shining like bright
stars in a lonely galaxy.
He loved them through
times dark,
frightening and cold.
They stood proudly
in face of harsh
reality
like a gaurdian he
watched over them
day and night.

His
name
was

Janusz
Korczak

Youth Courts and Postcards: Incorporating Korczak and Principles of Restorative Justice in a School Youth Court

Ira Pataki, Sharpsville Middle School, PA

Introduction

THE YOUTH COURT and its emphasis on the concept of restorative justice offers an ideal way to promote individual responsibility and constructive group
interaction with the transformative potential to change and empower our student
body as stakeholders in the school community. In this model, the student-driven
tribunal fosters the foundation of self-confidence, fairness, and empathy that we
as educators are striving to cultivate in our students.

For nearly a decade, I have been involved with a program that pairs students
from our district with Israeli students to read and discuss the Holocaust through
literature and online academic forums. This particular program was originally
supported by a foundation connected to the legacy of Janusz Korczak and his
Warsaw orphanage. In my previous career as a lawyer, I recognized that Korczak's
progressive view involved a Children's Court that functioned very much in the
way the Youth Courts of today operate. Modern youth court models follow in the
tradition reflecting the child-centered mechanism that embodies the very best of
Korczak's progressive vision, namely that children are not people of tomorrow,
but of today.

SKY (Sharpsville Korczak Youth) Court arose as an organic hybrid of Korczak's
progressive vision and the concept of restorative justice. Through SKY Court, we
hope to reinforce the core concepts of community, culture, communication, and
collaboration. The model we embraced teaches our student-participants the courtroom roles such as judge, bailiff, jury foreman, and advocate, and they are trained by

practical, hands-on activities that encourage questioning skills, mentoring, public speaking, and critical thinking. The overarching goal, however, remains the focus on restorative principles that connect the individual to the school community in a meaningful way.

Included here are examples of constructive dispositions (templates for guiding "jury" decisions) based on individual school culture and initiatives. As a language arts teacher, I have also explored the concept of restorative justice through young adult literature, including the writings of Korczak as well as stories such as "A Retrieved Reformation" by O. Henry.

Along with Korczak's Children's Court, another Korczakian element that Sharpsville has added to our youth court involves incorporation of Korczak's awarding of postcards in our proceedings. Specifically, each session of our SKY Court begins with the recognition and awarding of postcards based on the Six Pillars of Character. These postcards are noted in the court records and awarded on the basis of positive acts by students in the school community submitted to the court director by faculty. A template about this aspect of Korczak's ideas within the youth court framework is also part of this Appendix.

While our district as a whole and our middle school building in particular are not characterized by excessive discipline nor school-to-prison pipeline issues, our embracing of this Youth Court program nevertheless represents a deep commitment to promote leadership, role models, critical thinking skills, and the positive engagement in the daily affairs that leads to success in high school and beyond.

SHARPSVILLE YOUTH COURT PROCESS AND SCRIPT

Bold print indicates lines that should be spoken by the student holding the indicated court position.

BAILIFF has collected all forms containing the facts of the case. Bailiff has ensured that the judge, jurors, respondent, and youth advocate are to begin the hearing.

JUDGE: Bailiff, please escort the respondent and youth advocate into the court.

BAILIFF escorts respondent and youth advocate into court.

JUDGE (to respondent and youth advocate): **Please remain standing.**

BAILIFF: All rise. Youth court is now in session. The Honorable Judge_____(name of Student Judge) presiding.

JUDGE: Bailiff, please read the 6 Pillars of Character.

BAILIFF: Trustworthiness, Respect, Responsibility, Fairness, Caring, Citizenship

JUDGE: Bailiff, please announce the SKY Card recipients for this court session.

BAILIFF: Our SKY Card (Sharpsville KOOR-CHUK) Youth Card recipient(s) is/are:_____

JUDGE: Congratulations and well done to our honorees. Bailiff, please continue.

(Bailiff returns to script to read case number)

BAILIFF: Case Number_____ (read number from court forms), **the case of_____** (Respondent name). **Would everyone in the entire courtroom please stand.**

1) (Swear in everyone in room). **Please raise your right hand and repeat after me. I swear or affirm/** (wait for court to repeat) **that everything I see or hear/** (wait...) **in youth court today/** (wait ...) **shall be kept confidential/** (wait...). **Everyone, please be seated except the jury.**

2) (Swear in jury). **Please raise your right hand. Do you solemnly swear or affirm that you will objectively weigh the issues in this case and render a disposition according to the evidence and guidelines of youth court?** (Jury responds, yes). **Please be seated.**

3) (Swear in respondent and youth advocate). **Respondent and youth advocate, please rise and raise your right hand. Do you solemnly swear or affirm that the testimony you are about to give will be the truth, the whole truth, and nothing but the truth?** (Both respond, yes). **Please be seated.**

JUDGE: In youth court we maintain the same level of respect found in any courtroom. There will be no gum chewing, eating, or drinking. No cellphones or electronic devices are allowed. No laughing, talking, or inappropriate behavior is permitted while court is in session. If there is improper behavior, either the Bailiff or I will order the behavior to cease. If verbal warnings are unsuccessful, bad behavior on the part of a spectator or juror will result in their removal from the courtroom and the hearing will continue without them. If the respondent's behavior disrupts the proceeding, they will be removed, a mistrial will be declared, and the case will be referred back to the referring official. Does everyone understand? Bailiff, please read the facts of the case.

BAILIFF: (reads BOTH statements). 1) School Referral written by school personnel who referred the respondent and 2) the respondent's written statement (the Statement of Fact).

(after Bailiff finishes reading .. .)

JUDGE: Youth Advocate, please make your Opening Statement.

YOUTH ADVOCATE makes Opening Statement

(After the Opening Statement)

JUDGE:_____(respondent's name): **Do you wish to say anything before the jury begins the questioning?** (Respondent usually says no).

JUDGE: At this time the jury may begin questioning the respondent.

JURY FOREPERSON to the judge (after questioning is complete): **We have no further questions, Your Honor.**

JURORS proceed with questioning.

JURY FOREPERSON ensures sample juror questions are followed (if needed) and that all issues are explored and all jurors have participated.

JUDGE: At this time the Youth Advocate may make his/her Closing Argument.

YOUTH ADVOCATE makes Closing Argument.

JUDGE: Bailiff, please escort the Respondent and Youth Advocate out of the courtroom.

BAILIFF escorts respondent and youth advocate out of the courtroom. Bailiff returns to courtroom.

JUDGE (to Jury): **At this time the Jury may begin its deliberations.**

JURORS deliberate until a decision is reached and Jury Foreperson completes the Hearing Report form.

JURY FOREPERSON: Your Honor, we have reached a Disposition.

JUDGE: Bailiff, please escort the Respondent and Youth Advocate into the courtroom.

BAILIFF escorts respondent and youth advocate into the room and tells them:

BAILIFF: Please remain standing.

JUDGE: (to the entire Jury). **Please stand and read the Disposition to the Respondent.**

JURORS rise.

JURY FOREPERSON: We, the members of Sharpsville Youth Court, have reached the following Disposition for your case: (read Disposition to court).

> **JUDGE: _____(Respondent's name), Do you understand the Disposition? (Wait for response). Do you plan to complete it?** (Wait...) **Do you understand that if you do not complete it, your case will be returned to the referring source for further action?** (Wait for response).

> **JUDGE: Court is now adjourned.** (Taps gavel). **Bailiff, please escort Respondent and Youth Advocate from the room to complete the Disposition Contract.**

BAILIFF escorts respondent and youth advocate from the room.

YOUTH ADVOCATE completes Disposition Contract with Respondent.

APPENDIX II.2

Sharpsville Korczak Youth Court

Restorative Dispositions

Goals:

- Does it repair the harm done to the respondent or others?
- Does it take steps toward preventing the respondent from repeating the offense?
- Does it help respondent address his/her specific challenges? (Academic and/or Personal)
- Emphasize that NO part of the disposition should seek to punish the respondent.

1. Review the facts and circumstances of the case
2. Think about impressions that you had of respondent during the hearing
3. Identify who was affected by the respondent's actions and how they were harmed
4. Identify the needs of everyone who was harmed
5. Identify the challenges and needs of the respondent
6. Think about what activities and resources youth court can connect the respondent to that may keep him/her out of trouble
7. Explain your decision.

2

Hearing Report Form (Completed by jury foreperson during deliberation)

Respondent Name:_____ Case#_____

Offense date:_____Hearing Date and Time:_____(am/pm)

Restorative Disposition Assigned (Options and Considerations) Apologies:

Written/Oral (Circle)

Jury Duty Service: Bailiff, Observer, Juror (Circle)

Research and/or other Written task: Article Reflection, Journal, Essay

Personal Goal Sheet: Revising and Revisiting Goals

If Home/Family Issues noted during hearing, then Guidance Participation Required Internal:

House Big, Little, Activities, Posters, Planning, Committees_____

School Clubs _____

Study Halls _____

Yoga/Meditation_____

TED Talk with Reflection/Girl Talk_____

Time Management with Natural Helpers (high school peers)_____

Teacher Shadowing _____

Tutoring _____

Other Adult or Peer Mentors _____

Community Service Options:_____

Custom:_____

Assigned Peer Mentor: _____

Signature of Jury Foreperson (indicating full jury agreement):_____

Signature of Adult Supervisor:_____

Signature of Judge:_____

Sharpsville Korczak Youth Court

FOREPERSON SHEET

FACTS:

-
-
-
-
-

What was the **REAL** Reason for the behavior?

HARM

What was the HARM caused?   Who was harmed?

  Others?

You?!

BACKGROUND HISTORY

· · · · · · ·

REMORSE

Why should we believe you won't repeat this behavior?

Have you apologized?

What could you have done differently?

Constructive Disposition

REPAIR & BUILD UP:

PREVENT from Happening **AGAIN**

-
-
-

1

Youth Court   ©Pataki, 2018

PERSUASIVE STRATEGIES—**FCOP**

F   C   O   P

FAIRNESS	CONSEQUENCES	OVERCOMING OBJECTIONS	PRECEDENT
Appeal to fairness by referring to unequal or inequitable treatment in similar situations.	*Exploring favorable or positive results* of your position or noting unfavorable or negative results—develop and elaborate with several consequences.	*Identify reasonable contrary positions or opinions.* Answer by demonstrating that your position is still more logical, efficient, or prudent.	*Refer to a similar positive or negative situation,* fact, or occurrence as a supportive or contrary example.
Don't overuse!	Very important to develop in a several sentences, perhaps with cause and effect, both positive and negative!	Raise and respect the obvious weakness in your argument, then turn it into your strength by overcoming through logic and the benefits of your position notwithstanding.	Necessary for building a solid foundation as you begin to convince.
And avoid beginning with an appeal to fairness.		Absolutely essential for your credibility!	Use **FRED**: Facts, Research, Examples, and Details.

1

Sharpsville Korczak Youth Court

Juror Questions ©Pataki

FACTS:

 : What happened to cause you to be referred to Youth Court?

 When did the incident take place?

2

Where: _____

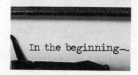

Who saw what happened?

In the beginning....

What was happening BEFORE the incident took place?

The Beginning

3

What happened immediately AFTER the incident?

What was said?

What did you do?

4

How did things *escalate* or get intense?

_____

Dial it Down?

How could you have prevented it from escalating?

How could you have "Dialed it Down?"

_____

Did you seek assistance? Did you ask for help?

How did you feel *DURING* the incident?

How did you feel *BEFORE* the incident?

5

What was the *REAL REASON* for the Behavior?

6

HARM What was the HARM caused?

Teachers?

Classmates?

7

HARM What was the HARM caused?

(continued)

Parents?

Others?

8

You?!

HARM What was the HARM caused?

(continued)

School?

9

Neighborhood?

Describe the harm caused by your behavior or the incident

10

What is your favorite subject in school?

What is your least favorite subject?

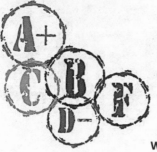

What is your GPA?

11

Do you participate in after-school activities?

   **Do you have a job?**

   **What do you like most about the school?**

12

What do you like least about the school?

What would be your dream job?

Are problems at home affecting your school behavior?

13

If so, and you are comfortable in sharing, what are they?

REMORSE

Have you been written up before?

If yes, when/for what?

14

Do you deserve to be written up?

Do your parents know what you did?
If not, how would they react?

Why should we believe you won't repeat this behavior?

15

Have you apologized?

What could you have done differently?

16

Constructive Disposition

What disposition would repair the harm

and *keep it from happening again?*

How can you Repair the Harm and Not Hurt Feelings of others?

17

APPENDIX II.6

Respondent Statement of Fact
(Completed by respondent during intake)

Respondent Name: _____ Respondent ID: _____ Case #:_____

Offense Date:_____ Hearing Date and Time: _____ at _____ AM/PM Offense
Category: _____

Please list below the facts of your case as you understand them to have happened. Include
any information you think is important to understanding how the incident occurred or
why you acted as you did.

Please be aware that your written statement will be read at the hearing.

_____

_____

_____

_____

_____

_____

_____

_____

_____

Student Signature and Date   Youth Advocate Signature and Date

_____   _____

2

Witness Impact Statement (Example)

On my afternoon route, I have a loud, rowdy group on the bus. I have to watch out for drivers-because I am always afraid that that they will drive through the stop. And I am also concerned about who is behind me, tailgating and what not. It's a lot to keep track of. With a more than a couple of dozen kids cooped up for a day and itching to get home, it takes all I got to watch the road, watch my speed, and monitor the road conditions.

You know it, and you heard it before-you got to have eyes in the back of your head. And I know it's part of the job, but these kids need to mind their behavior on the bus. It's all about safety. If they don't behave, I don't want to risk losing my edge or attention to the road. The risk is too big.

That afternoon was wild. I tried to tell the new kid to calm down, but she wouldn't. The next thing I know, there's a kid in the aisle! That's not a way to ride safely.

I can't have that. I don't want to be the bad guy. I just want to get these kids from point A to point B, and I am responsible to do it safely.

If a kid doesn't listen, then I can't have that kid on my bus route. It's plain and simple. Something needs to be done.

1

Sharpsville Korczak Youth Court

Dear Honored Postcard Recipient:

For many years, Sharpsville Language Arts classes have been participating in an experience of international cooperative learning about the Holocaust with students from several schools in Israel.

Together with our various Israeli partners over the years, we have learned about the Holocaust while simultaneously reading a book that documented the life of a youth in a Polish ghetto during Nazi occupation. As part of our studies, we have also learned about Janusz Korczak, a Polish pediatrician and well-known children's author, who ran a Polish orphanage and steadfastly remained with the Jewish children when they were ordered to relocate inside the walls of the Warsaw Ghetto. When the children were ordered to board the trains for the death camp Treblinka, Korczak again refused to abandon them, choosing instead to walk together with his beloved children, hand in hand, as they marched to the trains. Korczak and his children-nearly 200-all perished at Treblinka.

Although inspired by this timeless image of sacrifice, love, and courage, we are choosing to honor Korczak's *life* and his everyday practices of encouraging and empowering those children in his care. Korczak envisioned a children's republic, designed as a just community, in which its young citizens would have their own parliament, newspaper, and court of peers. Accordingly, we have established our own Sharpsville Korczak Youth Court in the tradition of Korczak's Children's Court.

In his Declaration of Children's Rights, Korczak stated that children have a right to be loved, respected, and given optimal conditions in which to grow. They have a right to be taken seriously. They are not people of tomorrow, but of today. They should be allowed to become whomever they are meant to be:

"The unknown person inside each child is the hope for the future."

To honor this legacy and continue Korczak's great practice of awarding Postcards as "encouragement cards" for good and virtuous behavior, the Sharpsville Korczak Youth Court hereby recognizes your efforts to make our school and community a better place.

In the words of Janusz Korczak: *"this card is not a reward, but a souvenir, a remembrance. Some will lose it on life's road. Others will treasure it forever."*

We at Sharpsville will treasure your contributions forever.

APPENDIX II.8

Lesson Plan: Academic Language Arts 7, Periods 1-2[1]

The Island on Bird Street, The Scar, Roll of Thunder, Hear My Cry

Using fiction, nonfiction, and poetry, this lesson is a culminating activity to help students understand the setting, characters, conflicts, plots, points of view, voices, and themes in the novels: *The Island on Bird Street, Roll of Thunder, Hear My Cry* and the short story *The Scar*, and apply their understanding to a deeper awareness of the social concerns and attitudes during the Holocaust and the Great Depression and make relevant and meaningful connections to their world today in terms of school, family, and the global community of which they have been a part of through their year-long work in the International Shared Reading Program.

Along with the novels, students will analyze nonfiction, a short story, and explicate poetry through figurative language and other literary techniques, and they will demonstrate their understanding of these topics by creating and designing a set of postcards according to the historical model of Janusz Korczak. These cards will demonstrate understanding of literary elements, themes, and traits, with a design that incorporates symbolism, visual metaphor, and close textual analysis to celebrate the positive impact of the Pillars of Character on the Sharpsville community and abroad. As an original extension of Korczak's practice, students will create cards that reflect their critical understanding and appreciation of literary elements, themes, techniques, and style.

Students will learn that their cards will also have an international presentation, as they will be given *in person* to their Israeli partners in mid-June, and discussed and shared at 2018 International Korczak conference (Seattle, WA).

Objectives:

- By close reading and critical textual analysis of novels, poetry, and other writings, students will analyze the use of literary elements by an author and a poet including characterization, setting, plot, theme, point of view, tone, and style to compare, contrast, and comprehend the impact of history and draw life lessons, relevant to daily life and learning.
- Students will demonstrate comprehension and understanding of themes, imagery, and other literary techniques that represent a variety of meaningful traits, behavior, conduct, and range of positive traits that connect with relevance to current relationships (partnerships) and daily interactions.

2

- By understanding and applying the lessons of history and literature, students will learn to take an active role in school leadership by identifying, recognizing, modeling, and celebrating the virtuous conduct of others.
- Students will comprehend the significance of the Pillars of Character and the role these qualities play in making our school environment and community safer and more tolerant.

MATERIALS:

- Postcard Templates
- Glue sticks
- Zits cartoon
- Short story *The Scar*, by Janusz Korczak
- Article, *Not in Our Town*
- Novel, *Roll of Thunder, Hear My Cry*
- Copies of Word Cloud poem from Langston Hughes
- Puzzle pieces of the picture (number of groups)
- Video, *Korczak of the Children*
- Korczak's postcards facsimiles
- Postcards Handout with Rubric

ANTICIPATORY SET:

Day 1: Korczak video: *Korczak of the Children*

Day 2: *Word Cloud* of Langston Hughes Poem with Puzzle pieces of symbol.

PROCEDURE:

Day 1: Show Korczak Video

1. Distribute the short story *The Scar* by Korczak
2. Read the story as a class
3. Divide students into the 5 International Shared Reading Project groups
4. Have students compare and contrast the themes, ideas, and imagery from *The Scar* with the 2 forums—**Upstanding** and **Easy To Hate a Stranger**
5. Instruct students to write connections (comparisons, contrast, and other reflections) among these works based on students' writing with partners and small group discussion

3

Day 2:

Divide students into International Shared Reading Groups from yesterday

1. Hand out Word Cloud of Poem and Clues sheet
2. While students work, hand out puzzle pieces
3. Read final version of poem, Justice
4. Discuss the idea of justice presented in the poem
5. Handout the quote by Korczak about the court
6. The court is not justice, but it should strive for justice
7. The court is not truth, but it should strive for truth
8. With these ideas in mind, distribute the article Not in Our Town
9. Read the article as a class
10. Instruct students to discuss the connection between Korczak's short story *The Scar* and *Not in Our Town*
11. Make connections to Forum discussions from yesterday
12. Show and distribute Korczak's postcards
13. Show the Zits cartoon about Postcards and distribute the postcard packet and rubric
14. Discuss culminating assignment that involves the design, creation, and presentation of 3 types of postcards: Partner cards, Defender cards, and Family cards
15. Show template and postcard model of appropriate card

CLOSURE & EXTENSION: *Where do we go from here? Presentation and Publication—and potential Participation!*

- Repeat deadlines and scheduling matters
- Review guidelines and requirements
- Repeat what a completed project must contain in order to satisfy the Rubrics
- Inform students that the Partner cards will be Hand Delivered in mid June when teacher visits partner school in Ra'anana near Tel Aviv, Israel
- In addition, inform students that their cards will be discussed and shown during a significant international conference organized by the Janusz Korczak Association of the USA in Seattle, Washington in August
- By introducing Korczak and his progressive methods and practices—namely the Children's Court—discuss with these students the potential for them playing an active role in our Sharpsville Korczak Youth Court going forward this year and next

ACCOMMODATIONS AND ADAPTATIONS:

- Groups have been pre-determined in order to focus on efficient collaboration and prior experience.
- Members of several groups already possess a variety of skills that will enable them to complete the task. Artistic, tactile, and more hands-on aspect of this project should be appealing.

4

- While there are certainly many opportunities for original work, enough material to complete the project satisfactorily will be given to each group, thereby leaving the majority of the time for assembly.
- All materials (other than the actual images for the collage) are provided by the teacher.
- Information will be presented slowly and clearly, with adequate time for notation, and I will continue to be available during Home Room, Academic Coaching, and Language Arts periods.

---

[1] Composed and used by Ira Pataki in Sharpsville middle school, PA, May 2018.

1

The Island on Bird Street, The Scar, Roll of Thunder, Hear My Cry

The Six Pillars of Character

Trustworthiness

Be honest • Don't deceive, cheat, or steal • Be reliable — do what you say you'll do • Have the courage to do the right thing • Build a good reputation • Be loyal — stand by your family, friends, and country

Respect

Treat others with respect; follow the Golden Rule • Be tolerant and accepting of differences • Use good manners, not bad language • Be considerate of the feelings of others • Don't threaten, hit or hurt anyone • Deal peacefully with anger, insults, and disagreements

Responsibility

Do what you are supposed to do • Plan ahead • Persevere: keep on trying! • Always do your best • Use self-control • Be self-disciplined • Think before you act — consider the consequences • Be accountable for your words, actions, and attitudes • Set a good example for others

Fairness

Play by the rules • Take turns and share • Be open-minded; listen to others • Don't take advantage of others • Don't blame others carelessly • Treat all people fairly

Caring

Be kind • Be compassionate and show you care • Express gratitude • Forgive others • Help people in need

Citizenship

Do your share to make your school and community better • Cooperate • Get involved in community affairs • Stay informed; vote • Be a good neighbor • Obey laws and rules • Respect authority • Protect the environment • Volunteer

Trustworthiness

Quotation/Example

_____

_____

_____

_____

_____

2

_____

_____

_____

_____

Explanation of Quotation/Example

_____

_____

_____

_____

_____

_____

Respect

Quotation/Example

_____

_____

_____

_____

_____

_____

Explanation of Quotation/Example

_____

_____

_____

©Pataki, Language Arts, Grade 7

3

_____
_____
_____
_____
_____

Responsibility
Quotation/Example

_____
_____
_____
_____
_____
_____
_____

Explanation of Quotation/Example

_____
_____
_____
_____
_____
_____

4

Fairness

Quotation/Example

_____
_____
_____
_____
_____
_____
_____

Explanation of Quotation/Example

_____
_____
_____
_____
_____
_____
_____

Caring
Quotation/Example

_____
_____
_____
_____

©Pataki, Language Arts, Grade 7

5

_____
_____
_____
_____

Explanation of Quotation/Example

_____
_____
_____
_____
_____

Citizenship
Quotation/Example

_____
_____
_____
_____
_____
_____

6

Explanation of Quotation/Example

_____

_____
_____
_____
_____
_____
_____
_____

_____

Partner Postcards Rimon Junior High, Ra'anana

**Review all of your International Student Lounge messages and your
Forum exchanges with your partner(s).**

Identify one of the Pillars of Character shown or demonstrated by Alex or
any other character(s) in _The Island on Bird Street_ and connect this positive
value or trait with what you have experienced with your partner or what you
have learned about during your yearlong communication in the International
Shared Reading Program. If possible, identify a detail or something specific
from your partner that makes the connection meaningful.

For each Postcard:

- Identify a Pillar of Character

- Find a quotation from the text that supports, illustrates, exemplifies,
  demonstrates, or otherwise highlights that selected Pillar. Your
  quotation should be at least three sentences.

- Provide an <u>explanation</u> that shows how the quotation demonstrates or
  is otherwise thoughtfully and meaningfully connected to the selected

7

Pillar. If and where possible, identify something specific from your partnership exchanges that makes the connection clear and meaningful. Required length: One Paragraph.

• Statement: Write one sentence according to the following Model:

"Your *Pillar* is an inspiration to your friends, family, and community." {Of course, you may personalize each Honor Statement for the particular recipient.}

Defender Cards: *Not in Our School*
The Scar, Not in Our Town
"Not in Our School!"

Your assignment is to make one postcard that honors or celebrates a Defender of our school and the role this person plays in making our school the special and safe place we want it to be for all members.

As you review the article *Not in Our Town* and the short story *The Scar* by Janusz Korczak, reflect upon the following quotation:

> "Don't bully anyone, neither him nor anyone. Defend the honor of this school. Let no one from [Our] school carry into the world, into life, such a scar as mine, neither on one's head nor on one's soul."
>
> *Teacher, from The Scar by Janusz Korczak*

Identify a Pillar of Character reflected in Korczak's story.

Explain how the quotation demonstrates or is otherwise thoughtfully and meaningfully connected to the selected Pillar. In your explanation, show how this Pillar and the ideas from the quotation relate to making our school a better place. Do not provide names, but try to make the connection very clear and relevant to the experience of school life at Sharpsville. Length: One Paragraph.

©Pataki, Language Arts, Grade 7

8

Honor Statement for Defender Postcard:

"Your {*Pillar* } defends the honor of our school."

When completed, identify a Defender and present the card to that person!

Community Cards: *Roll of Thunder, Hear My Cry*

Identify one of the Pillars of Character shown or demonstrated by any character(s) from *Roll of Thunder, Hear My Cry* and connect this positive value or trait with the powerful themes, life lessons, or significant ideas that we have discussed and explored in our reading of the novel. Be sure to consider our study of Segregated America, the poetry of Langston Hughes, and positive model and example set by Thurgood Marshall.

For each Postcard:

- Identify a Pillar of Character

- Find a quotation from the text that supports, illustrates, exemplifies, demonstrates, or otherwise highlights that selected Pillar. Your quotation should be at least three sentences.

- Provide an <u>explanation</u> that shows how the quotation demonstrates or is otherwise thoughtfully and meaningfully connected to the selected Pillar. Required length: One Paragraph

- Statement: Write one sentence according to the following Model:

"Your *Pillar* is an inspiration to your friends, family, and community."
{Of course, you may personalize each Honor Statement for the particular recipient.}

When completed, identify someone from your community or family to receive the card!

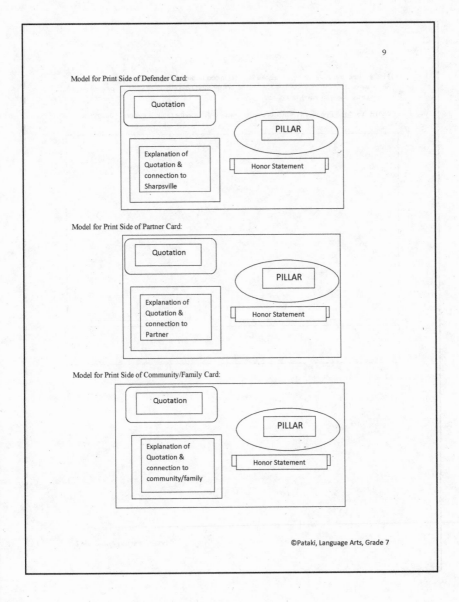

10

Find an event, scene, happening, or idea that has a big impact on one of the key characters or the action and draw or otherwise symbolize this event, scene, or happening (you may make a collage, panel sequence like a graphic novel, or a picture).

NOTE: You MUST provide a detailed quotation (exact words) from the text to accompany your picture.

Quotation:

Appendix II.10

The Island on Bird Street, The Scar, Roll of Thunder, Hear My Cry

Ira Pataki, Language Arts, Grade 7

4 Postcards Required: 200 Points

(If you have 2 partners, 2 of your cards must be Partner Cards. The rest of you may create a 2nd *Not in Our School Card* or a *2nd Community Card*)

Partner Postcard Rubric

Partner Postcard

	Trustworthiness	Respect	Responsibility	Fairness	Caring	Citizenship
Pillar	/2	/2	/2	/2	/2	/2
H/S	/3	/3	/3	/3	/3	/3
Quote	/4	/4	/4	/4	/4	/4
Exp:	/6	/6	/6	/6	/6	/6
Picture:	/35	/35	/35	/35	/35	/35
Total:	/50	/50	/50	/50	/50	/50

Note: Maximum possible "Picture" points for pencil or ink picture is 20/35 for every card type.

Picture materials (Note: Picture materials are the same for different card types)

- List A: cut paper, colored paper, tissue paper, "stained glass" effect, foil, stickers (limited and carefully/thoughtfully arranged), cloth, fabric, wallpaper, photos, postcards, "pieces", objects or tokens of appropriate width (ask me!), newspaper, comics, paint, other colors.
- Hint: Think of your picture as a collage or detailed symbol.
- No pencil and/or simple lined sketches or drawings.
- No stick figure drawings will be acceptable. Instead, think symbolically to incorporate pictures from magazines or other sources to represent your intended scene, event, symbol, or idea.
- If using colored pencils, markers, crayons, or similar materials, your drawing must also contain bits and pieces from List A to make the collage more detailed, symbolic, and developed.
- No metal may be used.

Total: /50   /50

2

"Not in Our School" Defender Card Rubric (Choose to do 2 if you do not have a 2nd Partner)

Defender Card

	Trustworthiness	Respect	Responsibility	Fairness	Caring	Citizenship
Pillar	/2	/2	/2	/2	/2	/2
H/S	/3	/3	/3	/3	/3	/3
Quote	/4	/4	/4	/4	/4	/4
Exp:	/6	/6	/6	/6	/6	/6
Picture:	/35	/35	/35	/35	/35	/35
Total:	/50	/50	/50	/50	/50	/50

Total:	/50	/50

Community Card Rubric (Choose to do 2 if you do not have a 2nd Partner)

Community/Family Card

	Trustworthiness	Respect	Responsibility	Fairness	Caring	Citizenship
Pillar	/2	/2	/2	/2	/2	/2
H/S	/3	/3	/3	/3	/3	/3
Quote	/4	/4	/4	/4	/4	/4
Exp:	/6	/6	/6	/6	/6	/6
Picture:	/35	/35	/35	/35	/35	/35
Total:	/50	/50	/50	/50	/50	/50

Total:	/50	/50

CONTRIBUTORS

Ken Bedell, Ph.D., is a former senior adviser in the Department of Education in the Obama administration, a writer and a passionate fighter for human rights and for the full elimination of racism in the United States.

Joop Berding, Ph.D., is a pedagogue and a retired professor of education at Rotterdam University of Applied Science. His publications are in the field of education, with a focus on Janusz Korczak, John Dewey, and Hannah Arendt. He is a member of the Dutch Korczak Association.

Mark Bernheim, Ph.D., is a writer and Professor Emeritus of Languages and Literature from Miami University in Ohio. He has extensive teaching experience in France, Austria, and throughout Italy through Fulbright awards and other affiliations.

Tonia Bock, Ph.D., is a professor and director of accreditation and assessment at the University of St. Thomas, MN. Dr. Bock is an educational and developmental psychologist who specializes in moral development.

Lillian Boraks-Nemetz was born in Warsaw, Poland, and is a child survivor of and witness to the Holocaust. She holds a master's degree in comparative literature, and is a published author of prose and poetry. She also serves as an outreach speaker for the Vancouver Holocaust Education Centre and Museum. Boraks-Nemetz is a board member of the Janusz Korczak Association of Canada.

Helma Brouwers, M.Ed., is a retired lecturer at the University of Amsterdam, Netherlands. She is the author of a widely used textbook for teacher training based on Korczak's and Vygotsky's ideas and an editor of several books on Korczak-inspired pedagogy. She is an active member of the Dutch Janusz Korczak Association.

Irina Demakova, Ed.D., is a professor and chair of the Department of Psychological Anthropology at the Institute of Childhood, Moscow State Pedagogical University (MSPU). She is also a vice president of the Russian Janusz Korczak Society, an academic adviser of the International Youth Korczak Center and of the International Integration Children's Korczak Camp "Nash Dom," and a head of the MSPU Academic and Research Korczak Center for Education of Children and Youth.

Shlomi Doron, Ph.D., is a senior lecturer at the Multidisciplinary Department of Ashkelon Academic College in Israel. He also works at the Korczak Education Institute of Israel (KEI).

Sara Efrat Efron, Ed.D., is a professor of education and director of the doctoral program in curriculum, advocacy, and policy at National Louis University in Chicago, IL. She is a widely published author who presents at national and international conferences.

Elisabeth Gifford studied French literature and comparative religion at Leeds University, UK. She worked for many years as a special needs coordinator specializing in literacy and dyslexia. She has an MA in creative writing. *The Good Doctor of Warsaw* is her third historical novel with a further two novels due to appear shortly.

Hillel Goelman, Ph.D., is Professor Emeritus at the University of British Columbia in Vancouver, Canada. Over his 35-year career at the university he taught courses in childhood education and research methods in the Department of Educational and Counseling Psychology, and Special Education, and chaired the Interdisciplinary Studies Graduate Program.

Shirane Halpérin was born in Geneva, Switzerland, in a family of dedicated Korczakians. She obtained a bachelor and master of law from the University of Fribourg, Switzerland, and serves as an active member of the Association Suisse des Amis du Dr Janusz Korczak.

Ewa Jarosz, Ph.D., is a professor at the University of Silesia in Katowice, Poland, and a researcher of problems of children's participation and violence against children. As a strong advocate for children's rights, she also served as the social advisor for the Polish Ombudsman for Children in 2011–2018.

Gilles Julien, M.D., is a pediatrician and social entrepreneur from Montreal, Canada. A pioneer in responsible and integrated medicine, Dr. Julien founded a model of Community Social Pediatrics to treat children whose development is compromised by the presence of toxic stress and complex traumas arising from difficult living conditions. He is also an author of several books and a recipient of prestigious awards, who continues to influence communities across Canada and elsewhere.

Ljubov Klarina, Ph.D., is a Leading Research Fellow at the Institute of the Study of Childhood, Family, and Education at the Russian Academy of Education in Moscow, Russia, and an author and coauthor of several books on preschool child development.

Angela M. Kurth, Ph.D., is a faculty member in psychology at the University of St. Thomas in St. Paul, MN. She has experience in early education contexts, and is interested in parent and teacher education.

Wojciech Lasota is an accomplished researcher of Janusz Korczak's theory and practice from Warsaw, Poland. He is a chairman and cofounder of the Polish Korczak Foundation. Lasota served as a general investigator on several projects aimed to promote Korczak's legacy in the world.

Jonathan Levy, M.Ed., is a pedagogue, teacher trainer, and trainer of child professionals (from Paris, France). His work is based on a pedagogical approach to children's rights. He is the program and scientific director of Child Rights in Action, and he also serves as vice president of the International Korczak Association.

Ewa Łukowicz-Oniszczuk served as the vice consul at the Polish Consulate in New York City from 2011-2013. Her interests include education for peace, human rights, and intercultural communication. She is a member of the Polish Korczak Association and works at the Polish Ministry of Foreign Affairs in Warsaw.

Tilar J. Mazzeo, Ph.D., is the Clara C. Piper Associate Professor of English at Colby College, in Waterville, ME. She is a *New York Times* bestselling author and holds more than 30 years of classroom teaching experience in American higher education.

Marek Michalak, Ph.D., is a special education teacher, Ombudsman for Children (2008–2018), chancellor of the International Chamber of the Order of the Smile, and chairman of the European Network of Ombudspersons for Children ENOC with its registered seat in Strasbourg in 2011–2012. He is currently an elected president of the International Korczak Association (IKA).

Caitlin Murphy is the communication and marketing manager of Wearthy (Australia). Caitlin is also a part-time actor and professional musician.

Darcia Narvaez, Ph.D., is a professor of psychology at the University of Notre Dame in South Bend, IN. She is a prolific writer, and her research explores issues of character and moral development. Previously, at the University of Minnesota and subsequently, she worked with educators to develop a framework for integrating moral character development into academic instruction.

Marta Santos Pais is the Special Representative of the United Nations Secretary-General on Violence against Children. She is a lawyer with 40 years of experience on human rights issues and a firm commitment to the rights of the child, and the author of a large number of publications on these issues. Marta Santos Pais also worked in UNICEF and at the International University in Lisbon, Portugal, and was a member of the UN Drafting Group of the 1989 Convention on the Rights of the Child and of its three Optional Protocols.

Ira Pataki, J.D., holds a law degree from Northwestern University and degrees in English language and literature from Oxford University and Columbia University. He currently serves as an instructor at Sharpsville Middle School in Sharpsville, PA.

Kristin Poppo, Ph.D., is the provost of Alfred State College. She is passionate about children's rights and has focused much of her work on how to develop compassion in children and young adults.

Peter C. Renn, Ed.D., serves as an assistant dean at Seattle Pacific University, Seattle, WA. An educator for over 25 years, his research interests include the role of critical pedagogy in schools and educational neuroscience.

Lukas Ritson is a sustainability educator and a cofounder of Wearthy (Australia), who developed and implemented successful outdoor programs that nurture sustainable development. He shares his findings at seminars, conferences, and private trainings across Australia and internationally.

Julie Scott, M.Ed., is an eighth-grade English/language arts teacher at East Valley Middle School/East Valley School District in Spokane, WA.

Marc Silverman, Ph.D., worked as a senior lecturer in the School of Education, Hebrew University of Jerusalem, for over 30 years. He has publications in philosophy of education and Jewish culture and education. He is the author of *A Pedagogy of Humanist Moral Education: The Educational Thought of Janusz Korczak* (2017) published by Palgrave-Macmillan.

Ralph Singh serves as the chair of the Wisdom Thinkers Network. He is an author, educator, storyteller, speaker, and community builder. For over 40 years, Ralph has focused on spirituality and values in education and in public life.

Amy Spangler, M.Ed., is an educational consultant and a former school principal with over 30 years of experience in public education in the United States and the international community of Japan.

Tamara Sztyma, Ph.D., is an art historian and curator of exhibits for the POLIN Museum of the History of Polish Jews in Warsaw, Poland, and an organizer of several exhibits, one of which in 2018 was inspired by Janusz Korczak's life and work. She is also an adjunct researcher at the Warsaw University, Artes Liberales Division.

Marcia Talmage Schneider is a writer and educator, and the author of *Janusz Korczak: Sculptor of Children's Souls*. She resides in New York City.

Mary S. Tarsha, M.Ed., is a graduate student in psychology and peace studies at the Kroc Institute for International Peace Studies in the Keough School of Global Affairs at the University of Notre Dame, South Bend, IN.

Hélène (Sioui) Trudel, J.D., is a certified mediator and social entrepreneur in Montreal, Canada, who designed the practice of integrated law in social medicine, focusing on the global health status and dignity of impoverished children through implementing the CRC as a whole, inspired by Janusz Korczak and Dr. Gilles Julien. She has received important awards and recognition for her work in Quebec and Canada.

Tatyana Tsyrlina-Spady, Ph.D., is Professor Emerita from Kursk State University (Russia) and an adjunct professor at Seattle Pacific University, Seattle, WA. She is an author of over 20 books and edited volumes, a visiting professor who taught the first Korczak-inspired Summer Institute at UBC (Vancouver, BC) in 2019, and who is considered a global expert in education. Her career was largely inspired by Janusz Korczak.

Agnieszka Witkowska-Krych is an anthropologist and sociologist who served for years as a fellow at the Korczakianum Research Center. She is currently pursuing her Ph.D. at the University of Warsaw and preparing a thesis about orphaned and/or abandoned Jewish children in the Warsaw ghetto.

INDEX